JEM SULTAN

The Adventures of
a Captive Turkish Prince
in Renaissance Europe

JOHN FREELY

HARPER PERENNIAL
London, New York, Toronto and Sydney

Harper Perennial
An imprint of HarperCollins*Publishers*
77–85 Fulham Palace Road
Hammersmith
London w6 8jb

www.harperperennial.co.uk

This edition published by Harper Perennial 2005
1

First published by HarperCollins*Publishers* 2004

A catalogue record for this book is
available from the British Library

ISBN 0-00-715067-9

Set in PostScript Linotype Minion with Spectrum display
by Rowland Phototypesetting Ltd,
Bury St Edmunds, Suffolk

Printed and bound in Great Britain by
Clays Ltd, St Ives plc

For Toots, Brendan and Ulrike
in memory of our journey together in search of Jem

Note on Turkish Spelling and Pronunciation

Throughout this book, modern Turkish spelling has been used for most Turkish names and for things that are specifically Turkish, with a few exceptions for Turkish words that have made their way into English. Modern Turkish is rigorously logical and phonetic, and the few letters that are pronounced differently than in English are indicated below. Turkish is very slightly accented, mostly on the last syllable, but all syllables should be clearly and almost evenly accented.

Vowels are pronounced as in French or German, i.e.: **a** as in father, **e** as in met, **i** as in machine, **o** as in oh, **u** as in mute. In addition, there are three other vowels that do not occur in English; these are: **ı** pronounced as the **u** in but, **ö** as in German or the **oy** as in annoy, **ü** as in German or as the **ui** in suit.

Consonants are pronounced as in English, except the following:
c as **j** in jam, e.g.: *cami* (mosque) = jahmy
ç as **ch** in chat, e.g.: *çorba* (soup) = chorba
g as in get, never as in gem
ğ is almost silent and tends to lengthen the preceding vowel
ş as in sugar, e.g.: *çeşme* (fountain) = cheshme

Acknowledgements

I would like to express my gratitude to those who helped me in various ways in my work on this book: Anthony E. Baker, Ulrike Ammicht and Dolores Freely for their photographs; Emin Saatçi for help with translations; Ulrike Ammicht for help with translations and computer graphics; Sinan Ozay for his help with computer problems; Ronald Newburgh for the photograph of Jem's *akçe*; Dr Anthony Greenwood, Director of the American Research Center in Istanbul, and Professor Gün Kut, Head Librarian of Bosphorus University, for making all of the resources of their libraries available for my research; Meral Bayülgen, and Professor Talat Halman for translating poems; Roderick Conway-Morris and Roderick O'Connor for many illuminating discussions about Jem; Marcel Chaussade for sharing with me his knowledge of Jem's life in Bourganeuf. Marcel in particular is to be thanked for having preserved the local traditions concerning Jem and for bringing them to life in the museum he has created in the Tower of Zizim. I would also like to express my thanks to my agent Derek Johns and my editor Michael Fishwick for their help in bringing this book into being, and to Kate Johnson for her very helpful editorial suggestions. I am also grateful to Cem Kozlu of Turkish Airlines, and to Peter and Rose Lauritzen for their hospitality at the Palazzo da Silva in Venice.

Contents

Illustrations

VIII, copy of the original by Mantegna; Pope Alexander VI, detail of fresco by Pintoricchio in Borgia Apartments in the Vatican; King Charles VIII of France, terracotta bust by an unknown Florentine sculptor of the late fifteenth century, in the Bargello, Florence.

The Tour de Zizim at Bourganeuf. (*Author's private collection*)

La Dame à la Licorne, detail of one of the tapestries at Aubusson.

Jem Sultan, pen-and-ink drawing by anonymous artist, c.1488. (Arras Library)

The Martyrdom of St Ursala, by Hans Memling, 1489.

(*top*) Jem Sultan being presented to Pope Innocent VIII by Guy de Blanchefort, the Prior of Auvergne, by Caoursin.

(*bottom*) Sant' Angelo, Rome, mid-nineteenth century.

Jem Sultan, detail of *The Disputation of St Catherine*, by Pintoricchio, Hall of the Saints in the Borgia Apartments, the Vatican.

(*top*) The Muradiye and its imperial tombs, Bursa. (*Author's private collection*)

(*bottom*) Interior of Jem's tomb, Bursa. (*Photograph by Anthony Baker*)

'... most of the events of the past, through lapse of time,
have fought their way, past credence,
into the country of myth'

Thucydides, *History of the Peloponnesian War*

PROLOGUE

The Tomb in Bursa

THE ANCIENT TOWN of Bursa is built on the lower slopes of Ulu Dağ, the Greek Mount Olympus of Bithynia, whose snow-capped and cloud-plumed summit can be seen from Istanbul on the clearest of winter days, an intercontinental view that extends from the easternmost peninsula of Europe to the westernmost mountain of Asia.

I first saw Ulu Dağ from Istanbul on such a day early in 1961, but it was mid-April before I could travel to Bursa on my spring vacation. By then the mountain had lost most of its snow and its lower slopes were ablaze with flowering judas trees, whose pink to purple and magenta blossoms had carpeted the cobbled streets of Bursa as if for a bridal procession. Aside from the occasional bus or communal taxi along the main avenues, the only vehicles were horse-drawn carts of itinerant pedlars, who hawked their fruits and vegetables to women peering from the latticed windows of old wooden houses, flanking the winding back streets along which I was strolling. A white-bearded patriarch astride a donkey greeted me gravely as we passed, touching his heart with his right hand and saying 'Selamünaleyküm' ('Peace be with you'), to which I responded with the same gesture and said '*Aleykümselam*' ('Peace be upon you').

At that moment I felt that I had rediscovered the vanished world of the imperial Ottoman era, which had ended with the founding of the Turkish Republic in 1923. Its ways still lingered on in the back streets of Bursa, where time is told only through the *ezan,* or call to prayer, which a *müezzin* makes five times a day from the minaret of every mosque in town, though imperfectly coordinated. The *ezan* for the mid-afternoon prayer was echoing from the minaret of the Muradiye, the mosque toward which I was headed, and I used the *müezzin*'s call as a directional signal to make the last stretch of my way there.

I had come to look at the Islamic architecture of Bursa, the first capital of the Ottoman Empire, which at its outset was limited to a small part of north-western Asia Minor. The first six Ottoman sultans were buried in Bursa, which the Turks had captured and made their capital in 1326. The thirty sultans who followed them were, all but the last one, buried in Istanbul, Greek Constantinople, which became the Ottoman capital after it was taken by Sultan Mehmet II in 1453.

The last of the Ottoman sultans buried at Bursa was Murat II, father of Mehmet II, who was laid to rest in 1451 in the garden of his imperial mosque complex, the Muradiye. Murat had died at Edirne, the second Ottoman capital, but he had written in his will that he wanted to be buried in Bursa:

> Bury me in Bursa near my son Alaettin. Do not raise a sumptuous mausoleum above my grave . . . but bury me directly in the ground. May the rain, sign of the benediction of God, fall on me . . . If I do not die in Bursa, transfer my remains there; see that they arrive on a Thursday in order that they be interred on a Friday.

Despite his wishes, Murat was buried in a large mausoleum, though the crown of the dome was left open so that the rain could fall on his tomb, an earth-filled catafalque above the actual grave. During the century after Murat's death another dozen tombs were erected in the Muradiye, the last resting places of Ottoman princes and princesses, along with the wives, concubines and slave girls of various sultans, all of them buried in the garden behind the mosque and its associated *medrese,* or theological school.

The funerary monument that I had particularly come to see was the domed octagonal tomb just to the south-west of the Muradiye's *medrese.* Among those interred there were two sons of Mehmet II, the princes Mustafa and Jem, the first of whom had died in 1474 and the second in 1495, as noted in the signs at the head of their earth-filled, marble catafalques, built to the same design as that of their grandfather Murat. Theirs is the most richly decorated of the tombs at the Muradiye, revetted in late-fifteenth-century ceramics, dark blue with a delicate overglaze of floral designs in gold, the dome decorated with a firmament of star-shaped tiles to represent the heavens in which the deceased now presumably dwell.

But it was not the tiles that had drawn me here, beautiful though they were, but rather the grave of Prince Jem himself, for in all my years of study of Ottoman history I had found him to be the most fascinating character in the whole imperial line. So do most Turks, who still refer to him as 'Jem Sultan', though he ruled for just twenty days. For over five centuries the story of Jem's life, romantic enough in itself, has been embellished by fabulous legend and folklore. In France, for instance, where Jem spent much of his exile, local traditions of his adventures and love affairs have inspired poems and novels, as well as a museum devoted to his memory. In Turkey, as the immortal Jem Sultan, he is the heroic prince and gifted poet who died before his time, the symbol of what might have been had he and not his brother Beyazit succeeded to the throne.

Despite all this Jem is virtually unknown in the English-speaking world, where, aside from short sections in historical works, little has been written about him. The primary source that tells us most about Jem's life remains the *Tacü-i-tevarih* of Sadüddin, a history of the Ottoman Empire down to 1520. Sadüddin drew his information from the *Vakiat-i-Sultan Cem*, a biography of Jem written by one of his faithful companions. The author preferred to remain anonymous, saying that his motive was to tell the true story of his master so that Jem's memory would be cherished and prayers would be recited for his soul, but it is thought that the author was Jem's secretary, the poet Haydar Bey, who remained with him throughout his exile and brought his possessions back to Turkey after his death.

The first comprehensive work on Jem to appear in a Western language was L. Thuasne's *Djem Sultan* (1892) which used a French translation of Sadüddin together with contemporary Western sources. Ismail Hikmet Ertaylan's *Sultan Cem* (1951), the most important modern Turkish book on Jem, is based on contemporary Ottoman sources as well as an important collection of documents preserved in the archives of the old imperial palace, Topkapı Sarayı. And the most authoritative recent work to appear has been Nicolas Vatin's *Sultan Djem* (1997), which includes French translations of both the *Vakiat* and the contemporary account of Jem's stay on Rhodes with the Knights of St John by the knight, Guillaume Caoursin. Many of the myths associated with 'Jem Sultan' are told in full by the seventeenth-century Turkish chronicler Evliya Çelebi, whose *Seyahatname,* or *Narrative of Travels,* is a fabulous description of the Ottoman Empire in the days of its glory.

However, all that I had read in my research, principally in French and Turkish, indicated that Western observers of Jem were looking at him through somewhat different lenses from those of scholars from the East, the perspectives on both sides subtly coloured, and sometimes distorted, by the cultural background of its author. Having spent much of my life straddling the continental divide in Istanbul, where Europe meets Asia, I hoped that I might be able to tell the story of Jem with far less cultural bias. But throughout I found myself reluctant to cast aside the layers of legend that had accumulated around Jem, for these myths have become part of his persona, even in my own mind, as well as in those of others who have fallen under his spell.

My travels in search of Jem took me through Turkey – where in Istanbul I discovered the existence of a talismanic gown made for the young prince and of a man who claimed to be one of Jem's descendants – and on through the Middle East to Cairo, across the Mediterranean to Rhodes, France and Italy, studying archives and looking for traces of his presence in the various fortresses, castles, chateaux and palaces where he had been imprisoned. The trail at its end inevitably led me back to Bursa, completing my quest where it began half a lifetime before, at Jem Sultan's tomb in the garden of the Muradiye.

But even when I finished my writing and research I knew that the tale would have no end, for Jem Sultan has crossed the border that separates history from myth, a tragic hero whose story will continue to capture the imagination of romantics, adding new aspects and dimensions to this epic of a captive Turkish prince in Renaissance Europe.

And so here is the story of Jem Sultan, looking back at him through the night of fading memory and the gathering mist of legends.

1

The Grand Turk

O<small>N</small> 29 J<small>UNE</small> 1453 a fast galley from Corfu arrived in Venice, bringing a letter to Doge Francesco Foscari from the Venetian *bailo,* governor of the Ionian Islands. The *bailo* reported that on 29 May of that year the Ottoman Turks had captured Constantinople, capital of the Byzantine Empire, the Christian continuation of the Roman Empire in the East. According to the *bailo,* the last Byzantine emperor, Constantine XI Palaeologus, had died in the final hour of the battle, when the Turks had broken through the city walls which had withstood invaders for more than a thousand years. The ancient imperial city had been sacked and was now firmly in the hands of Sultan Mehmet II, known to the West, like his ancestors before him, as the Grand Turk.

The following day the doge wrote to Pope Nicholas V in Rome, informing him of the 'horrible and most deplorable fall' of Constantinople. The pope received the letter a week later, by which time word of the fall of Constantinople had spread throughout Italy and on into northern Europe; church bells tolled mournfully, echoing the universal lamentation. Marino Sanudo, the Venetian diarist, later wrote of how 'The news of the loss of Constantinople caused a great terror among Christians.' The pope called the

catastrophe the 'shame of Christendom', since the rulers of
Europe, preoccupied by their own internecine struggles, had done
little to help their fellow Christians at Constantinople in their
final struggle against the Turks.

Cardinal Bessarion, a Greek who had left Constantinople for
Rome fifteen years before the fall of Byzantium, described, in a
letter to the doge, what he called the 'barbarism' of the Turkish
conquerors:

> A city which was so flourishing . . . the splendour and glory
> of the East . . . the refuge of all good things, has been
> captured, despoiled, ravaged and completely sacked by the
> most inhuman barbarians . . . by the fiercest of wild beasts
> . . . Much danger threatens Italy, not to mention other lands,
> if the violent assaults of the most ferocious barbarians are
> not checked.

ॐ

The conqueror of Constantinople, Mehmet II, the seventh sultan
of the Osmanlı dynasty, stood at the head of the great House of
Osman. The Ottomans were descended from Osman Gazi who
ruled over a small principality in Bithynia, the north-westernmost
region of Anatolia, the subcontinent better known in the West as
Asia Minor, in the early fourteenth century. A Gazi, or 'Warrior
for the Faith', was, in the words of the fourteenth-century Turkish
chronicler-poet Ahmedi,

> the instrument of the religion of Allah, a servant of God
> who purifies the earth from the filth of polytheism . . . the
> Gazi is the sword of God, he is the protector and the refuge

of the believers. If he becomes a martyr in the ways of God, do not believe that he has died; he lives in beatitude with Allah, he has eternal life.

The Osmanlı were Turks from central Asia who had settled in Bithynia as vassals of the Seljuk Turks. After defeating the Byzantines at the battle of Manzikirt in 1071 the Seljuks overran Asia Minor, ultimately founding the Sultanate of Rum with its capital at Konya. When the Seljuks were defeated by the Mongols in 1242, their sultanate was replaced by a number of independent Türkmen emirates. The most powerful of these were the Karamanid, who by 1300 had established themselves in the old Seljuk capital at Konya, creating a principality known to the Turks as Karaman and in the West as Karamania. The Osmanlı were the least of the emirates, but they had the great advantage of bordering on the Byzantine Empire, which was by then in the final throes of decline, comprising little more than north-western Asia Minor and the southern Balkans.

Osman Gazi expanded his little realm westward by raiding the Bithynian possessions of the Byzantines. Originally he would have been a *bey*, or lord, but as his territory expanded he would have been considered an emir. Osman's son and successor, Orhan Gazi, captured the Bithynian city of Prusa, Turkish Bursa, in 1326. Bursa became the first Ottoman capital, and Orhan used it as a base to conquer the rest of Bithynia and cross the Dardanelles into Thrace, the south-easternmost region of Europe. Orhan's son and successor, Murat I, began his reign in 1352 with the capture of the Thracian city of Adrianople, Turkish Edirne, which then replaced Bursa as the Ottoman capital. (Murat was also the first Osmanlı ruler to take the title of sultan, though Osman Gazi and Orhan Gazi are generally listed first and second in the line of Ottoman sultans.)

As the Osmanlı armies marched across Asia Minor and Europe they attracted new recruits, both Christian and Muslim, lured by the prospect of plunder from the Turks' many victories. During the fourteenth century the Ottomans penetrated deep into the Balkans, while at the same time expanding eastwards, conquering the Germiyan emirate in western Anatolia and continuing eastward to take part of Karamania. By the century's end Christendom's leaders, desperate to stop the Ottoman advance, organized two crusades against the 'Infidel Turk'. Both of these expeditions were crushed: the first by Murat I at Kosova in 1389, the second by Beyazit I at Nicopolis in 1396.

In 1402 the Ottoman Empire was almost destroyed when its forces were defeated by the Mongol conqueror Tamerlane and Beyazit I was killed at the battle of Ankara. A war of succession between the sultan's four surviving sons ensued, with the youngest, Mehmet I, emerging as the sole survivor in 1413. Mehmet ruled until his death in 1421, when he was succeeded by his son Murat II, who soon afterwards resumed the Ottoman push through Europe.

It was recognized, especially in the courts of Europe, that Murat II's military successes were due in no small part to the new elite corps, the Janissaries. The corps, which would form the nucleus of Ottoman armies, had a reputation for brutality that made it the terror of Christendom. This was despite the fact that every Janissary had been born a Christian. The corps comprised Christian youths whom it conscripted in a periodic levy known as the *devşirme*; they were then converted to Islam and trained to take their place in the Ottoman military. Each Janissary company had its own *kazan*, or bronze cauldron, from which they ate their meals and which they carried into battle as their

4

standard, guarding it as European soldiers would their regimental colours. They were instantly recognizable by their distinctive headdress, with a long white fold down the back, known as the 'sleeve of Hacı Bektaş', after the founder of the Bektaşi order of dervishes to which they all belonged. Like their Bektaşi brothers, the Janissaries were free-thinking, free-drinking and free-spirited and they lived as hard as they fought. Until the eighteenth century Janissaries were forbidden to marry as they were slaves of the sultan and owed their loyalty to him and him alone, but their frequent insurrections often made them a threat to the sultan they served and they often had to be pacified with bribes.

Many Janissaries rose to the highest positions in the Ottoman service, including that of grand vezir, or first minister, an office created by Murat I. The grand vezir held the title of pasha, another innovation of Murat I. Later the commanders of the army and navy were awarded the rank of pasha, as were the military governors of the European and Asian provinces, who were also given the title of *beylerbey,* a '*bey* who rules over *beys*'. The chief of the Janissaries was made an *ağa,* a rank that was later given to the Chief Black Eunuch and the Chief White Eunuch, the first of whom was in charge of the sultan's harem and the second the supervisor of the *selamlık,* the male quarter of the imperial palace. Christian captives were used here also, as concubines, since under Islamic law it was forbidden to enslave a Muslim. The sultan was restricted to four wives, although he could have as many concubines as he pleased.

During the early years of the Ottoman Empire the sultans contracted dynastic marriages with the Türkmen emirs as well as with Christian rulers, the most notable example of the latter being when Murat I married a daughter of the Byzantine emperor

John V Cantacuzenos. John had formed an alliance with Murat in the course of a civil war in Byzantium, a fatal mistake, since it gave the Turks their first opportunity to cross into Europe and establish a foothold there. Later, after the Ottomans had absorbed all of the Türkman emirates, the sultan's wives were chosen almost exclusively from Christian slave girls, and thenceforth there are very few known cases of Muslim women in the imperial harem. The highest-ranking of the sultan's wives was normally the mother of the sultan's first-born son, although she might be supplanted by a *haseki,* or favourite. The hierarchy of women in the harem was headed by the queen mother, known as the *valide sultan,* who in some cases became the power behind the throne.

૨૦૧

Early in Murat II's reign he ordered a new palace to be built in Edirne called Edirne Sarayı. And it was here, on 30 March 1432, that his third son, the future Mehmet II, was born. The sultan's first son, Ahmet, had died in infancy, and his second son, Alaettin Ali, had been murdered in 1443: both children were buried by their father at the Muradiye in Bursa, leaving Mehmet as sole heir to the throne.

At the age of five Mehmet was sent off to be provincial governor of Anatolia, first in Amasya and then in Manisa. In 1444, at the age of twelve, he was recalled to Edirne by his father to help him face a serious threat to the empire. Pope Eugenius IV had called for a new crusade against the Turks, announcing that 'by the inspiration of God, we intend to prepare a fleet and a land force . . . to snatch the Catholic flock from the yoke of miserable servitude'. A large Christian army mustered at Buda under the Hungarian nobleman John Hunyadi, who led them southwards into the Balkans. Murat marched his army north to meet the crusaders, leaving young Mehmet in charge of the capital at Edirne. Murat's army virtually annihilated the crusaders at the battle of Varna on 10 November 1444, with Hunyadi being one of the few Christians to escape with his life.

After his victory Murat returned to Edirne. Soon afterwards he astonished the court by announcing that he intended to abdicate in favour of his son, who on 1 December 1444 succeeded to the throne as Mehmet II. Murat, who was only forty at the time, then went off to his place of retirement in Manisa, leaving Mehmet, who was not yet thirteen, to rule the empire, with Halil Pasha as his grand vezir.

During the months that followed, Halil Pasha sent repeated messages pleading with Murat to return, insisting that Mehmet was too young and immature to rule. By September 1446 Murat, yielding to his loyal grand vezir's requests, ended his retirement and returned to Edirne. Halil Pasha persuaded Mehmet to abdicate in favour of his father, and Mehmet was sent back to Manisa.

Meanwhile, John Hunyadi had been organizing a second crusade, and in September 1448 he led his army across the Danube. Murat summoned Mehmet to join him in Edirne and mustered his army to confront the crusaders. The two armies met on 23 October of that year at Kosova, on the same field where Murat I had defeated the Serbs in 1389. The second battle of Kosova had the same outcome as the first: the Turks routed the Christians in a three-day battle in which Mehmet received his baptism of fire, as he led the Anatolian troops on the right flank of his father's

army. Once again Hunyadi escaped with his life, living on to fight
against the Turks for a further eight years.

Young Mehmet became a father for the first time at the age
of fifteen when, in January 1448, his concubine Gülbahar
(meaning 'the Rose of Spring') gave birth to a son, the future
Beyazit II. In 1450 another of Mehmet's concubines, Gülşah, gave
birth to his second son, Mustafa. Later that same year Sultan
Murat had a third son by the princess Halime Hatun, daughter
of the emir Ibrahim II, ruler of the Çandarıd Türkmen tribe in
Anatolia. The boy was named Ahmet, but nicknamed Küçük, or
Little, to distinguish him from Murat's first son who had died in
infancy.

On 3 February 1451 Sultan Murat died suddenly in Edirne
Sarayı, stricken by apoplexy after a long bout of drinking. Halil
Pasha kept his death secret in order to allow Mehmet enough
time to travel from Manisa to Edirne to claim the throne. He
arrived fifteen days after his father's death and was acclaimed by
the army as sultan, one month before his nineteenth birthday.

Mehmet kept Halil Pasha as his grand vezir, although he loathed
his father's old advisor, who he felt had sabotaged his first attempt
to rule as sultan. He also retained another of his father's old
vezirs, Ishak Pasha, whom he appointed as *beylerbey* of Anatolia,
ordering him to conduct his father's remains to Bursa for burial
in the Muradiye.

Succession issues had long plagued the Ottoman dynasty, the
most devastating instance being the civil war that ensued after
the death of Beyazit I. Mehmet decided to nip any potential threat
in the bud, and went straight to the harem of Edirne Sarayı,
where his concubines and children and those of his deceased
father both resided. Here he ordered the execution of Küçük

('Little') Ahmet, the son of Halime Hatun, the highest ranking of his father's four wives. Mehmet justified the murder of his half brother in terms of the Ottoman code of fratricide, used in similar circumstances by his forefathers. Appropriate verses of the Kuran were quoted, such as: 'The execution of a prince is preferable to the loss of a province,' and 'Death is better than disquiet.' Mehmet later had the code enacted into law, as stated in his imperial edict: 'Whichever of my sons inherits the sultan's throne, it behooves him to kill his brothers in the interest of the world order. Most of the jurists have approved this procedure. Let action be taken accordingly.'

Later that same summer Mehmet would have Halil Pasha arrested on a charge of treason. The elderly grand vezir was tortured for forty days and finally executed. Ishak Pasha took over Halil Bey's duties as head of the government for the following year, when the sultan appointed Mahmut Pasha as grand vezir. Mahmut Pasha was of noble Greek and Serbian lineage, and having been captured by the Turks as a youth, had become a Muslim and joined the Ottoman service.

Soon after establishing himself at Edirne Mehmet began preparations to attack Constantinople, which had been bypassed during the main Ottoman advance into Europe due to the difficulty in breaching the city's walls. After a seven-week siege Constantinople fell to Mehmet's forces and the sultan entered the city in triumph on 29 May 1453, two months after his twenty-first birthday. Thenceforth Mehmet II was known as 'Fatih', or the Conqueror, and the name of the city he had taken became Istanbul, a Turkish corruption of the Greek '*eis stin poli*', meaning 'in (or to) the city'. Fatih then gave his soldiers permission to sack the city for three days, as was the Muslim custom for places that were taken by storm. However he ordered his troops to stop before the first day had finished, after seeing the death and destruction that had already been visited upon the imperial city. Kritovoulos of Imbros, Fatih's Greek biographer, writes that,

> When he saw what a large number had been killed, and the wreckage of the buildings, and the wholesale ruin and desolation of the City, he was filled with compassion and repented not a little at the destruction and plundering. Tears fell from his eyes as he groaned deeply and passionately: 'What a city have we given over to plunder and destruction!'

Istanbul would be the Ottoman Empire's new capital and Fatih appointed Karıştıran Süleyman Bey to oversee the work of restoring and resettling the city. One of Fatih's first instructions was that Haghia Sophia, the Church of the Divine Wisdom, should be converted into a mosque, and the first Islamic service was held here on Friday, 1 June 1453.

In the weeks that followed Fatih received a succession of visitors at Edirne Sarayı, from Venetians, Serbs, Albanians, Greeks, Egyptians, Persians to the Karamanid Türkmen, all of them seeking to establish friendly relations with the young conqueror. One of the Venetian emissaries, Giacomo Languschi, recorded his impressions of Fatih (overestimating the sultan's age by five years):

> The sovereign, the Grand Turk Mehmet Bey, is a youth of twenty-six, well built, of large rather than medium stature, expert at arms, of aspect more frightening than venerable, laughing seldom, full of circumspection, endowed with great

generosity, obstinate in pursuing his aims, bold in all under-
takings, as eager for fame as Alexander of Macedonia.

When he heard of the fall of Constantinople Frederick III, the
Holy Roman Emperor, is said to have broken down in tears and
shut himself away in his quarters for several days of prayer and
meditation. When he re-emerged his advisor, Bishop Aeneas Silvio
Piccolomini (the future Pope Pius II), convinced him that he
should take direct action and lead a holy war against the Turks.
Piccolomini wrote to Pope Nicholas V with this same proposition
on 12 July 1453, pointing out the terrible threat posed by the
Grand Turk: 'Already Mehmed rules among us ... Already the
sword of the Turks hovers over our heads; already the Black Sea
is closed to us; already Wallachia is in the hands of the Turks.
Thence they will invade Hungary and then Germany.' Pointing
out the shameful disunity of Europe, he urged Nicholas to lead
Christendom in a crusade:

> Meanwhile we live in discord and enmity. The Kings of
> England and France have taken up arms against each other.
> Seldom is all Spain at peace and the Italian states can never
> find peace in their struggle for hegemony. How much better
> would it be if we were to turn our weapons against the
> enemies of our faith! I can think of nothing that might be
> more to Your Holiness's desire, Holy Father.

Frederick also wrote to the pope in this regard, promising to rally
all the princes of the empire and lead them against the enemies
of the 'cross of salvation'. Inspired, Nicholas issued a bull calling

for a crusade against the Grand Turk. His encyclical, dated 30 September 1453, referred to Mehmet as the 'son of Satan, perdition and death', and described the sultan as the forerunner of the Antichrist, comparing him to the red dragon of the Apocalypse, a monster having seven heads with seven diadems and ten horns.

The pope's appeal was answered with particular enthusiasm by Philip III 'The Good', Duke of Burgundy, whose father, John of Nevers, had been one of the leaders of the crusade defeated by Beyazit I at Nicopolis in 1389. Philip himself had contributed four ships to a fleet that had been organized in response to the crusade called for in 1444 by Pope Eugenius IV, but which had been defeated by Murat II at Varna. At Lille in February 1454 Philip held a spectacular feast, 'Le Banquet du Faisan', to excite enthusiasm for the crusade among the nobility of Burgundy. At the end of the feast a live pheasant, the symbol of knightly virtue, was brought into the banqueting hall and Philip took an oath on the bird that he would embark upon a crusade if at least one other ruler would take the cross. More than two hundred Burgundian noblemen pledged that they would accompany the duke, and Philip set to work organizing his contingent of the crusade. However, when the other Christian princes failed to agree on a programme of joint military action against the Turks, and when Pope Eugenius died on 24 March 1455, the proposed crusade was abandoned.

Fatih had now moved the headquarters of his government from Edirne to Istanbul, which had been rebuilt and repopulated to

befit its role as the capital of a Muslim empire. The city had been
founded as the Greek colony of Byzantium in around 660 BC on
the European shore at the southern end of the Bosphorus, the
strait that separates Europe from Asia between the Black Sea and
the Sea of Marmara. Constantine the Great made it capital of the
Roman Empire in AD 330, renaming it Constantinople. Then in
447 Theodosius II enclosed it with the great defence wall whose
magnificent ruins still stand today, extending along the landward
side of the city between the Marmara and the Golden Horn, the
scimitar-shaped estuary that joins the Bosphorus at the southern
end of the strait. The Theodosian walls enclosed seven hills, the
first of which was crowned by Haghia Sophia, at the confluence
of the Bosphorus and the Golden Horn, where their waters meet
and flow together into the Marmara, enveloping the city in what
the Byzantine historian Procopius called 'a garland of waters'.

Among the new buildings that Fatih erected was an enormous
mosque complex known as Fatih Camii, the 'Mosque of the
Conqueror', which he built atop the Fourth Hill on the ruins of
the church of the Holy Apostles. He also began construction of
an imperial residence in the centre of Istanbul, on the Third Hill,
which came to be known as Eski Saray, the Old Palace, for later
Fatih would erect a further palace called Topkapı Sarayı on the
First Hill, at the confluence of the Bosphorus and the Golden
Horn.

Fatih still spent part of every year at the old palace of Edirne
Sarayı, for Edirne was the mustering place for the campaigns that
he mounted almost every summer into the Balkans. From Edirne
in 1456 he invaded Serbia and put Belgrade under siege, but he
was defeated by John Hunyadi and forced to withdraw. This was
the first reverse in Fatih's meteoric career, with 24,000 of his

troops killed and he himself wounded in the thigh by a javelin. The news that Belgrade had been saved gave rise to jubilation throughout Western Europe, the new pope, Callistus II, calling it 'the happiest event of my life'. Talk followed of organizing another crusade against the Turks, but after John Hunyadi died a month later from the plague all thoughts of a crusade were shelved.

After his withdrawal from Belgrade Fatih marched his army back to Edirne, where he remained for a year. The following year he sent messengers throughout the empire and Christian Europe to announce the celebration of the circumcision of his two sons, Beyazit and Mustafa (the invited guests included the Doge of Venice, Francesco Foscari, who sent his regrets, probably because it would have seemed inappropriate for the head of a Christian state to be attending such an event).

The circumcision festival is described by the chronicler Aşıkpaşazade, who wrote that for four days there were continuous festivities at Edirne Sarayı and in the countryside around. The festivities included wrestling matches and other athletic events, performances of Turkish folk dances, music and competitions in poetry, the latter being among the wandering minstrels known as Aşıklar, or 'lovers', who perform in the villages of Turkey to this day, singing their love songs to the accompaniment of the stringed instrument known as the *saz*. Throughout the celebration Mehmet was said to have remained in the highest of spirits, showing no sign that he had suffered a serious military defeat less than a year before.

After the festivities both princes returned to their posts as provincial governors, Beyazit in Amasya and Mustafa in Manisa, to which they had been appointed earlier in 1457. Beyazit was then nine and Mustafa only seven, so they were accompanied by their mothers as well as by advisors and *lalas*, or tutors, just as Fatih had been when he had been sent off at the age of five to serve as governor in Amasya. The young princes were instructed in literature, history, geography and science, their books including works in Turkish, Persian and Arabic. Young Beyazit took great interest in his studies, taking particularly to contemplative philosophy, to the extent that he came to be known as Sufi, or the Mystic.

Fatih returned to action in 1458, mounting campaigns that in the following year resulted in the conquest of Serbia and southern Greece, including Athens. After the capture of Athens he went to see the ruined monuments of the ancient city, for his own childhood studies had imbued him with a deep reverence for classical culture, leading Kritovoulos to call him a 'Philhellene'. Three years later Fatih visited the site of ancient Troy on the Asian shore of the Dardanelles, which he knew from his reading of Homer. Kritovoulos writes that Fatih's conquest of Byzantium made the sultan feel that he had evened the score with the Hellenes for their victory over the 'Asiatics' at Troy, and that he only regretted that he did not have a poet like Homer to immortalize his heroic exploits.

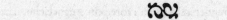

Eski Saray, the palace on the Third Hill of Istanbul, was completed in 1458, but Fatih continued to spend much of his time in Edirne Sarayı. One of his concubines, a girl named Çiçek, or Flower, possibly a Serbian princess, gave birth there to Fatih's third son on 22 December 1459. The boy, celebrated as the first of the Osmanlı line to be born after the conquest of Constantinople, was named Jem (written in modern Turkish as 'Cem'). Jem was the first and only son to be sired by Fatih after he became sultan. Thus Jem could claim that he was *porphyrogenitus*, or 'born in the purple', the term that had been used in referring to the Byzantine crown princes who were born in the Great Palace of Constantinople. Fatih was not pleased to have sired another son because of the dynastic complications this might cause, and palace tradition claims that he kicked the baby's cradle in anger causing Jem to fall and hit his head, an injury that may have caused the squint that is remarked upon in some descriptions of the prince.

Early in the spring of 1460 Fatih mounted a major campaign into the Morea, or Peloponnesus, where Thomas and Demetrius Palaeologus, the two surviving brothers of the late Emperor Constantine, were still ruling as despots. Demetrius surrendered to Fatih at Mistra, his capital, on 29 May 1460, seven years to the day after the fall of Constantinople, while Thomas fled to Italy, dying in Rome in 1465. Demetrius accompanied Fatih back to Edirne and was allowed to settle on an estate in Thrace, where he died in 1470. By that time the only other surviving fragment of Byzantium had vanished with the fall of Trebizond, the capital of the empire of the Comneni dynasty on the Black Sea coast of Anatolia, which surrendered to Fatih's forces in August 1461. The last emperor of Trebizond, David Comnenus, was imprisoned in Edirne, where Fatih had him executed on 1 November 1463.

Meanwhile Fatih's campaigns had led to the Ottoman conquest of Wallachia, Bosnia and Herzegovina, as well as the Aegean isle of Lesbos. Fatih's campaigns in Greece and Albania had resulted in the capture of a number of Venetian fortresses and colonies, which led Venice to declare war on the Ottomans, a decision taken on 28 July 1463 by the Signoria, or Council of State. The Venetians counterattacked in the Peloponnesus, and that autumn they established an alliance with King Mathias Corvinus of Hungary, son of the late John Hunyadi, who invaded Bosnia and captured two Ottoman-held fortresses. The news of this victory reached Venice at a time when the Signoria was making plans to attack the Ottomans on a third front, in Anatolia, by establishing an alliance with Ibrahim Bey, the emir of Karaman, as well as with Uzun Hasan, chieftain of the Akkoyunlu, a powerful Türkmen tribe in eastern Anatolia.

The Venetians sought to broaden their anti-Turkish coalition by exploiting the crusading enthusiasm of the new pope Pius II, the former Bishop Piccolomini. The pope summoned the college of cardinals to call for a crusade, praising the Venetians, 'who alone keep watch, who alone labour, who alone come to the aid of the Christians. They alone prepare to take vengeance on the enemy of Christ.'

Pius announced that he would lead the crusade himself, and he set out for Ancona, where he had outfitted and manned five galleys at his own expense. He arrived in Ancona on 30 July 1464, but died fifteen days later while awaiting reinforcements from Venice; he would be succeeded by the Venetian Paul II. The crusade was abandoned, but the Venetians and Hungarians fought on, aided in Anatolia by the Akkoyunlu and the Karamanid, the latter now ruled by the emir Ishak, son and successor of Ibrahim Bey. That same summer Fatih defeated the Karamanid and killed Ishak. Ishak was replaced as emir of Karamania by his brother Pir Ahmet, who surrendered to Fatih and became his vassal.

Fatih's next major campaign began in the spring of 1466, when he left Edirne at the head of a huge army to attack the Albanian chieftain Skanderbeg. After a hard-fought campaign that lasted for two years Fatih defeated Skanderbeg and conquered all of Albania except for five Venetian enclaves. Skanderbeg died the following year, taking with him to the grave the last hopes of an independent Albania, which remained under Ottoman control for the next four and a half centuries.

In 1468 Fatih turned his attention eastward, mounting a campaign intended to attack the Mamluks of Egypt, whose territory at that time extended as far north as Syria and south-eastern Anatolia. His move was prompted by the instability of the Mamluk regime, for that past winter there had been two successive usurpations, the last of which brought to power Kaitbey, who was to rule as sultan until 1496. Pir Ahmet was supposed to join the expedition as an Ottoman vassal, but he reneged and so Fatih attacked the Karamanid Türkmen instead of proceeding against the Mamluks. By the end of the campaign the Ottoman army had captured most of the Karamanid territory north of the Taurus range. Fatih assigned his son Mustafa to govern Karamania from the provincial capital at Konya, after which he returned to Istanbul with his army.

Jem, meanwhile, was sent to be provincial governor of Kastamonu, in northern Anatolia. Because he was only eight Jem was accompanied by his mother, Çiçek, and his two *lalas*, Kara Süleyman and Nasuh Bey. According to Jem's contemporary biographer Sadüddin, Fatih ordered the *lalas* to school Jem in the 'science of common men', and to teach him literature, history and science as well as Persian and Arabic.

Three years later Jem was brought back to Istanbul temporarily for his circumcision. The two eldest sons of Beyazit, Abdullah and Şahinşah, were circumcised at the same time as Jem, in a ceremony that is mentioned in passing by only one of the Ottoman chroniclers. Fatih's failure to put on lavish celebrations for the coming of age of his son and two grandsons seems to have been due to his preoccupation with his military campaign in Karamania. The previous year he had besieged the great Venetian fortress at Negroponte on the Greek island of Euboea, which surrendered to the Turks on 14 July 1470. The Karamanid emir Pir Ahmet had taken advantage of Fatih's absence in Greece to reoccupy some of the territory taken from him by the Ottomans two years earlier, and at the same time his brother Kasim Bey attacked the Turkish forces in Ankara. Thus, as soon as Fatih captured Negroponte he set out to take action against Pir Ahmet and Kasim Bey, whom he defeated later in the summer of 1470, forcing both of them to flee and take refuge in Azerbaijan with the Akkoyunlu chieftain Uzun Hasan.

By 1471 Paul II died and was succeeded by Pope Sixtus IV. Sixtus, a member of the powerful della Rovere family, filled all of the administrative posts in the papal hierarchy with members of his family, provoking a war with the Medicis of Florence. The war spread through the papal states, disrupting the unity of Christendom at the same time that the new pope was calling for a crusade against the Turks, whose capture of Negroponte he saw as the beginning of a new Ottoman offensive against the West.

Jem was called back to Istanbul in February 1472 to serve as regent for Fatih, whilst he and his sons Beyazit and Mustafa left for campaigns against Uzun Hasan. During the following winter forty days passed during which no news of the Ottoman expedition reached Istanbul. It was rumoured that Fatih had been killed and his army destroyed. After being persuaded by his advisors Jem declared himself sultan. But then news came that Fatih had been victorious over Uzun Hasan and he and his sons were all alive. Jem was terrified of his father's wrath, and fled, though needlessly, for when Fatih returned to Istanbul he forgave his son, probably because he saw in him something of the impetuosity that he himself had often exhibited in his youth.

Jem returned to Kastamonu as provincial governor in 1473, while his brothers also resumed their posts, Beyazit in Amasya and Mustafa in Konya. That winter Mustafa became seriously ill, and Fatih sent his Jewish physician Maestro Iacopo to try to save him, but the prince passed away in June 1474. Fatih was heartbroken by the death of his beloved son, whom he buried in the Muradiye at Bursa. He then had his grand vezir Mahmut Pasha executed, unjustly blaming him for Mustafa's death, and appointed Gedik Ahmet Pasha to replace him. Jem was transferred to Konya to replace his deceased brother as provincial governor of Karamania.

During the next few years Fatih's empire grew apace: in 1475 Gedik Ahmet Pasha captured the Genoese colony of Caffa in the Crimea. Then in 1476 Fatih himself led an expedition into Moldavia, while he ordered the army under Bali Pasha to invade Hungary, both campaigns ending victoriously for the Ottomans. Later that same year Fatih sent a raiding party into Friuli, at the northern end of the Adriatic. The Turks headed south, pillaging and burning everything in their path until they were stopped within sight of Venice, the fire and smoke of burning villages clearly visible to observers atop the campanile of San Marco. According to the chronicler Tommaso Malipiero, the Venetian nobleman Celso Maffei cried out in despair to Doge Andrea Vendramin: 'The enemy is at our gates! The axe is at the root.

Unless divine help comes, the doom of the Christian name is sealed.'

Early in 1478 Fatih launched an expedition against the Venetian fortress at Shkoder in Albania. Gedik Ahmet Pasha had advised against this, feeling that the fortress was invincible, and so Fatih dismissed and imprisoned him, appointing Karamanı Mehmet Pasha as his new grand vezir. Gedik Ahmet's assessment proved to be right, for the Ottomans lost 12,000 of their best men trying to capture Shkoder; they were forced to break off their siege and move their attack to other Venetian fortresses in Albania. Fatih subsequently freed Gedik Ahmet and appointed him admiral of the Ottoman fleet, though he retained Karamanı Mehmet as grand vezir.

Meanwhile the Venetian doge received reports that the sultan was preparing to send a large army to invade Italy through Friuli. Thus on 4 January 1479 the Senate met and decided to send an envoy, Giovanni Dario, to Istanbul to seek peace with the Turks. On 25 February word reached Venice that Fatih had agreed to the terms offered by Dario, in which the Venetians surrendered to the Turks almost all of their territory in Albania and the Greek mainland. In April, Lutfi Bey was sent as envoy to Venice to ratify the treaty. His party was greeted at the Bacino by forty Venetian noblemen in gilded gondolas, with the doge and the *collegio* looking on from the windows of the hall of the Great Council in the Palazzo Ducale. Weeks later, on St Mark's Day, Lutfi Bey took an oath confirming the treaty, after which the doge swore that he would abide by the terms agreed upon, ending sixteen years of war between the Serene Republic of Venice and the Ottoman Empire.

Fatih had triumphed in both Europe and Asia. He decided not

to go off on campaign during 1478–79, the twenty-fifth anniversary of his conquest of Constantinople, preferring instead to take his ease in his newly completed palace of Topkapı Sarayı, secure on his throne and with all of Europe living in terror of the Grand Turk's next move.

2

Death of the Conqueror

During the summer of 1479 Fatih sent a fleet under
Gedik Ahmet Pasha into the Ionian Islands, the archipelago
between Greece and Italy that had long been part of the Venetian
maritime empire. Despite the peace treaty between Venice and
the Ottomans, Gedik Ahmet went on to take Cephalonia, Ithaka
and Zante, completing his campaign with the destruction of a
Venetian fortress in Epirus. Next he mounted an expedition into
the Black Sea to attack Georgia and other areas of the Caucasus,
while other Ottoman forces raided Hungary and Transylvania.

The following year the Conqueror launched an expedition that
he had been contemplating for a quarter of a century: the invasion
of Rhodes. Rhodes was the headquarters of the Knights Hospitallers of St John, who had been blocking Ottoman expansion
through the Mediterranean, from their formidable fortress on the
northern tip of the island, just opposite the south-westernmost
promontory of Asia Minor. After his conquest of Constantinople
in 1453 Fatih had demanded tribute from the Knights of Rhodes,
but they had refused. Fatih responded by sending an expedition
to attack the island under the command of Admiral Hamza Bey.
But the invasion was repulsed and Hamza Bey was forced to

report to his sultan that the fortress of the knights could not be taken without a major expedition. Fatih knew that he would have to bide his time before being able to open up the Mediterranean. Now, after two decades of almost ceaseless Ottoman expansion, the time was ripe.

സെ

The Order of the Knights Hospitallers of St John was founded in the eleventh century in Jerusalem to operate hospitals and hospices for pilgrims who came to visit the Holy Land, but it also sent men to fight in the crusades against the warriors of Islam. Their emblem, the white cross of St John on a red field, contrasted with the red cross on white of the Knights Templars and the black cross on white of the Teutonic Knights, both of the latter two being purely military orders. The Knights of St John moved headquarters frequently during the Middle Ages: from Jerusalem to Lebanon in 1188, to Palestine in 1191, to Cyprus in 1291. Finally, after taking the island from the Byzantines in 1309, they established their headquarters on Rhodes. The knights captured and fortified several other islands of the Dodecanese, and later built a fortress on the south-western coast of Asia Minor at Halicarnassus, Turkish Bodrum. During the next century and a half the Knights of Rhodes would battle against the Ottoman Turks and the Mamluks on both sea and land, sometimes alone and sometimes in coalition with other Christian armies, such as the time they suffered defeat at the hands of Murat I at Nicopolis in 1396.

The grand master of the Knights of St John was Pierre

d'Aubusson, a French knight who had been fighting against the Turks for a quarter of a century. At the time of his election as grand master, on 17 June 1476, he had been given dictatorial powers to prepare the defences of Rhodes against what was seen as the inevitable Turkish attack. Two years later the knights received word that Fatih was preparing an expedition against Rhodes. In anticipation, on 28 October 1478, d'Aubusson signed a peace treaty with the Mamluk sultan Kaitbey, who had no desire to see the Ottomans established on Rhodes. Then, to gain time, d'Aubusson entered into negotiations with Fatih, who was only too pleased to do so, since he needed months to fully prepare his army and navy.

Normally such negotiations would have been conducted by the sultan's grand vezir, whose office, known as the Sublime Porte, came to be synonymous with the Ottoman government. But on this occasion Fatih summoned his son Jem from Konya to take charge of the situation, and in the late summer of 1479 a truce was signed between the Ottomans and the Knights of St John. During their correspondence concerning the negotiations d'Aubusson cultivated a friendly relationship with Jem, whose outgoing nature led him to respond positively to the grand master's approaches.

Earlier that summer Fatih had sent out invitations to celebrate another circumcision feast, this time for his nine-year-old grandson, the future Selim I, son of Prince Beyazit. Again Fatih requested the presence of the Doge of Venice (now Giovanni Mocenigo), but he, like his predecessor, politely turned down the offer. Fatih then asked whether the doge could send him a 'good painter'. The Venetian Senate decided on Gentile Bellini, who was sent to Istanbul in September 1479, where he remained until mid-January 1481. It was during this time that Bellini painted the famous portrait of the Conqueror which has become the iconic image of Mehmet II, completed on 23 November 1480. The portrait shows the Conqueror in three-quarter profile: deep-set brown eyes, a long aquiline nose, a pointed reddish beard; the sultan's head is crowned with a multi-layered white turban with a red conical top and he is dressed in a red kaftan trimmed with a collar of fur. Gian Maria Angiolello, an Italian captive in the Ottoman service who was living in Topkapı Sarayı at the time, described the sultan similarly:

> The emperor Mehmet, who, as I said, was known as the Grand Turk, was of medium height, fat and fleshy; he had a wide forehead, large eyes with thick lashes, an aquiline nose, a small mouth with a round copious reddish-tinged beard, a short, thick neck, a sallow complexion, rather high shoulders, and a loud voice. He suffered from gout in the legs.

A further portrait of Fatih attributed to Bellini was discovered around 1950 in a private collection in Switzerland. The painting shows Fatih in left profile facing a beardless young man, who is shown in right profile. A label on the back of the painting identifies the subjects as 'Mehmet II and his Son'. The son would appear to be Prince Jem, who was about twenty at the time, whereas Fatih's only other living son, Beyazit, was thirty-two, appreciably older than the youth in the painting. Both brothers were serving as provincial governors in Anatolia, Beyazit in Amasya and Jem in Konya, at that time, and so it was thought that neither of them could have posed for Bellini. However Jem did come back to Istanbul in 1479, when Fatih recalled him to take charge of the negotiations with d'Aubusson, and he would have been living in Topkapı Sarayı while Bellini was there.

The fact that Fatih chose Jem rather than Beyazit to conduct the negotiations with d'Aubusson was commented upon by insiders in the Ottoman court, who concluded that the sultan had decided that his younger son, he who was born 'in the purple', would be his successor. Jem was by far the more attractive of the two brothers, his generous and charismatic nature having made him a great favourite in Karamania, the central Anatolian region that he governed from the provincial capital in Konya. He was an enthusiastic sportsman and hunter, as well as being an accomplished poet in both Persian and Arabic. Stories of his romances with local women were legion: one miniature painting even depicts a woman throwing herself at Jem's feet whilst he was out hunting in the Karamanian countryside. Jem's boon companion, Aşık (or 'Lover'), compared young Jem resplendent in his court at Konya to the semi-mythical Persian king, Jemshid. The king possessed among other wondrous things a chalice known as the 'Cup of Jemshid', round the inside of which were engraved seven lines representing the seven climates of the earth and the greatest cities of each region. When Jemshid emptied the chalice the whole world was displayed to him. Thus the poets wrote of how the Cup of Jemshid could expand the heart of the drinker so that he felt that the entire cosmos was laid open before his eyes. Aşık wrote that Jem presided like the Persian king over a brilliant circle of poets and musicians at Konya:

> the Cup of Jemshid replaced the Seal of Solomon, and with
> him the voice of minstrelsy was heard for the drum of
> victory. The vapours of the wine of mirth were the diadem

on his head, and the flowing locks of the beloved were his
tugh [a symbol of rank] and standard.

While in Konya Jem visited the tomb of Mevlana Jelaleddin
Rumi, the revered mystic poet of thirteenth-century Anatolia. He
would have known and been inspired by Mevlana's poetry and
its message of universal love, particularly the immortal lines:

> *Long nights have I passed with the priests,*
> *And I have slept with pagans in the market places.*
> *I am the green eye of jealousy, the fever of sickness.*
> *I am cloud and rain, I have swept down over the meadows.*
> *Yet the dust of mortality never touched the hem of my garment.*
> *I have gathered a treasure of roses in the Field of Eternity . . .*

Jem's grandfather, Murat II, had endowed in Konya a *tekke*, or
lodge, of the Mevlevi dervishes, an order inspired by the teachings
of Mevlana renowned for their music and poetry and the hypnotic
dance that gave them the name the 'whirling dervishes'. It is quite
possible that Jem became a member of this brotherhood. However
there is also some reason to believe that Jem may have been,
perhaps secretly, a member of the Bektaşi dervishes, founded in
the thirteenth century by Hacı Bektaş. Many of the Ottoman
sultans were members of the Bektaşi, as were the Janissaries to a
man, though Fatih himself was strongly opposed to them and
indeed to all of the dervish orders. The Bektaşi were famous for
their love of wine and merriment, which would have suited Jem's
free-spirited and fun-loving character.

Beyazit, by contrast, was dour and withdrawn, and during the
years that he served as governor in Amasya, near the Black Sea
coast of Anatolia, he had little contact with the local people,
preferring to spend his time in study. He was drawn to and

became a member of the Halveti dervishes, a contemplative order who believed that their sheikhs had the power of divination. The Halveti sheikh at the time, Muhyidden Mehmet, told Beyazit that he would succeed his father as sultan, and this gave great comfort to the prince, who felt, with good reason, that Fatih had already decided on Jem as his successor. From early in his youth Beyazit had been an opium addict. When Fatih learned of this from Gedik Ahmet Pasha he was furious, though Beyazit assured his father that he had used the drug only as medicine during a period of illness. The grand vezir also told Fatih that the troops under Beyazit's command were poorly organized and disciplined. Beyazit denied this charge too and Fatih decided to let the matter pass. However from that point on Beyazit determined that he would one day have his revenge on Gedik Ahmet Pasha.

In 1479 one of the women in Jem's harem in Konya bore him a daughter, though the imperial genealogical records do not give the names of either the mother or child. The following year Jem's concubine Severid bore him his first son, Oğuzhan. The baby was brought back to Istanbul with his mother, ostensibly so that he could be raised in Topkapı Sarayı, but more probably so that Fatih could hold the boy as a hostage for Jem's good behaviour. Beyazit's son Korkut, who had been born in 1470, was also being raised in Topkapı Sarayı at that time, undoubtedly because he too was being held hostage. Later in 1480 another of Jem's concubines gave birth to his second son, Murat, who remained in Konya with his mother, whose name is unrecorded.

Fatih's inactivity in 1479–80 was due, in part, to his declining health. This was remarked upon by the French statesman and historian Philippe de Commines, who ranked Mehmet II alongside Louis XI of France and Mathias Corvinus of Hungary as the greatest rulers of the century. Mehmet, the diplomat noted, overindulged in '*les plaisirs du monde*' and no carnal vice was apparently unknown to this voluptuary. From his early years he suffered from gout (as Angiolello had also observed), and a series of other ailments brought on by his excesses. The sultan had a huge swelling and abscess in his leg that had first appeared in the spring of 1480. None of his physicians were able to explain or cure this malady, but Commines remarks that they looked upon it as divine punishment for the sultan's great gluttony (*'grande gourmandise'*). The Frenchman goes on to say that the sultan's illness kept him confined to his palace, for he was loath to show himself in public in such a condition: 'lest people notice his sorry state and his enemies despise him, he seldom allowed himself to be seen and remained secluded in his *serai*'.

Therefore when the much anticipated Ottoman advance on Rhodes began on 23 May 1480, the Conqueror remained at Topkapı Sarayı. In charge of the expedition was the commander, Mesih Pasha, a Greek of the imperial Palaeologus family who had converted to Islam. Mesih Pasha's fleet immediately established a blockade around Rhodes, but somehow Pierre d'Aubusson managed to smuggle out two letters on a fast galley. The first letter, to Frederick III, informed the emperor that during the first few days the bombardment had destroyed nine towers and had levelled the Palace of the Grand Master on Rhodes. The second was a circular letter to the members of the Order of the Knights of St John in Europe, informing them that their headquarters had been attacked by the Turks and calling on them to come to their aid. According to d'Aubusson, the invasion fleet was 'an Armada of one hundred and nine vessels', on which the sultan had 'brought a great many cannon, bombards and wooden towers with other engines of war, and has drawn up against us some 70,000 soldiers who assail us continually and press hard against us . . .'

The siege of Rhodes continued for more than two months, coming to a climax on the morning of 28 July with a Turkish bombardment with eight great cannon that almost reduced the fortifications to rubble, allowing the Turkish infantry to make their way to the tops of the ramparts. D'Aubusson personally led the defenders in a counterattack, and though he himself was seriously wounded his men drove the enemy from the ramparts in a two-hour battle in which, according to an account by Guillaume Caoursin, vice chancellor of the knights, some 3,500 Turks were killed.

At that point two ships sent by King Ferrante of Naples arrived, bringing news that aid would soon be on its way to Rhodes. But by then Mesih Pasha had decided that his losses were too great to continue fighting, and so that same day he lifted the siege, withdrew his troops and sailed away. The city of Rhodes and its fortress were in ruins, and half of the knights and the other defenders had been killed, the Turks having suffered far greater losses, with some 9,000 of their men dead and 15,000 wounded. According to Angiolello, Mesih Pasha's fleet returned to Istanbul 'not sounding instruments of joy, as they were accustomed to do on such occasions when the fleet came home'. Fatih angrily demoted Mesih Pasha, saying that if he himself had been in command of the expedition Rhodes would now be theirs.

On 27 July 1480, the day before the Ottomans were forced to lift their siege of Rhodes, Pope Sixtus IV had made an appeal to the princes of Italy to take united action against the Turks before it was too late. 'We have the enemy before our very eyes,' he wrote.

> He has already been sighted, poised to strike at the province of Apulia with a large fleet. If he should seize Ragusa or Rhodes (which God forbid!), nothing would be left of our safety ... Hear our paternal voice, consider the common peril, and judge for yourselves how great is the need to quicken our pace.

The next day an Ottoman fleet commanded by Gedik Ahmet Pasha was spotted crossing from Valona in Albania to the heel of Italy in Apulia. An army was landed near Otranto and the castle there fell to the Ottomans on 11 August, with more than half of the populace of 22,000 killed and the younger survivors carried off into slavery. The aged Archbishop Stefano Pendenelli remained to the last in the cathedral of Otranto, praying for divine deliverance as the Turks put his congregation to the sword. One account says that the Turks sawed the archbishop in two on the high altar, although a more reliable source suggests that he died of fright.

King Ferrante sent a courier to inform the pope that Otranto had fallen to the Turks. The king then mustered a substantial army that left Naples for Apulia on 8 September. His son Alfonso, Duke of Calabria, withdrew his troops from Tuscany, where Ferrante and the pope had been at war with Florence, and at the end of the month he set out for Apulia to join his father's forces.

According to Sigismondo de' Conti, the papal secretary, after the fall of Otranto, the pope was so terrified that he contemplated fleeing to Avignon: 'In Rome the alarm was so great as if the enemy had already been encamped before her very walls . . . Terror had taken such hold of all minds that even the pope meditated flight.' But Sixtus regained his nerve and realized that aid must be given to the Kingdom of Naples, even though Ferrante had recently betrayed him in the war they had fought with the Florentines. As Sigismondo commented:

> Sixtus IV would have witnessed with great indifference the misfortunes and losses of his faithless ally, had Ferrante's enemy been any one but the Sultan; but it was a very different matter when the common foe of Christendom had actually got a footing on Italian soil, and speedily the Papacy and Rome itself were threatened with utter ruin, unless he were promptly expelled . . . [The pope] at once sent all the money he could get together, permitted tithes to be levied from all the clergy in the kingdom, and promised a Plenary Indulgence to all Christians enlisting under the banner of the Cross.

Late in the summer of 1480 Sixtus issued a bull calling for united Christian action against the invaders before they took all of Italy: 'How perilous it has become for all Christians,' he wrote, 'and especially the Italian powers, to hesitate in the assumption of arms against the Turk and how destructive to delay any longer, everyone can see . . .' He went on to warn them that 'if the faithful, and especially the Italians, want to keep their lands, homes, wives, children, liberty, and the very faith in which we were baptized and reborn, let them believe us that they must now take up arms and go to war!'

King Louis XI of France indicated that he would give his

support to this anti-Turkish alliance. The Sforzas, the rulers of Milan, also offered the pope their support, but they said that peace must be established among the Italian states before the French king would help, 'for we confess that we cannot see how we may expect foreign aid if we make light of our troubles at home'. The coalition, the League of Naples, came into being on 16 September 1480, its members consisting of the papacy, the King of Naples, the King of Hungary, the Dukes of Milan and Ferrara, and the republics of Genoa and Florence. Representatives of the League gathered in Venice at the beginning of October 1480, and the envoys of King Ferrante led the pleas for Venetian help against the Turks. The Republic of Venice was exhorted to join the League, but the Signoria immediately declined, saying that for 'seventeen successive years' they had fought the Turks almost alone, with an unbearable cost in men and money, and now they could do no more.

Sixtus then began preparations to build a papal fleet in Genoa and Ancona, and appealed to England, France and Germany to join the coalition. Edward IV of England, because of internal political problems, declared that it was impossible for him to take part in the crusade. Louis XI assured the pope that France would participate in the war, but only if the other Christian states shared the burden. The Holy Roman Emperor, however, was too distracted by internal problems in Germany to participate in the coalition. The Sforzas of Milan wrote to their envoys in Rome that aid from the north would be long in coming, and that the united Italian states would have to make the effort themselves, even without Venice, 'because we are prepared to strive beyond our strength for the common safety and to defeat in war the barbarous, butcherly and savage Turks'.

On 8 April 1481 Sixtus issued a bull proclaiming the crusade, summoning all of the princes of Europe to arms against the Turks. But a general fear prevailed that once again nothing would come of this effort. The classical scholar Peter Schott, canon of Strasbourg, wrote that month from Bologna that he had gone to take one last look at Rome 'before the Eternal City was taken by the Turks'.

The Neapolitan army, with Alfonso in command, did not go on the offensive until the winter of 1480–81, but their presence in Apulia kept the Ottomans from moving westward, the Turks retiring within the walls of Otranto. Gedik Ahmet Pasha returned to Valona, leaving behind a garrison of 6,500 foot soldiers and 500 horsemen to defend Otranto under the command of Hayrettin Bey, a Greek convert to Islam who was fluent in Italian. King Ferrante demanded the surrender of Otranto, but Hayrettin refused to negotiate and demanded the submission of Brindisi, Lecce and Taranto. He warned Ferrante that if his demand was not met Fatih would personally appear in Apulia the following spring, with an army of 100,000 infantry, 18,000 cavalry, and a powerful artillery force, which he would use to conquer all of Italy.

Meanwhile Fatih had left Topkapı Sarayı in order to lead an army he had been mustering on the Asian shore of the Bosphorus. He had told no one of the goal of the campaign which had taken him out of his convalescence: some thought it would be another attempt to take Rhodes, while others believed he intended to conquer the Mamluk sultanate in Egypt.

On 25 April Fatih crossed the Bosphorus on his imperial caique to the Asian shore at Üsküdar, after which the grand vezir Karamanı Mehmet Pasha ordered the army to get underway. They proceeded slowly along the eastern coast of the Sea of Marmara, gathering further forces as they went, so that by 1 May they had only reached Gebze, at the head of the Gulf of Nicomedeia, where a halt was made at a place called Hünkar Çayı, or Emperor's Meadow. This was near where Hannibal had committed suicide in 183 BC, and where Constantine the Great had died in AD 338, though it is doubtful whether Fatih was aware of the historical significance of the site where his army set up camp.

Fatih had in fact called a halt here because he was stricken by severe abdominal pain. His Persian physician Hamiduddin al-Lari administered medicine which only made matters worse, and so Fatih's old Jewish doctor Maestro Iacopo was called in. Iacopo concluded that the ailment was a blockage of the intestines, but despite his frantic efforts he was unable to do anything more than alleviate the sultan's pain with powerful potions of opium. Mehmet II lingered on until late in the evening of 3 May 1481, when he passed away at 'the twenty-second hour', according to Gian Maria Angiolello. The sultan was forty-nine when he died, having reigned for more than thirty years, most of which he had spent in war. As the sultan's clerk Tursun Bey wrote in his biography of the Conqueror: 'Besides the gracious gift of the Conquest of Constantinople, Fatih wrested twenty or more independent lands from the enemies of His High Estate.'

The grand vezir Karamanı Mehmet Pasha tried desperately to keep the sultan's death a secret, but word soon reached Niccolo Coco, the Venetian ambassador in Istanbul. Coco immediately wrote to Doge Giovanni Mocenigo, sending the letter off with the captain of a Venetian galley, which reached Venice on 29 May, twenty-eight years to the day after the fall of Constantinople.

When the captain arrived at the Palazzo Ducale he was told that the doge was in conference with the Signoria, but without waiting the captain burst into the meeting hall and cried out, '*La Grande Aquila e morte!*' (the Great Eagle is dead). After the doge read the letter he gave orders to ring the *marangona*, the great bell in the campanile of San Marco that counted off the Venetian hours and was tolled on special occasions, usually to mark the death of a doge or the appearance of an enemy fleet. Now the *marangona* was for once bringing good news, and soon all of Venice was cheering the death of the Grande Turco. The doge sent a courier hotfoot to Rome to inform the pope, who had cannons fired from Castel Sant' Angelo, the great papal fortress on the Tiber. Church bells were rung to alert the populace, after which the pope led a procession, followed by his cardinals and all of the ambassadors, to the church of Santa Maria del Popolo. As night fell Rome was illuminated by a tremendous firework display, bonfires were lit and services of thanksgiving were held in churches all over the city, in celebrations that lasted for three days. As word spread that the Grand Turk had passed from the world, the scene was repeated throughout Italy and northern Europe. The Venetian chronicler Giovanni Sagredo reflected two centuries later: 'It is fortunate for Christendom and Italy that death stopped that fierce and indomitable barbarian.'

Nowhere was the news of Mehmet's death received with more joy than on Rhodes. On 31 May the order's vice chancellor, Guillaume Caoursin, delivered an oration entitled '*De Morte Magni Turchi*' before an assembly of the surviving knights and their grand master Pierre d'Aubusson. Caoursin exulted in the death of Mehmet, whom he referred to as 'this second Lucifer, this second Mohammed, this second Antichrist', and he explained how the Grand Turk's passing had been marked by extraordinary convulsions of nature:

For about the time of his departure from life frequent earth-
quakes occurred in Asia, Rhodes, and the islands round-
about, especially two of the most marked severity, which
were so great and terrible that they laid low many castles,
strongholds, and palaces.

Caoursin described the cataclysmic reaction of the earth itself on
receiving the foul remains of one guilty of such monstrous crimes:
'So abundant was the exhalation [of his corpse] and so great the
explosion within the caverns of the earth, that seven times it sent
through the earth its violent shocks and caused a sudden outflow
of the sea.'

Thus did the Western world receive the news of the Grand
Turk's passing, reviling his memory and rejoicing that Christians
need fear him no more. The princes of Christendom now waited
anxiously to learn which of Mehmet's sons would succeed him,
Beyazit or Jem, for Niccolo Coco's letter to the doge had said
there were rumours in Istanbul that the two princes were about
to contend for their father's throne.

3

Flight into Egypt

THE TURKISH CHRONICLER NESRI had been with Fatih's army when it camped at the Emperor's Meadow on 3 May 1481. After evening prayer he had bedded down near Fatih's imperial tent and fallen asleep. But in the middle of the night he was awakened by the sound of wagon wheels and neighing horses, only to find 'the wind whistling where the sultan's tent had been pitched'.

After morning prayer orders were given to break camp immediately, and to everyone's astonishment the officers sent the army marching back to Üsküdar at top speed. When the troops reached Üsküdar they found that all the boats that provided transport across the Bosphorus had been taken to the European shore on orders of the grand vezir Karamanı Mehmet Pasha, and so the army was forced to set up camp on the Asian side of the strait. By then a rumour had spread through the army that Fatih was dead and that his body had been taken back to Istanbul by the grand vezir.

Karamanı Mehmet had been present when Fatih passed away, and he had warned the doctors and all others in attendance to keep silent about the sultan's death under pain of execution.

Others outside the tent were told that the sultan was ill and was being taken back to Istanbul for treatment, and so the royal carriage was readied and horses saddled for the grand vezir and the others in his party. Fatih's body was bundled up and placed in the carriage, and the small caravan headed back to Istanbul surrounded by the sultan's bodyguard.

Karamanı Mehmet was one of the few in the uppermost levels of the Ottoman government who supported Jem as the successor to the throne. Gedik Ahmet Pasha, now the grand admiral of the Ottoman navy, was sympathetic to Jem, but he was in Valona, Albania with the Ottoman army there. Most others in the government were on the side of Beyazit, including the vezirs Ishak Pasha and Davud Pasha, the *beylerbey* of Anatolia Sinan Pasha, the *beylerbey* of Rumelia (Europe) Hersekoğlu Ahmet Pasha, and the commander of the Janissaries Kasim Ağa.

Before starting back to Istanbul Karamanı Mehmet sent three of his slaves on fast horses to Konya with instructions to inform Jem of his father's death, urging him to rush back to Istanbul so that he could claim the throne before his brother. But Sinan Pasha had ordered checkpoints to be set up on all the roads leading into Konya and the couriers were intercepted before they could deliver their message to Jem. At first the couriers would say nothing about their mission, but after Sinan Pasha had one of them impaled the other two revealed the news they were bringing to Jem. Sinan Pasha then sent his own courier to Amasya to inform Beyazit of his father's death, advising him to make all haste in returning to Istanbul to seize power before Jem.

Karamanı Mehmet had brought Fatih's body back to Topkapı Sarayı, where he had it packed in ice in a meat locker in the palace kitchens. By then the Janissaries with the army in Üsküdar had seized some rafts and crossed over to Istanbul, where under the leadership of Kasim Ağa they stormed the palace. After they discovered Fatih's body the Janissaries beheaded Karamanı Mehmet and paraded through the streets of Istanbul with his head on a pike, shouting 'Long live Beyazit!' The Janissaries took advantage of the absence of authority to sack the Jewish and Christian quarters of Istanbul, before they were finally subdued by Ishak Pasha, who had been left in charge of the city.

Ishak and Davud Pasha then summoned the other members of the government and met at the palace with Beyazit's son Korkut, who had been living with his mother in the harem of Topkapı Sarayı. Korkut, who was eleven years old, was raised to the throne as regent for his father, who was expected to arrive at Istanbul at any moment; meanwhile the vezirs secured the loyalty of the Janissaries and other elements of the army by promising them higher pay.

Beyazit was indeed en route, riding westward from Amasya with a bodyguard of 4,000 *sipahis,* or feudal cavalry. At Izmit, the ancient Nicomedeia, he paused in his journey and sent a trusted slave ahead to Istanbul, fearing that he might be walking into a trap. The slave reported back to Beyazit that he had seen Fatih's remains, and that his son Korkut had been made regent and was awaiting his arrival.

Thus reassured, Beyazit proceeded on to Üsküdar, where he arrived on 20 May, having donned a black robe as a sign of mourning for his father. At Üsküdar Beyazit was formally greeted by the pashas and conducted across the Bosphorus in the imperial caique, escorted by a flotilla of galleys and barges of all kinds. But when he reached the European shore he was confronted by a mob of Janissaries and *sipahis,* who demanded that he confirm the promises made to them by the vezirs in the name of his son Korkut. Beyazit placated the soldiers by promising them *bahşiş*, or a bribe, as well as a permanent raise in pay. But this did not satisfy them, and they made the further demand that Beyazit dismiss his uncle Mustafa Pasha, who had incurred their hatred. Beyazit had no choice but to remove Mustafa from his post and have him sent back to Asia. Beyazit resumed his progress toward Topkapı Sarayı but his path was again blocked, this time by a group of soldiers who demanded that all soldiers be given *bahşiş* and a raise in pay, to which he acceded. He was also made to promise that in the future he would appoint his vezirs only from among the officers of the Janissaries and *sipahis* and *içoğlan,* the imperial pages, for they wanted to prevent the rise to power of palace favourites such as Karamanı Mehmet Pasha from the *ulema,* or religious hierarchy. Again Beyazit agreed, but when the soldiers made still another demand, that they be given amnesty for their recent sack of the Christian and Jewish quarters, he remained silent and continued on his way to the palace.

The following day Beyazit took turns with the pashas and *ağas* in carrying the coffin of his father to Fatih Camii, the Mosque of the Conqueror. There Fatih was laid to rest in the splendid tomb that he had built for himself behind the mosque, the turban that he had worn till his last day placed at the head of his catafalque. The noted cleric Şeyh Vefa then led Beyazit and a crowd of 20,000 mourners in prayer for the repose of Fatih's soul, their devotions continuing until dawn.

The following day the Ottoman court assembled at Topkapı Sarayı, where Prince Korkut handed over power to his father, who ascended the throne as Beyazit II, the eighth sultan of the Osmanlı dynasty. Beyazit sat enthroned outside Bab-üs Saadet, the Gate of Felicity, the entryway to the Inner Palace, where he received the homage of the court in the ceremony known as *Biat*, or Allegiance, during which all the notables filed past to kiss the hem of the sultan's robe and swear fealty to him. There followed a meeting of the Divan, or Imperial Council, at which Beyazit announced the appointment of Ishak Pasha as grand vezir and of Davut Pasha and Hersekoğlu Ahmet Pasha as first vezirs. Messages were sent to governors and other officials throughout the empire to inform them of the new appointments, and all judges were ordered to publish the news of Beyazit's accession.

Some days later Beyazit proceeded to the suburb of Eyüp on the upper reaches of the Golden Horn, where Fatih had built a shrine around the tomb of Eba Eyüp, Companion of the Prophet Mohammed, who had been killed at that spot in the first Arab assault on Constantinople in the seventh century. There Beyazit was girded with the sword of his ancestor Osman Gazi, in a ceremony equivalent to a coronation, performed by the Nakib-ül Eşraf, Chief of the Descendants of the Prophet. He returned to the palace in a procession attended by the people of Istanbul, who cheered their new ruler with cries of 'Long live Sultan Beyazit!', while he distributed largesse to the crowd as he passed by. When the procession reached Topkapı Sarayı, Beyazit announced an additional increase of pay for the Janissaries, the *bahşiş* known as *Cülus Akçası*, or accession money, which was now customary for a new sultan to pay to his elite troops before they would serve him. Only then could Beyazit retire to the Inner Palace to receive the congratulations of the women in his harem, which was now headed by his mother Gülbahar, the new *valide sultan*, or queen mother.

Jem had by this time learned of his father's death and that his brother had stolen a march on him. After consulting with his advisors at Konya, he decided to fight for his throne. He assembled a mixed army which comprised *sipahis* from Anatolia, irregular infantry (*azabs*), Türkmen warriors from Karamania and from the tribes of Warsak and Turgud, together with dervishes and men of the *ahi,* the craft guilds of Konya and other cities. The latter were members of an autonomous religious and fraternal society known as the Ahi Brotherhood of Virtue, whose repu- tation for justice and hospitality was noted by the fourteenth- century Muslim traveller Ibn Battuta:

> Nowhere in the world are there to be found any to compare with them in solicitude for strangers, and in ardour to satisfy wants, to restrain the hands of the tyrannous, and to kill the agents of policy, and those who join with them. An *ahi,* in their idiom, is one whom the assembled members of his trade, together with other young unmarried men and those who have adopted a celibate life, chose to be their leader ... When we had taken our place among them, they brought in a great banquet with fruits and sweetmeats, after which they began their singing and dancing. Everything about them filled us with admiration and we were greatly aston- ished at their generosity and innate nobility.

The *ahi,* the dervishes, *sipahis, azabs* and Türkmen warriors, free-spirited and rebellious by nature, flocked to Jem's banner because Jem represented potential freedom from the rule of the tyrannous Ottoman sultanate. Many of Jem's followers were Alevi, a sect of the heterodox Shiite Muslims, as opposed to the orthodox Sunni Muslims who dominated the religious hierarchy of the Ottoman Empire and supported Beyazit.

Jem and his forces marched first for Bursa, by way of Akşehir,

Afyonkarahisar, Kütahya and Eskişehir. On 27 May his advance guard reached Bursa, where he was joined by a large number of *sipahis* and feudal troops known as *timarcis*, who originally had been mustered to join Fatih's final, aborted campaign. This brought Jem's force to about 20,000 troops, which he marshalled below the *kale*, or citadel, of Bursa, the ancient acropolis of Byzantine Prusa, where his ancestors Osman Gazi and Orhan Gazi were buried. Initially the people of Bursa refused to open the gates of the citadel to the rebels, fearing the wrath of Sultan Beyazit if they capitulated, and Jem was forced to camp outside the city to the west around the Beyazidiye, the hilltop mosque complex built by his forefather, Beyazit I.

Beyazit anticipated that his brother would attempt to establish himself at Bursa and so he sent orders to all of the European provinces to send troops to join the forces he was mustering in Istanbul. He also ordered the Ottoman navy to stop transporting troops to Valona in Albania, where Gedik Ahmet Pasha was waiting to reinforce the Turkish garrison at Otranto. Gedik Ahmet was instructed to return immediately to Istanbul with his army to join Beyazit.

Jem's forces made some probing attacks on the citadel at Bursa, after which his emissaries were able to persuade the Janissaries holding the garrison there to come over to their side. The people of Bursa then opened the city gates to Jem. Most of Bursa's citizens were sympathetic to Jem's cause, having also been influenced by a popular astrologer who predicted that Jem would be the next sultan. Many hoped that under Jem the city might regain its former status as capital of the Ottoman Empire. With Bursa as his base Jem could go on to conquer the rest of the empire, or at least to force his brother to divide it between them.

On 2 June, a month after his father's death, Jem had *akçe*, silver coins, struck in his name, and at the Friday noon service in the mosques of Bursa his name was praised as sultan in the *hutbe*, or sermon. These two symbolic acts meant that Jem had become the acknowledged ruler of the Ottoman state, if only the tiny part of it that his troops controlled.

Beyazit had by now crossed the Bosphorus to Üsküdar with the troops of the Istanbul garrison. He sent Ayas Pasha ahead with an advance force of 2,000 Janissaries from Mudanya to reinforce the Bursa citadel in anticipation of Jem's arrival. But when Ayas arrived at the city he found it already in the possession of the rebels, and after a brief battle he was forced to surrender to Jem. Beyazit now knew that Jem was at Bursa and sent more troops to help Ayas Pasha, under the command of his son Abdullah, governor of Manisa; but Ayas had by then succumbed and Abdullah was forced to retreat. A standoff ensued, and Beyazit was forced to wait at Üsküdar for the arrival of Gedik Ahmet and the army from Albania.

Jem chose this moment to send a deputation to negotiate with his brother, the principal envoy being his aged great-great-aunt Selçuk Hatun, a daughter of Mehmet I, who was accompanied by several members of the *ulema* from Bursa. Jem proposed that he and Beyazit divide the empire, with Beyazit retaining the European provinces, with Istanbul as his capital, and Jem taking Anatolia and ruling from the old Osmanlı capital of Bursa. But Beyazit rejected the proposal outright, quoting the old Islamic saying 'Kings have no relatives', and continued with his plans to marshal all the forces of the empire to attack Jem in Bursa. He also sent an agent to contact Jem's chamberlain, Astinoğlu Yakup Bey, whom Beyazit had corrupted with an enormous bribe and the promise of being made *beylerbey* of Anatolia. Beyazit's agent instructed Yakup to come over to Beyazit's side with his troops when a suitable opportunity presented itself, and the chamberlain readily agreed.

As soon as Beyazit received news that Gedik Ahmet and his army from Albania were approaching Istanbul, he marched his forces to Iznik, the Greek Nicaea, thirty miles north-east of Bursa. There he was joined by his son Abdullah, and together they continued on toward Yenişehir, ten miles to the south of Iznik, where they would rendezvous with Gedik Ahmet's army of over 16,000 men. This would bring the total force under Beyazit's control to about 40,000 – double the size of Jem's forces – and these were all troops of the imperial army, including the seasoned veterans led by Gedik Ahmet, the most capable commander in the Ottoman service. Jem's men were for the most part irregulars and Karamanian volunteers, whose commanders included men such as Jem's tutor Nasuh Bey, who had little or no military experience.

Jem met with his commanders to decide upon a plan of action. Most of his officers advised him to hold out in the citadel of Bursa and not to face the superior forces of Beyazit. But Feneri-oğlu Hasan Çelebi strongly recommended that they take their chances against the imperial army since they did not have the supplies to withstand a prolonged siege. In this he was supported by Yakup Bey, who knew that a battle in open country would give him the opportunity to switch sides at the right moment. Jem's natural impetuosity made him decide that he would rather fight than be besieged, and so he led his army out of Bursa to do battle with his brother.

Jem commanded the main body of his forces toward Yenişehir,

sending a detachment of Janissaries under Nasuh Bey to hold a
pass near Iznik. Sinan Pasha, the *beylerbey* of Anatolia, was sent
by Beyazit to attack Nasuh Bey, whom he quickly drove from the
pass and then marched on to the plain of Yenişehir, where the
sultan's other forces had now converged, including the Albanian
army under Gedik Ahmet. Jem's commander Uzğuroğlu Mehmet
led his army out onto the plain to confront Beyazit's forces early
on the morning of 22 June 1481. Jem led the first cavalry charge
himself, shouting 'Victory or Death!'

At the outset of the battle Yakup Bey rode off with his troops
on the pretext of making a flanking attack on the imperial army,
but as soon as he was out in the open he switched to the side of
Beyazit, who was waiting to welcome him. This quickly turned
the tide of battle. By noon Jem's forces had been routed and were
in headlong retreat. As the chronicler Nesri wrote in describing the climax of the battle of Yenişehir: 'The Karaman crows
scattered like young from the nest when they saw the eagles
of Beyazit.' Jem, who was slightly wounded in the battle, fled
for his life taking with him his family and a band of loyal followers. His reign as sultan in Bursa had ended abruptly after only
twenty days.

Jem and his companions rode with such desperate haste that
by the next morning they had reached Eskişehir, some sixty miles
south-west of Yenişehir. There they were set upon by the local
Türkmen tribesmen, who robbed them of all of their possessions.
They continued nonetheless across the barren Anatolian plateau,
foraging for food along the way, and sleeping under the stars.
On a particularly cold night one of Jem's officers, Sinan Bey, was
forced to borrow a sheepskin cloak from a local shepherd to
cover the young prince. On 26 June they finally reached Konya,

where for the moment they were safe among Jem's Karamanian supporters.

Jem and his party, by now numbering about forty, remained in Konya for three days. During this time they received word that Beyazit and his army were marching in pursuit of them. Jem decided their only chance was to head for south-eastern Anatolia, Mamluk territory. Beyazit would have to risk a war with the Mamluks if he entered this area, and Jem was sure that the Mamluk sultan Kaitbey would give him refuge.

They travelled south-east across the bleakest part of the Anatolian plateau, whose inhospitable landscape is vividly described by Gertrude Bell:

> barren save for a dry scrub of aromatic herbs or flecked with shining miles of saline deposit; naked ranges of mountains stand sentinel over the featureless expanse; the sparse villages, unsheltered from wind or sun, lie along the skirts of the hills, catching thirstily at the snow-fed streams that are barely enough for the patch of cultivated ground below; the weary road, deep in dust or mud according to the season, drags its intolerable length to the horizon.

As Jem and his party rode on they were joined by former members of his court in Konya and stragglers from the battle of Yenişehir, bringing the number of his company to about two to three hundred, many of whom were either ill or wounded. At each stage of the journey they were harassed by Türkmen tribes, whom they had to bribe in order to continue on their way. After stopping at Ereğli they left the Anatolian plateau and passed through the Taurus Mountains via the Cilician Gates – the same route that Alexander the Great had taken in 334 BC – and descended to the Mediterranean coast at Tarsus where they entered Mamluk territory.

Pausing in Tarsus, Jem sent word to Turhan Bey, the emir of the Ramazanoğlu Türkmen tribe in Adana, a vassal of the Mamluks and thus an enemy of Sultan Beyazit. The Ramazanoğlu emir welcomed Jem and his followers to Adana and granted them safe passage through Cilicia and on into Syria. From Iskenderun on the Mediterranean coast Jem's party made their way up through the Syrian Gates, and headed south across the Amık Plain to Antakya, ancient Antioch. The local *beys* treated Jem royally as he and his party passed through their territory, stopping at Aleppo, Hama, Homs and Baalbek before coming to Damascus.

At Damascus Jem and his followers were finally able to rest. The Mamluk *beylerbey* received Jem as his guest in the palace of Kasri Ablak, where he stayed for six weeks, exhausted from the ordeal of the battle and his subsequent flight. Jem visited the Ummayad mosque and other historic Islamic sites in the city, including the tomb of the prophets Houd and Hızır. All eyes were on Jem, and his visits to these sacred places aroused favourable comment, the populace feeling honoured that a son of the Conqueror was staying as a guest in their city.

From Damascus Jem and his companions resumed their journey, pausing at 'blessed Jerusalem' for a few days before moving on to Hebron and Gaza. In the last days of September they crossed the Sinai peninsula and entered Egypt, heading toward Cairo.

Meanwhile Beyazit had led his army eastward across the central Anatolian plateau, arriving at Konya four days after Jem's departure. Beyazit remained in Konya and ordered Gedik Ahmet to continue in pursuit of Jem. Gedik led the imperial army south-eastward as far as Ereğli, where he gave up the chase, for to continue farther would have taken him into Mamluk territory. He then led his army back to Konya where he reported his failure to Beyazit, who felt that Gedik could have caught Jem had he moved more swiftly, an incident that only added to the resentment that he felt toward the pasha.

For now there was nothing more that Beyazit could do. He appointed Abdullah provincial governor of Karamania, and having ordered Gedik Ahmet to follow him with his army, he started back for Istanbul. As the imperial army proceeded westward the Türkmen tribes along the way petitioned Beyazit that they be absolved of their taxes, saying that they should be rewarded for having harassed Jem and his followers on their flight after the battle of Yenişehir. But Beyazit would not commit himself and told them to present their case before the Divan in Istanbul. When they subsequently did so, Beyazit had the Türkmen chieftains executed for having interfered in royal affairs.

When Beyazit reached Bursa the Janissaries in his bodyguard demanded that they be permitted to sack the city to punish those who had supported Jem. Beyazit restrained them with bribes, but nevertheless they put to the sword a number of dervishes who had been supporters of Jem, taking revenge for their fellow Janissaries who had been killed in the Bursa garrison. Beyazit then returned to Istanbul, and eight days later Gedik Ahmet Pasha and his army reached the capital. As soon as Gedik Ahmet arrived he was summoned to Topkapı Sarayı, where Beyazit had him arrested and imprisoned without explanation. Beyazit probably knew that Gedik Ahmet favoured Jem, and he also felt that he had deliberately dallied in pursuit of his brother, and had allowed him to escape. Beyazit hated Gedek Ahmet for having maligned him to Fatih and had been waiting for a chance to take revenge upon him.

When news of Gedik Ahmet's arrest broke the next morning the Janissaries stormed the palace and threatened Beyazit, demanding that he free Gedik Ahmet. The old general, who was of Serbian origin, had been taken up in the *devşirme* as a youth and enrolled in the Janissaries during the reign of Murat II. He had risen to the position of vezir under Fatih, for whom he had commanded the Ottoman army in many victorious campaigns, most recently in the capture of Otranto. He was a heavy drinker but never let this dull his ability as a commander, and he was highly respected by his men, beloved for his generosity and justice. The soldiers saw his arrest as another example of Beyazit's disregard for them and preference for the religious hierarchy and civilians, and they were outraged. The violence of their reaction alarmed Beyazit, who was still deeply worried that Jem might gain the support of the military. And so Gedik Ahmet was released from prison, reappointed vezir, and restored as commander-in-chief of the army.

Beyazit had another reason for reinstating Gedik Ahmet, for he was now faced with a serious uprising by the Karamanid Türkmen under Kasim Bey, who succeeded as emir on the death of his brother Pir Ahmet in 1475. Kasim Bey had attacked an Ottoman force commanded by Ali Pasha, the governor in Konya. Beyazit sent Gedik Ahmet with an army to aid Ali Pasha and put down the rebellion in Karamania. Kasim Bey attacked Ali Pasha near Mut, but on the approach of Gedik Ahmet he retreated across the Taurus Mountains to Tarsus. Gedik Ahmet then set up his winter camp at the town of Karaman, south of Konya, which he used as his headquarters to govern Karamania and keep an eye on Kasim Bey.

During June 1481, the Christian crusade proclaimed by the pope the previous summer showed signs of coming to fruition, spurred on by the death of Fatih and the civil war that was distracting the Ottomans. On the fourth of that month Sixtus wrote to the Marquis Federico of Mantua and others that God had shown the way to salvation from the Turks, 'revealing to us a light from on high to free us forever from the peril which for years past has struck the Christian commonwealth with so many calamities'. Now was the time to take action, before the Turks could recover from the civil war and the sons of the Conqueror could resume the barbarities of their father. 'We have our fleet ready in Genoa; thirty galleys and four ships splendidly equipped will soon be at the Tiber docks; at Ancona also we are arming others, and they will be joined in good course with the royal fleet [of Naples].'

Sixtus knew that interest in the crusade would subside now that the Conqueror was gone, and his fears were soon realized when the Bolognese informed him that they wished to withdraw their pledge of financial support, for 'with the Turkish tyrant's death necessity presses us no more'. The pope's envoys in Mantua had already told him that the Marquis Federico was withholding funds that had been collected for the crusade. Sixtus himself tried to set the best possible example by contributing most of his own silver plate and sending a large quantity of sacred liturgical vessels to the papal mint to meet his share of the expenses of the crusade.

He appointed Cardinal Campofregoso to command the papal fleet, summoning him to Rome along with the papal legate Cardinal Savelli. On 30 June the pope and his cardinals went to the church of San Paolo Fuori le Mura for the blessing of the papal fleet. After vespers the pope held a consistory at which he addressed Cardinal Campofregoso, telling him of the historic importance of his mission, after which, according to the chronicler Volaterranus, Sixtus 'gave him his Legate's ring and the banner which he had consecrated for the fleet'. Volaterranus writes of how the captains of the fleet then came in, kissed the pope's feet, and were signed with the cross on their breasts. The pope and the college of cardinals then went down to the Tiber, where the galleys were lying at anchor, and boarded each of the vessels to give the apostolic blessing. The crews stood fully armed on the decks and saluted when the pope appeared, whereupon, 'weapons were brandished, swords drawn and struck upon the shields, and military evolutions executed as in actual battle. Hundreds of hoarse voices shouted the Pope's name amid the thunder of the artillery; it was a feast for both eye and ear.'

On 4 July the fleet departed to join forces with the royal navy of King Ferrante of Naples in besieging Otranto, which had been isolated since Gedik Ahmet Pasha was recalled from Valona by Beyazit. The Turks in the Otranto garrison fought obstinately, but were forced to surrender on 10 September. Ferrante immediately informed the pope, and Sixtus in turn transmitted the good news to the other Christian princes in Europe.

Sixtus hoped that the recapture of Otranto would be the first step in the reconquest of Christian lands under Ottoman occupation: the papal fleet, joined by the ships of the other powers, would then sail across to capture the Turkish-held fortress of

Valona, and from there the allies would head south to begin the liberation of Greece. In August a Portuguese fleet of twenty-five vessels under the command of the Bishop of Elbora arrived to support the pope's cause and was immediately directed to begin the attack on Valona.

Central to the pope's plan to recapture Greece was his ward, Andreas Palaeologus, son of Thomas Palaeologus, former despot of the Morea and brother of the late Constantine XI, the last Byzantine emperor. When Fatih conquered the Morea in 1460 Thomas fled to Rome with his family, which included his sons Andreas, born four months before the fall of Constantinople in 1453, and Manuel, born in 1455. When Thomas Palaeologus died in 1465 Andreas became the pretender to the throne of Byzantium, supported first by Pope Paul II and then by Sixtus IV, who now saw a God-given opportunity to use him as the symbolic leader of his crusade.

On 15 September 1481 Sixtus instructed the Bishop of Elbora to assist Andreas Palaeologus in crossing the Ionian Sea to the Morea, so that the pretender could begin the reconquest of his father's despotate. Three days later Sixtus wrote to all the Christian rulers of Europe, telling them the glorious news of the recapture of Otranto, 'which we have been waiting for with all of our heart, and which has been most pleasing to us – today we have learned it from our people!' He then made an eloquent plea for united action: 'This is the time of deliverance, of glory, of victory, such as we shall never be able to regain if it is neglected now. With a little effort the war can now be brought to a successful conclusion which later on can be done only at the greatest cost and with the greatest injuries to ourselves.'

At the same time Sixtus sent a message to the commander of

the Christian fleet, Campofregoso, urging the cardinal to take swift action 'lest we prove unequal to the chance which heaven has offered us'. But the pope's plea came to nothing, for dissension in the Christian army at Otranto and an outbreak of plague in the papal fleet led the allied leaders to postpone their campaign indefinitely. King Ferrante informed Sixtus that Campofregoso was about to return with the fleet to Civitavecchia, near Rome, quoting the cardinal's statement that he had been instructed to do so by the pope himself. Sixtus replied to Ferrante on 21 September that he had, on the contrary, intended that the papal fleet should sail to Valona after the recapture of Otranto. He then sent strict orders for Campofregoso to set sail for Valona at once.

But by the beginning of October Sixtus heard the news that the papal fleet had docked at Civitavecchia. The pope hurried there at once in an attempt to persuade Campofregoso, the Neapolitan ambassador, and the ships' captains to turn around. Campofregoso reluctantly informed Sixtus that the planned invasion of Greece was for the moment impossible because of the outbreak of plague, an increasingly mutinous mood on the ships, the advanced season of the year and the escalating cost of the enterprise. Sixtus declared himself still resolute and prepared to make every sacrifice, according to Volaterranus, who wrote that though the pope 'would, like Eugenius IV, pawn his mitre and sell the rest of his silver plate, all was in vain'.

Sixtus conceded defeat for the time being, and returned to Rome on 17 October 1481 utterly disappointed but consoled by the knowledge that the Turks were not in a position to invade Italy whilst the two sons of Mehmet the Conqueror were embroiled in civil war. But his mood would shortly change when he heard the news that Beyazit had emerged victorious in the struggle, and that Jem had been forced to flee and was now in exile in Egypt.

4

Escape to Rhodes

ON 30 SEPTEMBER 1481 Jem and his party reached Cairo, the Mamluk capital, where he hoped to find refuge and possibly help in advancing his cause. The Mamluk sultan Kaitbey was the most powerful rival of the Ottomans in Islam, and through his *beys* and *beylerbeys* in south-eastern Anatolia and Syria he had assured Jem that he would be welcome in Cairo and that there he would be safe from his brother Beyazit.

The word *mamluk* in Arabic means 'owned' or 'belonging to', and in particular it applied to white male slaves who were taken as prisoners of war or purchased in the slave market. The practice of employing a large body of foreign slaves, particularly Turks, dates from the time of the Abbasid caliphs of Baghdad, beginning in the middle of the eighth century. The Mamluks seized power from the Ayyubid sultans in the middle of the thirteenth century. The first Mamluk dynasty, mostly Turkish and Mongol in origin, ruled from 1250 until 1382. They were known as the Bahri, from the isle in the Nile at Cairo where they lived when they were slaves of the Ayyubids. The Bahri were supplanted by the Burji Mamluks, the first of whom, Barquq, came to power in 1382. This dynasty took its name from the Burj, the citadel of Cairo, where they had lived under the Bahri sultans. The second dynasty of Mamluk sultans differed from the first principally in two respects: their ethnic origins and the absence of any hereditary succession. Except for two Greeks, the Burji sultans were Circassians, and none of them were able to establish the hereditary succession in their own family. The Burji dynasty ruled for nearly a century and a half over an empire that stretched from Egypt to south-eastern Anatolia. Their realm included the Arabian cities of Mecca and Medina, so that the Mamluk sultans, or 'Soudans', could lay claim to the titles of Caliph and Protector of the Holy Places.

El-Ashraf Seyfeddin Kaitbey was the last of the great Mamluk sultans. A Circassian, he had been purchased as a boy slave for 50 dinars by Sultan Gakmak, by whom he was eventually freed. Kaitbey's power and influence grew during the reigns of the next nine sultans until he finally seized power in 1468, beginning a sultanate that was to last for nearly twenty-nine years, the longest and most illustrious reign in the history of the Burji Mamluks.

At the very beginning of Kaitbey's reign he almost went to war against the Ottomans when Fatih mounted a campaign intended to invade Syria. But the conflict was averted when Pir Ahmet's defection led Fatih to attack the Karamanid instead. This was but one instance of the constant rivalry between the Ottoman and Mamluk sultans in the marchlands between their two empires in south-eastern Anatolia, through which Jem and his company had passed in their journey from Konya to Cairo. At the time of Jem's arrival in Egypt, Kaitbey would have been in his early seventies, but was still bristling with life, as shown in a portrait of him by Gentile Bellini (c.1480) – his imperious visage showing no weakening of the ruthless will that had enabled him to progress from slave boy to sultan.

As soon as Kaitbey heard that Jem and his followers were approaching Cairo he sent his principal officers, led by the chief eunuch of his harem, to greet them. The streets of the city were decorated as if for a fete, and the entire populace turned out to see the son of the great departed Mehmet the Conqueror. The party rode up into the citadel, the fortified palatine enclosure built in the last quarter of the twelfth century by the great Kurdish warrior Saladin. Jem and his family were led to their quarters, the mansion of Ibn Djulak, and here they bathed and rested, attended by the sultan's servants. At the sultan's palace Kaitbey greeted Jem warmly, saying that he looked upon him as his son and he would do whatever he could to help him.

During the holy month of Ramazan Jem dined nightly with Sultan Kaitbey in his palace, entertained by poets, musicians and dancers, and during the day they toured the sights of Cairo and its environs. The city's exotic atmosphere at this time is revealed in the Jewish physician's encomium in Scheherazade's *Tale of the Hunchback*:

> He who has not seen Cairo has not seen the world. Her soil
> is gold; her Nile is a marvel; her women are the damsels
> of paradise; her houses are palaces; and her air is soft,
> sweet-smelling as aloe-wood, refreshing the heart – and how
> could Cairo be otherwise, when she is the Mother of the
> World?

Jem took the opportunity to ask Kaitbey if he would be prepared to support him in his struggle against Beyazit, but the sultan would not be drawn, saying that he would have to consult with his vezirs. Kaitbey was secretly delighted to see the Ottoman state in such disarray over succession, and the longer this lasted the better: and so for the moment he prevaricated and advised Jem to be patient.

By mid-December Jem was growing restless and with Kaitbey's permission, he decided to make a pilgrimage to Mecca. Jem and his servants joined a caravan organized by a group of merchants who were making a pilgrimage to Mecca and Medina. The young prince's appearance in the Holy Places aroused considerable interest among the other pilgrims and the local residents. Jem was the only one of the imperial Osmanlı line to ever go on the *Haj* – the pilgrimage that every Muslim is expected to make once in his lifetime, culminating in a visit to the sacred Kaaba in Mecca – despite the fact that for four centuries the Ottomans controlled the Holy Places. This set Jem apart in the minds of many at the time and has since, and he is often referred to as *Hacı*, or the Pilgrim.

Although Jem was a good Muslim, his motives in making the *Haj* were probably more complex, having as much to do with his imperial ambitions as his piety. He wanted to project the image of a man who would not only rule the Ottoman Empire but would be the Caliph of Islam and Protector of the Holy Places. He is referred to as such in a poem written by Hasan ibni Mahmud-i Bayati, an Arab chieftain whom Jem had befriended on his pilgrimage.

At Mecca Jem circled the Kaaba for the customary seven times, the first four at a rapid pace, following the example of the Prophet Mohammed. He also went on to visit the tomb of the Prophet in Medina, arriving on 11 February 1482. He found the people of Medina still grieving over the destruction of Ulu Cami, the Great Mosque, which had burned down three months before after its minaret was struck by lightning. The morale of the populace was greatly improved by Jem's visit, and he encouraged them to begin rebuilding Ulu Cami, an incident that was long after remembered in Medina.

Jem returned to Cairo on 11 March 1482, having been away on the *Haj* for eighty-one days. During his absence Kaitbey had been in contact with Beyazit and had offered to mediate between the two brothers, but Beyazit had rejected his offer out of hand. When Jem discovered this he sent a letter to Beyazit, asking his forgiveness and swearing on the Kaaba that 'my place can be only at your door and at your feet'; but he ended the letter on a bitter note:

> While you lie on a bed of roses in sheer happiness,
> Why should I be covered by ashes in sorrow's furnace?
> If one observes piety, shouldn't justice favour him?
> Is that not a legitimate right claimed by the pilgrim?

Beyazit responded with a poem of his own, composed in exactly the same form, in which he based his right to the throne on predestination. At the same time he criticized Jem for using the pilgrimage to advance his very worldly imperial claim.

> Since from time immemorial we were given this state,
> Why then are you unwilling to accept preordained fate?
> 'I went on the pilgrimage', you say to advance your claim;
> Why then are these worldly gains and sovereignty your chief
>   aim?

In the same letter Beyazit offered to support Jem on an estate near Jerusalem, provided that he live there quietly. Enraged by his brother's responses, Jem determined to renew the civil war. Many offers of support had been sent to him in Cairo during his absence on the *Haj*, most notably from Kasim Bey of Karamania.

Kasim Bey, whom the Italians called the Gran Caramano, was known in the West as the King of Cilicia, since the territory of Karamania originally extended down to Cilicia on the Mediterranean coast. Kasim had spent the winter in Tarsus reinforcing and gathering supplies for his army in preparation for a spring campaign against the Ottomans in Karamania. In November 1481 he had requested help in this campaign from the Knights of St John, asking that they send five armed galleys to attack the Ottoman forces along the Mediterranean coast of Asia Minor, so as to divert Beyazit while his forces besieged Konya. But Pierre d'Aubusson replied that the knights were unable to help because they were still suffering grievously from the attack of Mesih Pasha the previous year, and could not risk offending the Porte. Beyazit was informed of Kasim's overture by his spies, and he immediately sent an envoy to contact d'Aubusson, who offered the knights a peace treaty.

Kasim Bey wrote to Jem from his headquarters in Tarsus, saying that many of the tribal leaders in south-eastern Anatolia wanted to switch their allegiances from Beyazit to Jem; they were willing to swear loyalty to the prince and would fight for him against Beyazit. Kasim proposed that they all join forces, promising that he would rule Karamania as Jem's vassal after they defeated Beyazit. He said that Gedik Ahmet Pasha was sympathetic to Jem's cause, as was Mehmet Ağa, the Ottoman commander at Ankara, who had been head of the Janissaries in Fatih's time. A number of Ottoman troops deserted from Gedik Ahmet's winter headquarters in Ereğli and crossed the Taurus to come down to Adana, where they joined forces with Kasim. Later in the winter they were joined there by Mehmet Ağa and his troops from Ankara, who had now openly declared their support for Jem.

Jem accepted Kasim's offer and once more asked Kaitbey for his support. Kaitbey was well aware of the changed situation in south-eastern Anatolia and reluctantly agreed to support Jem, even though many of the leaders in the Mamluk government were strongly opposed to becoming involved in the Ottoman war of succession – one opponent, Yashbegin, the Mamluk governor of Egypt, even going so far as sending assassins to murder the prince. Kaitbey gave Jem 40,000 gold sovereigns, around 2,000 soldiers, and the rights to a number of fortresses on the borders of Karamania. He also ordered the Mamluk governors of Damascus and Aleppo to give Jem 10,000 gold sovereigns each and to provide paid volunteers for his army. Thus supported, Jem left Cairo on 26 March 1482 with his followers, leaving behind his mother, his son Murat, his daughter Gevher Melek, and their mother, along with other women in his harem, having entrusted their care to the Mamluk sultan.

Jem did not know it, but this would be the last time he would see his family, though he kept in constant touch with his mother, who continued to write to him from Cairo for the rest of his days, doing everything she could to help him.

෨

Jem arrived in Aleppo on 6 May, his company now greatly augmented by the volunteers provided by the Mamluk governors. He then continued on to Adana, where he was joined by Kasim Bey and Mehmet Ağa and their followers, together constituting a larger army than the one that Jem had led in the first stage of the civil war. The combined forces marched up through the Cilician Gates on to the Anatolian plateau, and set up camp between Konya and the town of Karaman in southern Karamania.

Beyazit's spies had been keeping him well informed. He ordered Gedik Ahmet Pasha to return to Konya and bring Prince Abdullah to Afyonkarahisar, some 150 miles farther to the west, where they would have greater security while they waited for the main body of the imperial army to join them. Meanwhile Beyazit gathered together an army of 200,000 men and began marching eastward across Anatolia, heading for another confrontation with his brother, one that he hoped would end the war of succession once and for all. But even though Beyazit was in command of far greater forces than Jem, he was still insecure. There were rumours, for instance, that many of Beyazit's own men were secretly sympathetic to Jem's cause, and so he distributed a large quantity of money among them.

As the advance units of the imperial army approached, Kasim Bey and Jem set out to attack Gedik Ahmet before he could join forces with Prince Abdullah. Their hope was that if they could defeat Gedik before he reached Konya then they might be able to persuade him to switch to their side. Jem sent a cavalry unit under the joint command of Sinan Bey and Mehmet Ağa to attack the rear of the Ottoman forces, but Gedik drove them off and continued his march, picking up Abdullah in Konya and continuing on to Afyonkarahisar.

Mehmet Ağa rode on with his cavalry to besiege Konya, where he was soon joined by Kasim and Jem. But the Ottoman garrison under Ali Pasha put up such a strong defence that Jem's forces were unable to take the city. Mehmet Ağa then led his cavalry 150 miles to the north, to Ankara, where he had left his family for their safety. But a force of Ottoman troops under Iskender Pasha, the governor of Amasya, reached Ankara before he could. Mehmet Ağa was killed and his forces defeated, and the commander's severed head was sent as a trophy to Beyazit.

Jem and Kasim learned of Mehmet Ağa's defeat at the same time that they received reports of the approach of the imperial army. They retreated eastward to Ereğli, their forces melting away as every man among them sought to save himself. At Ereğli Jem sent a message to Beyazit, requesting a reconciliation, but before there was time for an answer he and Kasim were forced to flee before the advancing imperial army, taking refuge in the Taurus Mountains above the Mediterranean coast along with a small band of loyal followers. Beyazit sent Iskender Pasha to pursue the fugitives with a unit of cavalry, but the imperial troops lost their way in the trackless mountains and soon gave up the chase. The sultan followed this with another force under Hersekoğlu Ahmet Pasha, but to no avail. For Jem and Kasim had been taken by their Türkmen nomad guides into the highlands of Pisidia, which even Alexander the Great had failed to penetrate when he conquered Asia Minor in 334 BC. There they went to ground early in the summer of 1482, while Beyazit fumed at his inability to find Jem and rid himself completely of the war of succession that had so blighted the whole first year of his reign.

೧೧೧

From Pisidia Jem considered fleeing to Persia, but Kasim Bey persuaded him to seek refuge in Europe, where, he told him, the Christian princes would be sure to help him regain his throne, and it would be in their interest to have him with them in their struggle with the Ottoman sultan. But Kasim had his own interests at heart in giving this advice, for he knew that if Jem led a European army against the Ottomans then Beyazit would leave Karamania unguarded, whereupon he himself could regain power there.

Jem first sent a letter requesting asylum to Venice, but the Venetians refused, for they were at peace with the Ottomans and did not wish to provoke a war. At the same time the Senate forbade all Venetian *bailos* and naval officers to grant Jem asylum or give him any assistance. Beyazit knew at once from his spies in the Senate that Jem had approached the Venetians, and so he wrote to the Signoria reaffirming the peace treaty that had been signed between the Ottoman Empire and the Serenissima, and adding that he assumed Venice wished to preserve 'the good and sincere and faithful peace and friendship which we have between us'. The Senate responded by congratulating Beyazit on his 'glorious victory' in the civil war he had been forced to fight against his brother Jem, now a fugitive.

After his rejection by the Venetians Jem sent a similar letter to Pierre d'Aubusson, with whom he had established good relations during the peace negotiations three years earlier. But the messenger sent by Jem was captured by the imperial army, and thus Beyazit learned of his brother's intention to seek refuge on Rhodes. When no answer was received from Rhodes, Jem realized that his messenger had failed to get through. He then sent another letter in the hands of two of his trusted companions, Doğan Bey and Firenk Süleyman Bey. The latter was a European convert to Islam; his first name is a corruption of 'Frank', meaning 'French' or more generally 'European'. Firenk Süleyman spoke French and was thus able to communicate directly with d'Aubusson to describe Jem's perilous situation.

Jem's two envoys managed to elude the imperial troops and made their way down to a small port on the Mediterranean coast, where they found a galley that took them across to Rhodes. They arrived there on 10 July and were immediately taken to present Jem's letter to the grand master. D'Aubusson read the letter to the Council of Knights, who agreed to offer asylum to Jem and to bring the prince and his companions across from Asia Minor to Rhodes. The envoys urged the knights to hurry, for Jem was in danger of being captured by Beyazit. Once the details of the transfer were worked out, Doğan and Firenk Süleyman left to bring Jem the good news.

At Pisidia, Jem and Kasim parted, the two of them agreeing to meet again when and if they succeeded in regaining their thrones. Then Kasim rode eastward to Persia and Jem set out south for the Mediterranean coast of Cilicia. Jem's Türkmen guides led him and his companions through the Taurus Mountains down to the Mediterranean coast at Corycus, a port guarded by two fortresses, one at the entrance to the harbour and the other on a seagirt offshore isle. (The fortress on the islet is known in Turkish as Kız Kale, the Maiden's Castle, from a legend that the King of Cilicia had once used it to sequester his daughter in order to protect her, for a sorceress had predicted that the princess would be killed by a serpent. But the king's enemies smuggled an asp to the island in a bowl of fruit presented to the princess, who was bitten by the snake and immediately died.)

At Corycus, a Karamanian galley was waiting to take Jem and his companions to rendezvous with a squadron of the Knights of St John. Once Jem's party had boarded the galley they set sail immediately, but just in time, as a cavalry detachment of the imperial army had just arrived in Corycus in pursuit of them. The galley sailed for Anamur, a seaside fortress on the southernmost coast of Asia Minor controlled by the Karamanid, where arrangements had been made for a Rhodian squadron, commanded by Don Alvaro de Zuniga, Prior of Castile, to take the party on to Rhodes.

When the Karamanian galley was off Anamur it was spotted by the Rhodian flotilla. Don Alvaro had been given strict orders by the Knights' Council not to put any troops or passengers ashore on Asia Minor, since the knights did not want to unduly provoke Beyazit or draw attention to their activities. After signals had been exchanged, Don Alvaro sent a barque to fetch Jem and his party to transfer them to the *Grande Nef du Tresor*, the flagship of the flotilla – a magnificent galley that was said to be the finest vessel in the Mediterranean.

D'Aubusson and the Council of Knights had in the meanwhile drafted a letter of safe conduct for Jem, granting him asylum on Rhodes and the right to leave the island whenever he wished. Before boarding the barque, the letter was read out to Jem. At that point Firenk Süleyman took his master aside, telling him that he had serious reservations about the sincerity of the knights, whom he believed intended to use Jem purely to further their own interests. But Jem felt that he had no choice but to accept their offer of asylum, and so he boarded the barque, which took him and his companions out to the *Tresor*. Once again they were just in time, for as the barque pulled away Jem could see a detachment of Beyazit's army taking possession of the fortress at Anamur.

Jem was welcomed aboard the *Tresor* with a cannonade and a

flourish of trumpets, which doubtless raised his spirits. As the flotilla made ready to depart Jem wrote a farewell letter to his brother. He attached it to an arrow and fired it toward the fortress at Anamur, hoping that it would be found and delivered to Beyazit. The contents of the letter are quoted by the seventeenth-century historian Richard Knolles in his *Lives of the Othoman Kings and Emperors*. In it Jem expressed his deep resentment at how he had been forced to throw himself on the mercy of the Christians:

> Thou knowest, (most unkind and cruel brother), that I flie not unto the Christians, the mortall enemies of the Othoman family; for hatred of my religion and nation; but enforced thereunto by thy injurious dealing, and dangerous practices which thou incessantly attemptest against me, yea even in my extreme miserie. But this assured hope I carry with me, that the time will come when as thou the author of so great wrong, or thy children, shall receive the just guerdon [reward] of this thy present tyrannie against thy brother.

And so Jem left Turkey for an uncertain future, looking back at the mountains of Anatolia as they receded in the distance, wondering if he would ever again see his homeland.

5

The Castle of the Knights

O N 22 JULY 1482 the Rhodian flotilla headed due west from Anamur to Rhodes, a voyage of about 300 miles along the Mediterranean coast of Asia Minor. Don Alvaro, commander of the expedition, had already sent a fast galley ahead to alert Pierre d'Aubusson, so that the knights could prepare for Jem's arrival on Rhodes.

On the first evening of the voyage Don Alvaro invited Jem to have supper with him in the wardroom of the *Tresor*. At table Jem sat cross-legged on a divan in the Turkish fashion, while Don Alvaro sat on a bench facing him, with an interpreter between them. As the maître d'hôtel directed the servants bringing out the food, he carefully tasted each of the dishes that were set before the young prince. Puzzled by this, Jem questioned Don Alvaro who said it was the custom to have a taster sample the food being presented to a royal guest, to assure him that it had not been poisoned. According to the chronicle by Guillaume Caoursin – who refers to Jem alternatively as 'Zizim' and 'the barbarian' – Jem replied that there was no need for a taster as he had no fear of being poisoned when he was the guest of such noble and distinguished knights and that if he had been afraid he would not have put his life into their hands, and now that he was among such generous souls he would ask them to treat him as an ordinary guest and not a prince. Don Alvaro and the other knights applauded at this, and Jem proceeded to take food from all the dishes on the table, heaping it on to his plate and feeding himself with both hands, for he had had little to eat in the previous days.

One of Jem's companions, Ayas Bey, was in fact his *çaşnegirbaşı*, or chief taster, but Jem did not mention this to the knights, not wanting to spoil the gesture he had made. Ayas had been with Jem since the prince's childhood, as had others in his entourage: his tutor Nasuh Bey and one of his officers, Jelal Bey. Also accompanying Jem at this time were his secretary Haydar Bey, his *kapıcıbaşı* (chief doorkeeper) Sinan Bey, his *hazinedarbaşı* (chief treasurer) Hüseyin Bey, his maternal uncle Ali Bey, another Ali Bey who was his *imrahorbaşı* (chief equerry), his messengers Firenk Süleyman and Doğan, and seven others identified as Ahmet Bey, Mustafa Bey, Sirmment Ağa, Sofi Sadi, Salih, Yusuf Yazıcı, and Süleyman.

ରୋ

The 300-mile voyage took a week, during which time d'Aubusson made elaborate preparations for Jem's arrival. The city of Rhodes still bore signs of the damage from the Turkish siege of 1480, and d'Aubusson wanted to complete the repairs before Jem arrived, particularly to the great Palace of the Grand Master, which had been remodelled and expanded.

The fortified city of Rhodes, built at the north-eastern extremity of the island, comprised two main parts, the Kastello and the

Chora. The Kastello, or Castle of the Knights, was the smaller, northernmost part of the city. This was the preserve of the Order of the Hospitallers of St John of Jerusalem, its principal buildings being the Palace of the Grand Master, the Hospital, and the inns, the *auberges*, of the order, which lined the main thoroughfare of the Kastello, the Street of the Knights. The Kastello was separated by an inner wall from the Chora, or main town which included the commercial centre and the quarters of the Greeks, Jews and western Europeans.

Each of the inns housed knights from one of the *langue*, or tongues, into which the order was divided by nation. There were originally seven *langue*; these were, in order of seniority: Provence, Auvergne, France, Italy, Aragon and Catalonia, England and Germany. Then in 1462 an eighth *langue* was formed which included both Castile and Portugal. Pope Pius II wrote of the English *langue*, to which the Scots and the Irish also belonged, 'there was nothing the Scots liked better than abuse of the English'. The income of the order was originally derived from landed property throughout Europe, all of which had been bestowed on the Hospitallers by wealthy donors. Eventually these properties, which came to be called commanderies, were each placed under the supervision of a member of the order. The supreme head of the order, the grand master, was elected for life. During the last century of the order's occupation of Rhodes seven of the eleven grand masters were French, including four from the *langue* of Auvergne; the third of these was Pierre d'Aubusson.

D'Aubusson was born in 1423 in La Marche, in central France. His father was Renaud, Lord of Monteil-le-Vicomte and Viscount of La Marche, his mother the Lady Marguerite Chambon. D'Aubusson's family could trace their lineage back to both the

Dukes of Normandy and the Saxon kings of England, and had been semi-independent *seigneurs* in La Marche. Pierre d'Aubusson had fought against the Swiss in 1444 in the army of the Dauphin, the future Louis XI. He had taken part in the war between King Sigismund of Hungary and the Ottomans, after which he returned to France and served under Charles VII in the war against the English. When the latter war ended he journeyed to Rhodes and was accepted in the *langue* of Auvergne. He fought against the Turks at Kos in 1457 and in 1470 he commanded the Rhodian squadron that had been sent to help the Venetians defend Euboea against Fatih. The grand master Gianbattista Orsini appointed d'Aubusson as Prior of Auvergne. During the last three years of Orsini's grand mastership, 1473–76, he passed over virtually all of his responsibilities to d'Aubusson, who concentrated his efforts on strengthening the defences of Rhodes against the impending attack of the Turks.

When Orsini died in 1476 d'Aubusson was the natural successor and was unanimously elected grand master. According to a contemporary historian, d'Aubusson was 'of fine person and acute intelligence and easily captured the friendship of anyone who met him and whose affection he studied to win'. He went on to distinguish himself in the siege of Rhodes by the Turkish admiral Mesih Pasha in 1480, during which he personally led the defenders, battling hand-to-hand with the Turks even after he had been wounded five times.

Beneath d'Aubusson was a network of bailiffs, also known as the 'grand crosses'. There were three categories of bailiff: conventual, capitular and honourary. And it was the conventual bailiffs who were the elected heads of the eight inns at Rhodes, each holding important posts in the military hierarchy of the order.

The bailiff of the *langue* of Provence was the grand commander and president of the treasury, comptroller of the expenditure, superintendent of stores, governor of the arsenal, and master of the ordnance. The bailiff of Auvergne was the grand marshal and commander of all the armed forces, both military and naval. The bailiff of France was the grand hospitaller, serving as director of the hospitals and infirmaries. The bailiff of Italy was grand admiral, acting as second-in-command to the grand marshal. The bailiff of Aragon was commissary-general, while the bailiff of Germany was chief engineer. The bailiff of England was Turcopolier, or chief of the light cavalry, the so-called turcopoles, who were sons of Christian fathers by Turkish mothers. The turcopoles were brought up as Christians and were paid to serve as cavalrymen in the order, dressed in Islamic fashion and familiar with the ways of Turkish warfare. The English knight John Kendal was appointed Turcopolier in 1477 and fought in the defence of Rhodes in the siege of 1480 and served afterwards as envoy to the papal court.

The heroic defence of Rhodes had made d'Aubusson and his knights heroes throughout the Christian world. Guillaume Caoursin, the vice chancellor of the order, was made ambassador to the papal court in Rome, and the Knights of St John were excused from paying taxes to the papacy for the next five years. D'Aubusson immediately began rebuilding the city of Rhodes and repairing the damage to its fortifications, as well as constructing new ships for the Rhodian fleet, for he knew that it was just a matter of time before the Ottomans would make a renewed attempt to take the island. This was one of the reasons d'Aubusson had responded so quickly to Jem's request for asylum, for d'Aubusson realized that Jem could be used to keep Beyazit at bay, and that with Jem in his possession he could play on the sultan's fear that his brother would act as a figurehead in a new crusade against the Turks.

The *Grande Nef du Tresor* arrived at Rhodes on 29 July 1482, drawing up alongside a wooden jetty which had been designed so that Jem could ride ashore on horseback. The jetty was covered with carpets and cloths embroidered in gold and silver, and the stone pier of the port was strewn with flowers, as were the streets through which Jem was to pass. The entire population of the city lined the route along which the royal parade passed, together with Greek, Venetian, Genoese, Florentine, English, French and Flemish merchants, as well as seamen from all over Europe and North Africa. Many townspeople looked on from the gaily decorated balconies and rooftops of their houses, in a holiday atmosphere created by the excitement of the arrival of the son of the infamous Mehmet the Conqueror.

Jem rode ashore, on a 'most beautiful horse' which had been presented to him by the knights. A cannonade was fired from the island's fortress, a band of trumpeters and drummers struck up on the quay and the populace applauded enthusiastically. Looking out appreciatively on the huge crowd that had gathered to greet him, Jem remarked to one of his companions that 'it was with great justice that the Rhodian women were considered the loveliest in Asia', and he was pleased that they were not shrouded in veils and robes, as they would have been in Anatolia.

Representatives of the grand master and a troupe of sumptuously dressed pages greeted Jem and his companions and led them through the Marine Gate, the main entry point to the town from the port, and on to the piazza at the centre of the commercial quarter of the Chora, where d'Aubusson and the other knights were waiting to meet them. D'Aubusson, mounted on a magnificent charger in the centre of a group of knights, rode slowly to the centre of the piazza to meet Jem. Caoursin, in his account of this historic meeting, wrote that Jem put his right index finger to his mouth three times in a gesture as if requesting silence, for 'such is the custom of Turkish princes when they exchange solemn salutations'. D'Aubusson and Jem shook hands and, speaking through an interpreter, exchanged greetings. The grand master, accompanied by the interpreter, then rode with Jem at his side to lead a cavalcade to the Street of the Knights and the Auberge de France, an annexe of which was to be the residence of the prince and his companions during their time on Rhodes. Jem's accommodation was on a side alley off the Street of the Knights, opposite the main building of the Auberge de France, in a stone structure in two storeys over a vaulted basement, with a roof terrace shaded by grape vines. The residence thereafter became known as the 'Palace of Zizim', a name that it bears to this day.

D'Aubusson suggested that Jem might like to rest before dinner, and led the prince to the door of his lodgings. Jem thanked him for his hospitality, dismounted from his horse with 'great agility', and, flanked by a pair of his attendants, bounded up the exterior staircase of the inn. Jem's spirits seemed higher than they had been at any time in the preceding weeks, buoyed by the warmth of the reception he had received and the hope that the knights would help him regain the sultanate.

As soon as the knights had secured custody of Jem on Rhodes, d'Aubusson notified the pope, asking his permission to negotiate a 'true peace' with the sultan, using Jem as a powerful diplomatic tool. The pope readily gave his permission, and d'Aubusson began the negotiations, informing Beyazit that in return for taking custody of Jem the order would no longer pay tribute to the sultan, give annual gifts, or send an annual envoy to the Porte. The knights asked that the Rhodians be given the privilege of free trade throughout the Ottoman Empire, subject only to the normal tolls and customs duties. They also requested that the sultan pay the knights for the expenses they had incurred in keeping his brother. In return the knights promised that Jem would be kept 'quiet and pacific ... so that no war could be waged against Beyazit on his account'.

On Jem's first evening on Rhodes he was escorted to the Palace of the Grand Master, where d'Aubusson had laid on a lavish banquet in his honour. Jem and d'Aubusson sat at the high table and conversed through an interpreter, whilst musicians and singers entertained them throughout the successive courses of the banquet.

The following morning the two men met again at the palace, where Jem explained through the interpreter the reasons why he had sought refuge with the knights on Rhodes. Jem, as quoted by Caoursin in his chronicle, told d'Aubusson that he had been forced to flee 'by the evilness of my brother', explaining, 'My thoughts were to take refuge and I did not know where to go, until at long last I thought of you, noble hero, and I remembered your illustrious reputation, which has spread as far as the Indies.' Continuing, he told the grand master of how he 'knew that your generosity and great wisdom would not be affected by what my father did to you in the past, and that you would not despise the son of the tyrant who comes to take refuge with you, and, on the contrary, support him with your advice, help and protection'. Jem explained to d'Aubusson that his claim to the Ottoman throne was based on the fact that he was born after his father became sultan, whereas when Beyazit was born Mehmet was only the crown prince. He assured the grand master that, if the Christian princes helped him regain his throne, they would gain in him 'a friend instead of an enemy, a host instead of an adversary, a faithful ally instead of a treacherous foe'.

D'Aubusson thanked Jem for his compliments and reiterated that the knights had welcomed him to Rhodes 'as a guest and as a friend ... It is up to us to respect the laws of hospitality, benevolence and love.' He urged Jem not to be disheartened for Christendom would support his just cause:

> Do not lose your courage and confidence for we will do whatever will be mutually beneficial to you and the Christians, given our ability, means and sensibilities, as well as those of the pontiff of Rome, the kings and potentates of the Christians, who hold the reins of Christendom, and their powerful, wise and zealous love for the interests of Christianity ... [the Christian princes] will know how to use the possibilities given to them by your arrival here. As for us we will not abandon you, and you will find us favourable to your cause. We have understood your claim to your rights and it gives us the sense that we support the right cause.

Jem then asked for d'Aubusson's help in bringing to Rhodes a number of his officers and servants whom he had been forced to leave behind in Anatolia, along with some of his belongings.

D'Aubusson immediately had a galley equipped and ordered that it take Jem's uncle Ali Bey to the Cilician coast, so that he could supervise the retrieval of the prince's men and possessions. The new arrivals would bring the number in Jem's entourage on Rhodes to thirty-seven.

During the days that followed Jem was feted at a series of banquets and joined the knights on a number of hunting parties, as d'Aubusson did everything he could to make his guest feel secure and happy. The knights' vice chancellor Caoursin had the opportunity to observe Jem at close quarters day in, day out, and recorded a detailed description of 'the barbarian prince's character', in a section of his memoir he titled 'Zizim's Physical and Moral Portrait':

> The king Zizim is 28 years old [he was in fact twenty-three at this time]. He is quite tall and his health is excellent. His expression is fierce. His blue eyes are aligned obliquely and his brows almost touch at the root of his nose; the left eyebrow turns up towards his forehead, the right one turns down over his eye. His mouth is small and his thick lips are almost always twisted to the left by a twitch. At times he uncovers and then hides again his teeth, and at the same time lowers his left lid to lift it again soon afterwards. His aquiline nose, somewhat salient toward the middle, is diverted at its tip to the left. His chin is small, his skin chestnut coloured. He doesn't let his sparse beard grow but trims it with scissors.

Caoursin also observed that Jem was built heavily, but that 'his weight does not hinder his ability to jump, ride, hunt or in archery. In fact he moves as if he were slender . . .' If Jem was 'displeased by something', Caoursin continued, he would immediately show his anger by rolling his eyes and by speaking with a shrill voice. But when in the presence of an important person, he composes his face, and, smiling, indulges in a role of simulation and dissimulation. When he talks quietly his speech is grave, tempered and modest, but he is not very talkative. Even as an exile and a fugitive, he does not lose his aristocratic dignity.

Caoursin also noted Jem's eating habits, physical activities, dress, moods, peculiarities, attitudes and talents, all evidence of how closely the prince was observed during his time on Rhodes:

He doesn't accept wine when not flavoured, for he thinks that this changes its nature, like vinegar, made out of wine but different in character . . . He likes roasted meat, dislikes boiled food, and eats with great appetite melons, grapes, pears, apples and other fruits of all kind. He eats little bread and drinks water after dissolving sugar in it. He can't bear heat, cold, or being hungry . . . He has a taste for luxurious clothing. He frequently uses spas and baths, and after bathing he douses himself in cold water. He is a good swimmer and goes to swim every day in the sea, naked, without prudishness in sight of everybody. He observes those around him and always seems a little sad and pensive. If he has shown any signs of joy it is in the presence of the grand master. He shows great piety and follows Mohammed's rule strictly. If he sees one of his people drunk with wine, he jumps on him with fury. He is so fidgety that he can't stay long in one place: he chose to sleep in every single room of his apartments and not even despised the roof terrace of the house. On the contrary, after having brought his bed out onto the terrace, he spent several nights under the stars. Very skilled in the Turkish language, he has since childhood applied his spirits to literature, and thus developed a talent

as an historian and has composed a book on the great deeds
of his father.

Although Jem had made it known that he found the women of
Rhodes very attractive – and some who came into his presence
were quite aware of this and played on it – none was willing to
meet him in private. Jem had purchased twenty Muslim slaves
whilst on Rhodes, including three women. One of the women, a
beautiful girl named Alméida, was chosen by Jem to be his mistress. Neither Sadüddin or Caoursin mention Alméida, who did
not appear publicly with Jem but remained sequestered in his
residence, a one-concubine harem to make up for the unavail-
ability of the Christian women on the island.

ന്മ

All the while Beyazit had been distracted by the war of succession,
the pope had failed to take advantage of the Ottomans' difficulties
and move any further toward organizing a crusade. Instead Sixtus
had become embroiled in a new war which not only created dishar-
mony in Europe, but which would soon threaten Rome itself. Sixtus
had formed an alliance with Venice against King Ferrante of Naples,
who invaded the papal states in mid-April 1482, supported by allies
in Ferrara, Florence, Milan, Mantua and Urbino. On 28 November
1482 a truce was concluded, and two weeks later a treaty of peace
was signed between Rome on one side and on the other Naples,
Milan and Florence, with Venice abstaining from the agreement.
But this led to a bitter dispute between Venice and the pope, who
began organizing an expedition against the Venetians.

When d'Aubusson first announced Jem's arrival on Rhodes to the Christian princes of Europe, Sixtus responded by saying that the Christian world would gain much from the possession of Jem, and that he could possibly use him in a crusade to 'rid the world of Mohammed's descendants'. In letters to the commanders of the Knights of St John in Europe d'Aubusson underlined that Jem was free to come and go as he pleased, part of the promise of safe conduct they had made to Jem. He informed the commanders of the promises that Jem had made to him, in which the prince swore that if he regained the throne he would return all territories the Turks had taken from the Christians, reassuring him that the Ottomans would never again wage war against Christendom. And d'Aubusson concluded the letters by saying that the friendship and hospitality the knights were showing to Jem would enable Christendom to achieve its aim of driving the Turks out of Europe. But privately d'Aubusson had little confidence that the Christian powers would manage to unite in peace and use Jem in a crusade. So in the meantime, with all of Italy at war, he saw no reason why he should not use the prince to extract every advantage that he could from the situation.

It was not long before Beyazit made contact with d'Aubusson through his agent, Hacı Ibrahim. After first unsuccessfully trying to involve the Venetians in helping him kidnap his brother, Beyazit promised to return to the knights all the treasures and relics that had been looted from their possessions by Turkish corsairs, provided that they discuss with him the future status of his brother Jem.

Meanwhile the Council of the Knights had been deliberating about what to do with Jem. They knew that Beyazit would try to extradite Jem and that they could not allow this because it would violate their laws of hospitality. They also knew that Beyazit might very well try to have his brother assassinated. Some of the knights feared that Beyazit would attack Rhodes and try to take his brother by storm, and so wanted to send Jem to one of their commanderies in France. Others wanted to keep the prince confined to the Castle of the Knights so as to have more direct control of him.

Jem was aware of these discussions, and he now realized that he should have heeded Firenk Süleyman's warning and not have come to Rhodes. He began wondering if he should have accepted Beyazit's offer of an appanage, perhaps in eastern Anatolia, where at least he would have some freedom of movement. This led him to write a letter to his brother, an abject appeal for a reconciliation in which he threw himself on his brother's mercy and asked for his forgiveness. Doubts have been cast on the authenticity of this letter. Even if Jem did write it, he may merely have done so in order to put on record that he had tried to bring about peace with his brother Beyazit. Jem must have known that such an appeal would be refused, and this would then justify his effort to seize the Ottoman throne by force, with Christian help. In fact, without waiting for an answer from Beyazit, Jem spoke to d'Aubusson on 18 August and asked to be sent immediately to Western Europe.

Jem's plan was to travel to Hungary, where he would take refuge with King Mathias Corvinus at the capital, Buda. Jem believed that the Hungarian king was the best chance he had to regain his throne. Corvinus, the son of John Hunyadi, was the most powerful Christian ruler in the Balkans and had been fighting against the Turks across their common border for nearly a quarter of a century. He was married to Beatrice of Aragon, daughter of

Ferrante I, and had allied himself with his father-in-law against their common enemy Beyazit. The Hungarian army together with the Neapolitan fleet made up a formidable force which would be the core of any crusade against the Turks, and the great wealth of Corvinus would be a major contribution to financing the expedition.

At the same meeting on 18 August, d'Aubusson informed Jem that the Council of the Knights had come to a decision: Jem was to be moved to a commandery in France. D'Aubusson stressed that if Jem remained on Rhodes he was liable to be captured by Beyazit. Jem therefore agreed to the knights' wishes, hoping to move on from France to Hungary in due course. According to the account by Caoursin, the Council of the Knights had decided, almost to a man, to inform the pope, the emperor Frederick III of Germany, and all other Christian princes that Jem, whom Caoursin referred to as 'the King', would be moved to mainland Europe: 'He was a gift sent by God for the good of Christendom,' Caoursin wrote, 'and it seems best to bring the King to the West under the protection of the Grand Master and the Knights of Rhodes.' Ten days later d'Aubusson and the Council sent an envoy to the Porte, and informed them also of their plan to send Jem to Europe.

Orders were given to prepare the *Grande Nef du Tresor* to transport Jem to France, and the Council met again on 31 August and confirmed the decision. D'Aubusson thereupon appointed the members of the order who would accompany Jem and allocated the expenses of the journey. Jem and his entourage would sail the following day, this time under the command of Guy de Blanchefort, Prior of Auvergne and nephew of Pierre d'Aubusson. The itinerary was explained to Jem through interpreters 'skilled in Latin and Turkish', and Jem replied that he was satisfied with the plans and thanked d'Aubusson for having arranged his journey.

At d'Aubusson's urging, Jem composed three documents and left them with the grand master. The first document gave d'Aubusson the power of proxy to deal in Jem's name in all negotiations that the order might engage in with Beyazit and other rulers. The second stated that Jem was leaving Rhodes of his own free will and under no compulsion from the knights. The only stipulation that Jem insisted on was that his freedom of movement should not be restricted, as guaranteed by the original promise of safe conduct drawn up by the knights. The third document put in writing the promises Jem had already made to d'Aubusson, which would come into effect when he secured his inheritance. These included pledges that Jem would remain at peace with the knights; that all Turkish ports would be open to them without restrictions or taxes of any kind; 'that the Grand Master shall withdraw every year from my dominions 300 Christians of both sexes, and of such ages as he may select, to transfer them to the island of the order, or for any other purpose which he may think advisable', and that 'in order to make some return for the outlay which the Grand Master has made, and is making every day, with such liberality on my account, I agree to pay him in specie the sum of 150,000 gold crowns'.

Jem's final pledge stated:

> I promise upon oath to restore to him [the grand master] all the islands, all the lands, and all the fortresses which the Ottoman emperors have captured from the Order . . .
>
> In testimony that this is my will I have signed this deed with my hand, and have sealed it with my seal. Done at

Rhodes, and in the palace of the Auberge de France, on the 31st of August 1482.

The night before Jem's day of departure d'Aubusson threw a farewell banquet for him in the Palace of the Grand Master. Jem was seated at the place of honour, next to d'Aubusson at the high table, though he would have preferred to recline cross-legged on a divan in the Turkish fashion. Throughout the evening he sat hunched over the table, staring down at his plate, only lifting his eyes to cast discrete sidelong glances at d'Aubusson to observe his Western table manners. Singers and musicians entertained them during the meal, including a quartet of knights of the English *langue* who sang to the accompaniment of an instrument described by Sadüddin as having 'four joined flutes', perhaps a bagpipe played by a Scot or an Irishman. The song was applauded enthusiastically, though Jem paid little attention to this or any of the other entertainment. D'Aubusson, noticing this, called for a Turkish slave to be brought to the dining hall, where the man played a 'barbarous instrument', probably one of the traditional stringed instruments of Anatolia, such as the *saz*. According to Caoursin, this brought a faint smile to Jem's face.

The following morning Jem and his companions were escorted from their lodgings by the knights, who marched in procession with their guests to the harbour, where the *Tresor* was waiting to set sail. Jem and d'Aubusson said an emotional farewell to one another, as recorded by an anonymous Western observer: 'forgetting the proud reserve of his Asiatic nature ... Zizim fell at d'Aubusson's feet in a paroxysm of grief, bathing them in tears ... while the calm fearless d'Aubusson wept upon the neck of Zizim tears of paternal affection'. Thus did Jem end his stay with the man to whom he had entrusted his future, but who had already and would further betray him. Jem boarded the *Tresor* along with his entourage and soon afterwards the crew set sail. Jem had been on Rhodes just thirty-four days, the beginning of an exile that would last for the rest of his life.

6

Across the Mediterranean

T HE *GRAND NEF DU TRESOR* set sail from Rhodes on
1 September 1482 with Jem and his party, which now numbered fifty-seven, including the twenty slaves he had purchased on
Rhodes. Guy de Blanchefort had under his command 300 'knights'
servants' as well as the crew of the *Tresor*, and the Council had
elected two other knights to assist Blanchefort in conducting Jem to
France, namely Merlo de Piozzasco, Prior of Lombardy, and Charles
Allemand, *seigneur* of Rochechinard and commander of Avignon.
One Guillaume Archinault, a knight of the *langue* of Provence,
was elected to be Jem's maître d'hôtel, and he would henceforth
have responsibility for supervising the prince's household.

The first leg of the voyage took the *Tresor* westward from
Rhodes around the south-westernmost peninsula of Asia Minor,
passing the site of ancient Knidos. There the *Tresor* headed north
to head for Kos, the second largest isle of the Dodecanese after
Rhodes, where the knights had fortified the main town on the
eastern end of the island, just opposite their great fortress at
Bodrum on the coast of Asia Minor. The voyage took nine days,
more than twice as long as usual, the *Tresor* having been hampered
by a heavy storm and contrary winds.

Jem and his companions went ashore at Kos, the only time on the voyage that they were permitted to leave the ship, for the knights were concerned about the prince's security and were trying to keep his journey secret. Jem and his guardians were received there at the Castle of the Knights, erected by the Venetians in 1450 and enlarged by Pierre d'Aubusson after the siege of Rhodes in 1480, when the Turks also attacked Kos. After leaving the island the *Tresor* headed westward across the Aegean, sailing through the Cyclades, the 'encircling isles' scattered around the sacred islet of Delos, legendary birthplace of Apollo. The Cyclades had since the early thirteenth century been held by the Venetians, usually governed by a duke on Naxos, the largest isle of the archipelago, which the *Tresor* would have passed halfway across the Aegean. The *Tresor* then sighted Cape Matapan, the southernmost point of mainland Greece, and rounded the south-westernmost cape of the Peloponnesus, where it was now in sight of the two great Venetian fortresses at Koroni and Methoni, known as the 'eyes of the Republic' for all ships sailing that way passed under the eyes and guns of the Venetians, guarding the sea lanes of the Serenissima's maritime empire.

Once clear of the last Peloponnesian cape the *Tresor* headed westward across the open waters of the Ionian Sea toward Sicily, a distance of some 350 nautical miles. On 2 October the *Tresor* finally reached the Sicilian coast at Syracuse, where the knights stopped for two days to take on supplies.

The island was at the time under Spanish rule, which began in 1409 when it became part of the Kingdom of Aragon. Alfonso V of Aragon inherited Sicily in 1416 and used it as his base to conquer Naples and the southern half of Italy. When Alfonso died in 1458 he was succeeded in Aragon by his brother Juan II, who was also King of Navarre through his wife Blanche. Sicily reverted to Juan, while Alfonso's illegitimate son Ferrante inherited the Kingdom of Naples. Juan's son Ferdinand married Isabella of Castile in 1469. Isabella succeeded to the throne of Castile in 1474 and five years later, when Juan II died, Ferdinand became King of Aragon. Ferdinand's rise to power was noted by Machiavelli in *The Prince,* in which he commented: 'We have in our days Ferdinand, the present King of Spain, who may, not improperly, be called a new prince, since he has been transformed from a small and weak king into the greatest monarch in Christendom.' Ferdinand and Isabella, called by Pope Alexander VI the 'Catholic Kings', would be two of the players in the 'great game' that developed around the custody of Jem Sultan.

The knights kept Jem and his companions out of sight while they were in Syracuse, and again when they stopped for a day and a night in Messina. Blanchefort felt that King Ferrante would have agents watching for Jem, whose departure from Rhodes would have been noted by his spies there. One of Ferrante's spies did indeed leave Rhodes immediately after the *Tresor* departed. It would have been completely in character for Ferrante to have made an attempt to capture Jem en route, hoping to use him as a pawn in his intermittent war with Venice and the papacy and his negotiations with Beyazit.

The *Tresor* sailed out through the Strait of Messina, the narrow waterway between the north-eastern tip of Sicily and the toe of Italy. Seeing that night that the sea in the strait was calm, Blanchefort decided that he, his officers and Jem would dine on deck by candlelight. But their lights were spotted by a Venetian galley, which seems to have been patrolling the strait to keep watch on any movement by the Neapolitan fleet. At dawn the

Venetian ship closed in on them, whereupon the knights, thinking that they were being attacked by pirates, armed themselves and prepared to fight, sending Jem and his companions below deck. But then the two sides recognized one another's ensigns: the white cross of the Knights of St John and the winged lion of St Mark, patron saint of Venice, and they each put down their arms. A delegation of Venetians set out from their galley in a small boat and were invited aboard the *Tresor*, where they were greeted cordially by Blanchefort and his officers. The Venetians asked if Prince Jem was aboard, and Blanchefort said that he was not. After receiving presents from the knights the visitors departed. Blanchefort later learned from d'Aubusson that Jem's departure from Rhodes had been reported to Beyazit by agents of the Serenissima, who, without actually being disloyal to Christendom, took this opportunity to maintain the Republic's peace treaty with the Ottomans by informing the sultan of his brother's movements.

The following day they passed nineteen galleys in succession, all of them flying the ensign of the King of Naples, but none of them challenged the *Tresor*. Next day they passed through the Aeolian and Lipari Islands, a screen of islets off the north-eastern coast of Sicily. Sadüddin describes how the volcanic isle of Stromboli, the northernmost of the group, was in eruption when they passed, 'covered with smoke by day and at night transformed into a mountain of fire'. Sadüddin also says that Jem was profoundly impressed by the volcano, which evidenced to him the boundless power of the Creator.

Their course then took them north-north-west through the Tyrrhenian Sea, out of sight of land until they passed between the isle of Elba and Corsica. The knights passed the time trapping sea birds that alighted on the rigging, an activity that Jem thought to be cruel – though he himself was an avid hunter of wild birds. One day they spotted a whale that Jem compared to an overturned galley, spouting a stream of water 'as high as two pikes', according to Sadüddin. The knights told Jem how whales were caught using baited lines attached to floating barrels, and of how they were processed afterwards to give as much as 200 barrels of oil each.

North of Corsica they entered the Ligurian Sea, where they changed course to head westward, passing another spouting whale. Then on 16 October they landed at Villefranche-sur-Mer, just to the east of Nice, forty-five days after leaving Rhodes.

The following day Jem and his companions disembarked and were taken to Nice. Villefranche and Nice were then part of the Duchy of Savoy, an alpine principality within the sphere of influence of the French kingdom. Blanchefort had originally planned to land in Toulon or Marseilles but he received word that the plague was raging in France. Thus he had decided that he would land in Villefranche and wait in Nice while permission was obtained from Louis XI to transport Jem to one of the order's commanderies in France.

The royal governor of Nice, Antoine de La Foret, had been instructed by Duke Charles I, the ruler of Savoy, to do everything he could to make Jem comfortable during his stay. The governor transmitted these instructions to Gaspare Grimaldi, a wealthy Genoese merchant who would be Jem's host in Nice. But Grimaldi was secretly in the employ of Beyazit, one of a network of agents who would regularly report to the sultan on Jem's whereabouts and activities, as well as sending other news that might be of interest to the Porte.

Grimaldi put up Jem in his palace on Le Chateau, the acropolis in Nice, where he lived with his family, which included six daughters and, according to the French sources, 'a bevy of nieces'. According to the chronicles, on Jem's first night there Grimaldi's oldest daughter brought him a bed warmer and when she put this under his blanket she lightly touched his thigh, arousing him, and made no objection when he took her into his arms. Her younger sisters subsequently made themselves available to Jem, as did her cousins. Thus a family harem was created for Jem by Grimaldi, who perhaps hoped that one of his daughters or nieces might one day become a sultana.

Jem and his companions seemed to have greatly enjoyed the pleasures of Nice, whose way of life was so utterly unlike anything they had seen in Muslim Turkey. Sadüddin wrote of Nice that it has 'very amiable young men and women, innumerable gardens and vineyards'. He goes on to say that the knights brought

> pleasant virgins from Nice to dance for Jem. These girls did not wear veils to cover themselves like Turkish women. On the contrary, they took pleasure in flirting and kissing, and after dancing they went to sit on the laps of their lovers, with naked breasts. Amongst them there was one who was particularly charming, to whom Jem was strongly attracted.

But according to local tradition, the women who entertained Jem and his companions were not virgins brought from Nice by the knights, as Sadüddin supposed, but prostitutes from the bordellos of the port.

Jem wrote a number of pieces of verse soon after he arrived in Nice, one of them a couplet in which he simply expressed his delight in the town:

> *What a wonderful place is this city of Nice*
> *A man can stay there and do as he please!*

But the first lines of a more sombre piece expressed Jem's resignation to the fate that had brought him to France, which he calls Frengistan.

> *Oh take your cup, Oh Jem Jemshid*
> *We are in Frengistan*
> *Destiny has to decide*
> *No one can escape his fate*

In a later stanza of the same poem he speaks of the young (male) beauties he found in the city:

> *Eighteen charming well-made boys*
> *Each the son of a noble*
> *Hold in their lovely hands*
> *Golden glasses of sparkling wine.*

Despite such distractions, Jem was anxious to be on his way. He still believed his best hope lay with Mathias Corvinus, who might offer him the command of an army to help him regain his throne. But before he could make his way to Hungary he would have to obtain a passport from the French king. Guy de Blanchefort played along with Jem, and asked him to designate one of his own men to accompany the delegation of knights who were going to petition Louis XI to grant a passport to the Turkish prince. Jem asked how long the mission would take and was told that it would be about twelve days, whereupon he ordered Nasuh Bey to accompany the knights as his representative.

The knights brought Nasuh to a village a day's ride from Nice, where he was confined while they continued on their journey.

After twelve days had passed Jem asked for news of the mission, and Blanchefort put him off by saying that there had been unexpected delays, an excuse that he was to give in various forms over the weeks that followed.

The French-speaking Firenk Süleyman had managed to eavesdrop on the knights' conversations and found out that they were stalling. He informed Jem, who said that he had come to the same conclusion himself. The knights then had Süleyman arrested and imprisoned for spying, but Jem intervened and persuaded them to leave the servant in his custody. Süleyman managed to acquire some Western clothing to replace his robes, and at the first opportunity, with Jem's help, he escaped from Nice, promising his master that he would remain in touch and help him to gain his freedom. But Firenk Süleyman was never seen again, and his fate is unknown.

Jem was kept waiting in Nice for nearly four months, without any word as to whether Louis XI had approved his petition to travel through France. The knights prevaricated and said that the king would not grant an audience to Jem because he did not want to lay eyes on a Muslim, and he would certainly not allow a son of the hated Turkish Conqueror to travel across his kingdom. But the truth was that Guy de Blanchefort had sent an envoy to Plessis-le-Tours, where Louis XI was holding court, to ask the king 'if it was his pleasure to suffer Jem in his kingdom', which permission was granted readily. But Jem was never told of this, for Blanchefort had no intention of allowing his prisoner to see the king. Jem then asked the knights if they would help him contact Mathias Corvinus, but he was told that this was impossible, although they knew that Corvinus was keen to make contact with Jem.

Since Jem's departure from Rhodes, Pierre d'Aubusson had been busy writing letters asking the Christian rulers of Europe whether they would be prepared to unite in a crusade against the Turks. However, his efforts came to nothing: the papacy and Venice were too preoccupied with their war against Naples; Pope Sixtus merely congratulated d'Aubusson on successfully sending Jem to France, saying that this would surely be beneficial to Christendom, and King Ferrante replied that although he felt the grand master's possession of Jem gave Christendom a welcome opportunity to use the prince in a crusade against the Turks, he regretted that since he was at war with the pope and the doge he was not in a position to take part in a campaign against the Turks.

D'Aubusson also wrote to Beyazit to reassure him that he had 'sent Jem to France not to worry you but to guarantee his security'. The sultan responded by sending an envoy to Rhodes with presents for the grand master, and by writing to Louis XI offering him a huge annual subsidy to keep Jem in France, on condition that he did not pass him on to any other Christian ruler.

Beyazit and d'Aubusson had, in fact, been in constant communication since the day that Jem left Rhodes. On 2 September 1482 d'Aubusson sent two envoys on a mission to Beyazit. These were Guy de Montarnaud and Leonard de Prat, who were empowered to conclude the peace proposal that the knights had made to the sultan when they first took possession of his brother. The envoys left Rhodes on the same day that Jem sailed for France, and made their way to Edirne, where Beyazit was holding court. Beyazit received the envoys cordially, and called in Gedik Ahmet Pasha and Mesih Pasha to begin discussions with them.

Both of the pashas spoke Greek, and so the Rhodian envoys addressed them in that language. Montarnaud spoke first and said that they would negotiate as equals, and that there would be no mention of tribute or the obligation of sending annual envoys to the sultan. Gedik was offended by this, and said that he was surprised that the envoys of such a little state could presume to speak on equal terms with the representatives of a great empire. The Rhodian envoys kept calm and said that they were aware of the awesome power of the sultan, but their order relied on the Christian values of the knights and on divine protection, and they would rather die in arms than stain their honour with a cowardly peace. Gedik was about to answer in wrath, but Mesih, whispering to him in Turkish, said that the knights were indomitable and urged him to move on. Leonard de Prat, who understood Turkish, told Montarnaud what had been said, and they realized that they had gained an initial advantage in the negotiations, which then proceeded calmly. After several meetings the negotiators agreed on terms and a peace treaty was drafted. The document was submitted to the sultan, who agreed to its contents and gave orders to conclude the treaty with the knights without delay.

Contemporary sources refer to the treaty as the most favourable ever granted by a sultan to the Christians up to that time. When the document was ready Beyazit signed the treaty, which was to hold for the duration of his lifetime. After the two pashas left Beyazit invited the Rhodian envoys to see him. Speaking through an interpreter, the sultan asked after his brother and was told that he was in good health. He then gave them rich gifts as farewell presents, after which they departed for Rhodes with the Turkish envoy, Hayrettin Bey, a favourite of the sultan.

The envoys reached Rhodes on 2 December and gave copies
of the treaty to d'Aubusson, who after reading it to the Council
of the Knights made the document public. Hayrettin Bey met
with the grand master and the Council to present his credentials,
transmitting a message from the sultan expressing his gratitude
for their hospitality to Jem and stating that he would reimburse
all of their expenses. D'Aubusson responded by saying that Jem
had been received in accordance with the laws of humanity, with
no regard to his being an enemy.

D'Aubusson, using the proxy that Jem had left with him,
reached an agreement with the Turkish envoy over the prince's
situation on 7 December 1482. As part of the agreement, the
sultan was to send the knights on 1 August of each year a payment
of 45,000 ducats (of which d'Aubusson himself apparently kept
10,000), and for the present year the same amount was to be paid
in forty days.

ର୍ଯ୍ଦ

Soon after the peace treaty between the Knights of Rhodes and
the Ottomans was signed, Beyazit attended to some unfinished
business: the elimination of the aged Gedik Ahmet Pasha. Late
in the autumn of 1482 Beyazit invited Gedik and all of his other
pashas to a festive dinner at Edirne Sarayı, at which wine was
served openly and everyone present had a great deal to drink,
including the sultan. All the talk at the dinner was about Jem,
and it greatly annoyed Beyazit to see how interested the pashas
were in his brother's adventures, which were already beginning
to take on legendary aspects. Beyazit deliberately provoked Gedik

by saying that he had reduced the budget of the army and was going to eliminate some of the top ranks. Gedik, who was quite drunk, responded scornfully: 'If you provoke the army your throne will be in danger. A sultan with a living brother will find it difficult!' But Beyazit let this incident pass, since he had already prepared his next move.

When the other guests got up to leave Beyazit told Gedik to remain, saying that he had something he wanted to tell him in private. As soon as they were alone Beyazit summoned his guards, who arrested Gedik and carried him away to the palace dungeon, where he was tortured, presumably to reveal what he knew about whether Jem's supporters were plotting a revolt. As soon as the Janissaries in Edirne learned of this they rioted, as they had done before, for Gedik Ahmet Pasha remained their hero. Beyazit had Gedik brought to the palace gate to show that he was alive, which reassured the Janissaries. But as soon as the Janissaries had left Beyazit had Gedik killed by his executioners, thus ending the illustrious career of the greatest Turkish general of his time.

Beyazit then took the opportunity to order the execution of Jem's two-year-old son Oğuzhan, who had been held as a hostage in the Ottoman court since the last days of Mehmet the Conqueror. The sultan sent a secret message to Iskender Pasha in Istanbul, telling him to have the infant killed quietly, making it appear as if the prince had died a natural death. Iskender subsequently wrote back and told Beyazit that his orders had been carried out without disturbance.

When Jem learned of Oğuzhan's death months later, he was heartbroken, and later composed a *mersiye*, or threnody, in which he refers to the rich man Karun mentioned in the Kuran:

We heard that our son Oğuzhan had been martyred
And Jem was filled with sorrow in Frengistan.

I should not be crying out in sorrow
But the loss of Oğuzhan has put me in burning fire

I would not have exchanged a single hair of my Oğuzhan
For all the wealth of Karun and the empire of Osman.

Jem knew in his heart that his son had not died of natural causes. He had no doubt that his brother would try to eliminate him too, for as long as Jem was alive Beyazit would never feel secure as sultan.

Having made peace with the Knights of St John, Beyazit sent his envoy, Iskender Bey, to Venice to conclude a peace treaty with the Serenissima. Iskender told the Venetians that the sultan would like to see Jem in their custody, regardless of cost. If that could be managed Beyazit would give the Morea to the Venetians, and Venice would soon thereafter be 'the mistress of all of Greece'. The Venetians responded through Jacomo de Mezo, the interpreter for the Council of Ten, the doge's cabinet, who said that the Venetians would do everything they could to satisfy the desires of the sultan, and that they would so inform all the *bailos* of their maritime empire, and that the governors would contact Mesih Pasha, who was in charge of this matter. But the truth was that the Serenissima had no intention of helping Beyazit over Jem, and that they would move as the situation developed, and according to their own interests, avoiding direct action.

Early in 1483 Guy de Blanchefort decided that the plague had abated to the point where he could risk moving Jem from Nice. The women who had given solace to Jem during his stay were sad to see him leave: Turkish tradition has it that the prostitutes of Nice gave Jem two farewell presents to remember them by, a chimpanzee and a white parrot. Both creatures were credited with having exceptional talents: the chimpanzee could play chess and the parrot had been taught to speak in Turkish and Arabic, and included in his repertoire the ability to recite verses from the Kuran. The Turkish tradition goes on to say that the chimpanzee and the parrot remained with Jem for the rest of his days, cheering him up in his long years of exile. European sources do not mention the chimpanzee or the parrot, and here history and myth part company in their accounts of the life of Jem Sultan.

❧

7

La Belle Hélène

JEM AND HIS COMPANIONS left Nice on 6 February 1483, the knights deciding to head inland to the north-east, to Chambéry, the heart of the Duchy of Savoy, where they would wait until they received word of Louis XI of France's attitude toward their holding of the Turkish prince. The knights took an indirect route in the hope that they would attract less attention, for they knew that Jem was now being sought after by several of the Christian princes of Europe.

The party initially followed the course of the main highroad between Nice and Turin. According to Sadüddin, their first stop was at the village of l'Escarène, about thirty miles from Nice. There Jem and his companions were rejoined by Nasuh Bey, who had been sent by his master some three months before to make contact with the King of France. Nasuh told Jem that the knights had confined him to a house in the village while they continued on their journey to the French court. This confirmed Jem's suspicions that the knights had never intended for him to contact the King of France, and he now knew for certain that he was their prisoner.

On 8 February the group passed through the village of Coni,

which is not mentioned by Sadüddin, but the passage of Jem and his companions is mentioned in a local chronicle by an anonymous scholar who was obviously impressed by the sight of a Turkish prince and his retinue, now forty in number, all of them, he wrote, robed and turbaned. The chronicler noted that there were three women in the entourage and that one of them seemed to be the prince's mistress. The latter was doubtless the slave girl Alméida, who now had Jem to herself again having had to share him with so many women in Nice.

South of Turin the party turned westward to traverse the Alps at the Col du Mont Cenis at an altitude of 2,083 metres, passing from Piedmont into Savoy. They made the crossing in the dead of winter, under extremely hazardous conditions. Sadüddin wrote that they made their way down from the pass on sleighs:

> As it is impossible to descend this mountain on horseback, they put travellers who don't want to descend on foot onto sledges on the snow. The sledge-man launches the sledge into the void and leaps on. They get to the bottom in a flash. They bring their horses down by a roundabout way.

After crossing the Alps the party stopped in the villages of St-Jean-de-Maurienne and Aiguebelle before reaching Chambéry, capital of the Duchy of Savoy.

The House of Savoy had first come to prominence in 1046, when Countess Adelaide, heiress of a line of French counts of Savoy, married Oddone, son of Humbert 'the White-Handed', uniting the cisalpine and transalpine possessions of the two families. The Savoyard dynasty was intertwined with the Houses of Anjou and Burgundy, and at the time of Jem's arrival Charlotte of Savoy was married to Louis XI of France, whose heir apparent was the future Charles VIII. The reigning Duke of Savoy, Charles I, had succeeded his brother Philibert on 22 April 1482, at the age of fourteen, ruling from his palace at Chambéry. Charles was a nephew of Charlotte of Savoy and a ward of Louis XI.

At Chambéry the knights were told that Charles was away visiting his uncle, Louis XI, but that he was expected to return soon. After resting for a day or so the party moved a day's journey southwestward to les Échelles, where on 20 February Jem was placed in a commandery of the Knights of St John in a tower directly under le Grand Chartreuse, the spectacular massif that dominates the landscape between Chambéry and Grenoble. Hearing that the son of the late Grand Turk was in their midst, people from the surrounding area flocked to les Échelles to see Jem. One of them, whom Sadüddin refers to as 'a man of religion', brought Jem a present of a chain of onions, so that he should lack nothing he needed.

A letter Beyazit received from one of his spies during this time reported the fact that Jem was receiving numerous visitors at les Échelles, and that some of them wanted to join him in taking up arms against the sultan. One of Jem's visitors was an agent of Mathias Corvinus who requested that Jem come to Hungary to join with the king in a crusade against Beyazit. Jem asked the knights to allow him to send two of his officers, Mustafa Bey and Ahmet Bey, to meet with Corvinus in Buda. The knights agreed and the two envoys departed for Buda. However nothing was heard of Mustafa or Ahmet Bey again.

Early that spring the Duke of Savoy returned to his chateau in Chambéry, where he learned that Jem was at the knights' commandery in les Échelles. At the first opportunity he rode down to meet the prince, about whom he had heard so much in the past year. The two young men were greatly taken with one another and immediately established a strong bond of friendship. Jem gave the duke an antique Arab weapon, a bronze ball and chain he had purchased in Damascus for fifty gold pieces. Charles, who was then only fifteen, looked upon Jem as a hero, and Jem was deeply touched by the attentions of the impressionable young duke in the flower of his youth. Sadüddin, underestimating Charles's age by more than a year, wrote that 'the young duke was as beautiful as a cypress tree, one for whom you would give your soul. He had no equal in the garden of beauty, and he was not yet fourteen.' On leaving the duke pledged to Jem that he would not rest until he had freed him from the Knights of St John.

Charles went to René, Duke of Lorraine, with whom he was close friends, and together they plotted to join forces to liberate the Turkish prince. But on 26 June 1483 Jem and his companions were abruptly moved from the commandery at les Échelles. The knights had learned of the dukes' plot and were so alarmed that they decided to move Jem from the Duchy of Savoy immediately. The group was taken south to Grenoble, where they crossed the River Isère, a tributary of the Rhône, bringing them to the village of St-Quentin-sur-Isère. Here they boarded a ship that took them down the Isère to its confluence with the Rhône at Valence, and then south to Montélimar. After a day's journey eastward they arrived at another commandery: le Poet-Laval, a hilltop village in the Dauphiné. Jem's new prison looked out over the beautiful valley of the Jabron, a tributary of the Rhône flanked by undulating and thickly forested hills, which to the north-east give way to the much higher and barren crags of the Vercors, south-west of Grenoble.

In Istanbul Beyazit had heard rumours that Jem had died whilst in Europe and an imposter was being prepared to take his place (he would later discover that this story was in fact misinformation planted by the Mamluk sultan Kaitbey, who was also plotting to gain control of Jem). So an envoy was dispatched to France with instructions to find Jem, report on his health and conditions of confinement and to give him a letter from the sultan. The envoy was accompanied by Paolo da Colle, a Florentine merchant long resident in Istanbul, who acted as his guide and interpreter.

At Turin, Beyazit's envoy was detained at the court of the Duke of Savoy, and so Paolo da Colle determined to press on with the mission on his own. Paolo soon discovered that Jem was being held at les Échelles, and that he had been taken there by an 'Admiral of the Knights' – this would have been Merlo di Piozzasco, one of three officers of the Knights of St John responsible for Jem's custody. But when Paolo arrived at les Échelles he was told that the prince had been moved, escorted by over a hundred and fifty mounted knights, to another commandery, at le Poet-Laval.

In Paolo's report to Beyazit he states that the new castle to which Jem had been taken was on 'the river which divides the kingdom of France from that of the Savoy, because this place where they have put him is off any road, so that nobody chances to arrive there save one who goes on purpose'. At le Poet-Laval, Paolo handed over Beyazit's letter to the knights, but does not appear to have been allowed to see Jem in person since he does not mention the state of the prince's health in his report.

The letter Jem now read was a reply to the one he had sent to Beyazit on the eve of his departure from Rhodes. After greeting Jem as his 'dear and honoured brother', Beyazit addressed the accusations made by Jem in his letters:

I acknowledge your letter of supplication which has arrived at my court and my ministers have advised me of its contents. Violent oaths have been expressed in this letter, and you accuse us of hardness and indifference about your situation. We protest with all of our energy against this accusation.

Beyazit repeated that Jem's idea of sharing the Ottoman Empire was completely out of the question, for, he wrote, the sultanate 'is absolute and cannot admit any partner, for this is the will of God and men's actions cannot change this institution'. He then acknowledged the letter that Jem had sent him from Mecca, and offered him an appanage there, despite the fact that the Holy Cities were under the control of the Mamluks: 'I have decided that if you take residence in those regions we would provide you a yearly income of 1,000,000 aspers for your subsistence. If you agree to put yourself apart you will enjoy the sweetness of repose.' Beyazit then warned Jem of the consequences of turning down this generous arrangement.

But if you refuse our offer and let yourself be subject to foreign instigators and your ambition, and if you keep the fires burning and fan the flames of disorder and rebellion we will have to take measures dictated to maintain public order. And as that has been done you have to suffer the consequences.

But Beyazit closed on a more conciliatory note: 'We can't do anything for the moment,' he wrote. 'Later we will think about a way to change your circumstances. Meanwhile we will send you without default every year the pension we have agreed upon. Let the will of God be accomplished.'

The second part of the mission of Beyazit's envoy was to deliver a letter from the sultan to Louis XI of France. In the letter Beyazit promised that he would send the king a haul of sacred Christian relics if he promised to keep Jem in France and not allow him to be used in a crusade against the Turks. Louis was suffering from a serious illness and was terrified by the prospect of his impending death. This had led him to acquire the relics of saints from many countries in the hope that he could be cured by divine help. He had also employed quacksalvers to cure him, one of whom had prescribed the blood of infants as a remedy for the king. But even in this desperate state Louis ignored Beyazit's offer, and at Ruiz in Provence the Turkish envoy received a royal command not to proceed any farther. For Louis had put his last hopes in Françoise Paule, 'a man of holy life', who was brought from Italy to see him in Lyon. The presence of this renowned thaumaturge did not prolong the king's life, but it did at least soothe his spirit in his last moments. Louis finally passed away weeks later, on 30 August 1483, apparently with courage and resignation, or so say the French chroniclers.

Louis was succeeded by his only son, who came to the throne as Charles VIII. Charles was only two months past his thirteenth birthday at the time of his accession, which led to discussions about whether a regent should be appointed until he came of age. The question was settled when control of the throne was effectively taken by Anne de Beaujeu, the late king's eldest child, who was nine years older than her brother Charles. Anne had been married for ten years to Pierre de Bourbon, Sire de Beaujeu, heir presumptive of the House of Bourbon. 'Madame de Beaujeu' had been described by her father as 'the least foolish of a sex which contained no wise ones', and she was said to have inherited all of the late king's virtues and none of his many defects, her principal fault being her avarice. Thus Anne de Beaujeu became the power behind her brother's throne, as was evident from the moment of Charles's coronation. Jean Foulquart, a court official at the time, wrote in his memoirs of a scene in the banquet hall following the coronation, when 'Madame de Beaujeu came through the Chapel door, and entered the hall, to see how the king was behaving himself'. Their uncle, the Duke of Orleans, saw how overawed the young king was by his elder and much more intelligent and capable sister, and cautioned him: 'Madame de Beaujeu, your sister,' Orleans said, 'wants to keep you in leading-strings and to have rule over you and your kingdom.'

With the accession of Charles VIII of France, the knights feared that the French regime might become unstable, and that someone might take Jem from them, particularly the Duke of Savoy. And so to tighten security they separated Jem from the majority of his companions, who now numbered almost fifty. A cavalry unit of 800 knights was brought in to le Poet-Laval to take away twenty-nine of Jem's entourage, leaving him with eighteen or nineteen. Among those removed were Ayas Bey, Jem's taster, and Sinan Bey, his chief doorkeeper. The twenty-nine Turks were taken to Aigues-Mortes, a port on the Mediterranean east of Montpelier, from where they were put on a ship to Villefranche. There they were joined by Beyazit's envoy, who accompanied them back to Rhodes, where they arrived on 27 January 1484. After conferring with Pierre d'Aubusson, the envoy returned to Istanbul, where he immediately reported to his master, the sultan.

The Duke of Savoy had been away on a journey when the knights moved Jem out of the duchy. When he heard the news he went again to the Duke of Lorraine, and on 18 July 1483 they petitioned Venice to help them free Jem. The Venetians were embarrassed by the proposal and therefore did not respond until 6 August, apologizing for the delay, which, they claimed, was due to the difficulties of their war with Ferrara. They assured Savoy and Lorraine of their goodwill, saying that whatever came of their enterprise they would receive the gratitude of Venice, but asked the dukes to postpone action saying that they would reconsider the proposal in due course.

Indeed Venice's war against Ferrara was but one of a series of outbreaks of hostilities which made a Christian crusade against the Turks, in which Jem was now seen as the central figure, ever less likely. On 25 May 1483, as part of the simmering dispute between Rome and Venice, Sixtus had placed the Venetian Republic under an interdict. This should have suspended all operations of the Roman Catholic Church in Venice, but the Venetians opted to ignore the sanction. The pope therefore prepared for war against the Serenissima – putting aside his own pleas for peace in Christendom and with it his own hopes for a crusade – and joined the anti-Venetian alliance with Naples, Ferrara, Florence and Milan. After more than a year of inaction the allies came to terms with the Venetian Republic, by which time Sixtus would be on his deathbed.

Mathias Corvinus's forces had meanwhile been making continuous attacks against Emperor Frederick III. Sixtus tried to intervene by sending Bishop Bartolommeo de' Maraschi to ask Corvinus 'to desist from war upon the emperor'. Bartolommeo arrived in Buda on 16 October 1483 and was received by Corvinus the following day. He assured the bishop that he did not want to make war against Frederick, and that he would do everything he could to come to terms with the emperor. Corvinus then raised the subject of Jem, 'who is held by the Knights of Rhodes'. He told Bartolommeo that he still wanted to use Jem against Sultan Beyazit, who he believed was very unpopular among his subjects. He had been told that some of the leading pashas had conspired to assassinate Beyazit, but their plot had failed. One of them, a renegade pasha who had escaped from a Turkish prison, was now in Buda and had offered his services to Corvinus in a renewed effort to overthrow Beyazit in favour of Jem. The king proposed to send the pasha to Rome with a member of the bishop's household, and Bartolommeo readily agreed, writing to the pope 'whom I ask in the king's name to admit the Turkish pasha into his presence', and that arrangements be made for the pasha to see Jem. Nothing, however, came of this plan, and there is no further mention of the renegade pasha in the papacy's diplomatic correspondence. From this point Corvinus realized that Sixtus had no intention of helping him gain control of Jem, and his relationship with the pope was embittered thereon. That same year a peace treaty was agreed between Hungary and the Ottoman Empire which was to last for five years.

∽∾

At the beginning of November 1483 the knights moved Jem again, taking him back up the Rhône to Valence and then up the Isère to Rochechinard. There they imprisoned him and his remaining companions in a commandery of the order belonging to

Barrachin Allemand, nephew of Charles Allemand, commander of the Knights of St John in Avignon. Here Jem would remain through the winter of 1483–84, while the knights carefully watched events at the French court.

At Rochechinard it seems that Jem was allowed a greater amount of freedom. He was frequently seen hunting in the surrounding countryside, though always accompanied by a group of 'guardian knights'. It seems Guy de Blanchefort still thought he needed to keep up the pretence that the prince was the knights' guest rather than their prisoner, although Jem was now fully aware that he was a captive. Jem rebelled against the continuous presence of the knights and persuaded Blanchefort to let him make his daily excursions alone, though secretly observed, the prince having given his word that he would not try to escape. According to local tradition, on one of Jem's first solitary excursions, dressed as always in his Turkish robes and turban, he dismounted in a forest clearing to enjoy the morning sunshine. After a while he was surprised when another rider appeared and stopped at the edge of the clearing to look intently at him. At first he thought the stranger was a knight, but then he saw that it was a young woman with long fair hair. He called out to her in greeting, but she remained silent. When she turned to ride away he shouted after her, but she spurred her horse and disappeared in the forest. Jem returned to the clearing the next day but no one appeared, nor in the days that followed.

A fortnight later Jem was playing chess with Guy de Blanchefort when word came that visitors had arrived. Blanchefort rose to greet them, a young couple whom he addressed as Jean de Sassenage and his sister Philippine. Jem immediately saw that Philippine was the young woman he had seen in the forest, and he could tell from her look of surprise that she recognized him too. Their father, Blanchefort told Jem, was the Baron Jacques de Sassenage, a knight of the Order of St John, whose chateau was half a day's ride to the north on the River Isère. Blanchefort introduced Jem to the visitors, saying that he was the son of Mehmet the Conqueror and brother of Sultan Beyazit, whose throne he claimed as his own. After an hour or so the guests departed. According to French tradition, as Philippine rode off she turned to smile at Jem. Blanchefort, seeing Jem's evident interest in Philippine, remarked that because of her beauty she was known locally as La Belle Hélène, since she was said to be as fair as Helen of Troy.

Some days later Jem accompanied Blanchefort to the chateau at Sassenage, where they were guests of Baron Jacques. The baron greeted Jem with great civility, inviting him to stay at the chateau as his guest. Some of the sources say that Jem was moved to Sassenage by the knights, but almost certainly he was not, for Blanchefort would have wished to keep him at Rochechinard, where he could guard his prisoner much more securely.

Before the end of his first visit to Sassenage Jem took the opportunity to speak to Philippine privately, asking when he might see her again. She had answered with a smile, but said nothing. The following day Jem rode alone to the forest clearing where he had first seen her, and before long she appeared, saying that she knew he would be there, whereupon she dismounted and fell into his arms. At that and subsequent meetings their love developed into a deep passion, Jem promising Philippine that if he regained his throne he would make her his empress. Sadüddin wrote of the affair:

The *chatelain* of Sassenage had a daughter who was an admirable beauty, and she was taken by a passion for the prince, so that they came to a secret commerce and exchanged love letters. Their tenderness and mutual affection knew no limit, and they enjoyed numerous meetings and conversations.

Sadüddin claims that their love was never consummated, although French sources say that it was a deeply passionate romance. Their relationship became the source of a novel written in 1673 by Guy Allard, an ancestor of Stendhal, who entitled it *Zizime prince ottoman, amoureux de Philippine-Hélène de Sassenage.* In his prologue Allard notes that the story was based on an actual historical incident perpetuated by local tradition. Allard claimed to have seen a portrait of Philippine-Hélène in the chateau at Sassenage, and described her as having 'a semi-oval face, a small mouth, nicely-shaped eyes, a witty look, a fortunate physiognomy'. Jem's French biographer, Thuasne, compares the love affair with Philippine to that of Desdemona and Othello, quoting the Moor's words from Act I, Scene III of the play: 'She loved me for the dangers I had pass'd,/ And I loved her that she did pity them.'

But then at one of Jem's meetings with Philippine she began to weep, saying that she could no longer see Jem, and that her father had arranged for her to be married to a French nobleman. Jem could not bring himself to speak, and he waited for Philippine to continue. She told Jem that she was pregnant with his child, and she put his hand to her so that he could feel the baby kicking. After a final embrace, Philippine tore herself away and rode off into the forest.

Philippine's marriage to the nobleman was celebrated at Sassenage a month later, after the publication of the banns for three successive Sundays. Jem accompanied Blanchefort to the wedding and presented the bride with a magnificent emerald, after which he excused himself on the pretext of a severe headache. He never saw Philippine again, for soon afterwards he was informed by Blanchefort that the knights would be moving him and his companions from Rochechinard the following day. One of Jem's poems is believed to have been inspired by his undying love for Philippine, written after he had given up hope of ever seeing her again.

> Ah, for the time when my star rode triumphant, good fortune its
> mount,
> Keeping abreast with the dream of your fleetly elusive embrace . . .
> Ah, for the time when your threshold was residence, also, for Jem!
> How good a time it was we never knew until lost without trace.

Local records confirm that Baron Jacques was the *chatelain* of Sassenage while Jem was at Rochechinard, and that his daughter Philippine bore a son out of wedlock in 1484. Tradition has it that the Turkish prince 'Zizim' had fathered the boy, and that he was raised by Philippine as a Christian and married to a relative of the family.

The nineteenth-century historian Alphonse de Lamartine tells a version of this tale in his *Histoire de Turquie*:

> The chronicles of the province of Dauphiné assure that an offspring was born of these clandestine lovers in the castle of Sassenage; that the child brought up by the beautiful Philippine under the appearance of a page, espoused in turn, a relative of this noble house, and that the blood of Othman flows, perhaps, still in the veins of an obscure Christian family.

Such is the story of Jem and Philippine, whose affair lives on in the folk traditions of Rochechinard and Sassenage, where the lovers are still referred to as Prince Zizim and La Belle Hélène.

8

La Dame à la Licorne

EARLY IN 1484 Pierre d'Aubusson wrote to Guy de Blanche-fort telling him to move Jem from Rochechinard to La Marche in central France. The grand master felt that the order would have greater control of Jem there, where the knights had their most powerful commanderies as well as the loyalty of the local population.

Sadüddin provides a few details on the route taken by the knights in their journey from Rochechinard to central France. The first stage took them westward for about two days to a mountain fortress at St-Antoine, between the Isère and the Rhône. There Jem visited the abbey at St-Antoine and conversed with the abbot, who showed him the sacred relics in the church. They also stopped at Vienne, on the Rhône, south of Lyon, where 'blind destiny' caused a fire in the house where they were spending the night. From there they travelled westward from Lyon to Clermont, the old provincial capital of Auvergne, where Pope Urban II had preached the First Crusade, at the Council held there in November 1095.

Continuing westward, the knights and their captives passed from Auvergne to La Marche, whose eastern part is now known

as the Creuse. There they stopped at Aubusson, the town that
gave its name to the family of Pierre d'Aubusson. Then, a day's
journey west of Aubusson, they came to Bourganeuf, at that time
capital of the order's *langue* d'Auvergne, where the knights and
their prisoners arrived toward the end of March 1484. This was
the homeland of the d'Aubusson and de Blanchefort families,
who had chateaux not only at Bourganeuf and Aubusson but also
at the nearby towns of Le Monteil-au-Vicomte, Morterolles and
Bois-Lamy. All of these chateaux were commanderies of the
knights, and Jem would be confined in each of these in turn over
the next four years, beginning and ending at Bourganeuf.

The town and chateau of Bourganeuf belonged to Guy de
Blanchefort, Jem's keeper, who became Prior of Auvergne in 1485.
The town, surrounded by a defensive wall, was inhabited entirely
by the vassals of Guy de Blanchefort, who was both their temporal
and spiritual lord. Jem and his group were confined to the Tour
de Lastic, then the largest tower in the chateau, built in 1420. But
Blanchefort felt that this tower was not strong and capacious
enough for the purpose, and so he ordered construction to begin
on a more suitable tower in which to confine Jem and his companions, deciding to move them elsewhere until it was completed.
Besides, an agent of the knights had just brought Blanchefort a
worrying message: Mathias Corvinus was plotting to kidnap Jem.
And so after twenty days Jem and his companions were moved
from Bourganeuf, leaving Jelal Bey behind, for he had fallen ill
during their stay.

The knights rode with their captives a day's journey eastwards
to Le Monteil-au-Vicomte. The commandery of the order into
which they moved had been the home of Renaud d'Aubusson,
Lord of Le Monteil-au-Vicomte and Viscount of La Marche,

whose son Pierre d'Aubusson had been born there in 1423. At the time of Jem's stay the *chatelain* was Antoine d'Aubusson, a brother of Pierre, who had been one of the heroes of the siege of Rhodes in 1480.

Sadüddin says that Jem and his companions stayed in Le Monteil-au-Vicomte for two months. They then moved to the commandery of the knights at Morterolles, another day's ride, south of Bourganeuf. According to the records of the Order of St John, the chateau at Morterolles was a square fortified structure with three towers bordered by moats and surrounded by a defensive wall, its citadel approached by a bridge and a drawbridge. In mid-August 1484 the knights moved their captives once more, mindful of Corvinus's plot, this time several days' ride north-west to Bois-Lamy, above the east bank of the Cher river. There they took over another chateau belonging to Antoine de Blanchefort, described by Sadüddin as 'a place very difficult of access', where Jem would languish for two years.

At Bois-Lamy the possessions that Jem had left behind at various stages of his flight were restored to him. Here Jem seems to have found a degree of inner calm, and he began to write verse again. One of the poems reveals that his spirits were reasonably high, at least at the beginning of his sojourn there, in tune with the music of France, and he writes of: 'Harp and tambourine and organ dulcimer-like sweet resound,' and of how 'Beauties sing in their own language songs and carols passing sweet ... golden caps upon their tresses, bare their arms for all to see.'

At some time in 1484 the Florentine, Paolo da Colle, who was now working as an agent for Lorenzo de' Medici, visited Jem. Paolo brought Jem a copy of a geographical treatise published in 1482 by the renowned Florentine scholar Francesco

Berlinghieri. The treatise was based on the *Geographia* written in the mid-second century AD by Claudius Ptolemaeus (Ptolemy) of Alexandria, the basis for all subsequent work in geography up until the European Renaissance, both in Islam and the West. Jem's father, Mehmet the Conqueror, had made a careful study of Ptolemy's *Geographia* and had undoubtedly included it among the books from which his sons were to be tutored, for a thorough knowledge of geography was essential for anyone ruling an empire that encompassed so much of the *oikoumene,* or 'inhabited world', as that of the Ottomans.

Berlinghieri originally made a copy of his treatise for Jem's father (which is now preserved in the Topkapı Sarayı archives), and inscribed it: '*To Mehmet of the Ottomans, illustrious prince and lord of the throne of God, emperor and merciful lord of all Asia and Greece, I dedicate this work.*' But before Berlinghieri could send the volume to Istanbul word reached Florence that the Conqueror had died and that he had been succeeded by his eldest son. Berlinghieri then hastily added a dedication to Beyazit, and asked Paolo da Colle to present it to the new sultan. Eighteen months later Berlinghieri made another copy of his work with a dedication to Jem, praising him in almost exactly the same words as those he used to address Beyazit, ending with the wish that the prince would not forget him when he regained his throne. This was the copy that Paolo da Colle now presented to Jem, who was delighted, for he had been deeply interested in geography since his youth, and he would have undoubtedly studied Berlinghieri's maps in considering the prospects of regaining his lost empire.

Soon after Jem arrived at Bois-Lamy news came that Pope Sixtus IX had died. He was succeeded seventeen days later by Cardinal Giovanni Battista Cibo, who took the name of Innocent VIII. The new pope was from a distinguished Genoese family which had long had connections with the Levant, one of his ancestors having been governor of Chios in the mid-fourteenth century. Cibo was fifty-two years old at the time of his election. His secretary Sigismondo de' Conti wrote that 'He was above middle height, strongly built, and his face was full, his complexion strikingly fair, and his eyes weak.' He had fathered two illegitimate children, a daughter Teodorina, and a son Franceschetto, but, as Ludwig Pastor wrote of him in his multi-volume history of the papacy: 'it is certain that from the moment Giovanni Battista entered the ecclesiastical state, all the accusations against the purity of his private life ceased'. Sigismondo wrote of Innocent that, 'Nobody left him without being consoled; he received all with truly fatherly kindness and gentleness; he was the friend of high and low, of rich and poor.'

Among the embassies that came to Rome to congratulate the new pope on his accession was that of the Knights of St John. A document in the Venetian archives, dated 4 November 1484, records a note from Pierre d'Aubusson to Pope Innocent VIII, in which he 'accredits his ambassadors'

> to tender obedience to the pope's accession, the venerable religious brothers, Edward de Carmedino, preceptor of Langon, and John Kendal, turcopolier of the Order and procurator general at the Roman court, and the notable man the grand master's secretary Guillaume Caoursin.

The Rhodian envoys swore obeisance to the new pope on 26 January 1485 in the name of Pierre d'Aubusson. In his address

Sultan Mehmet II (Fatih) by Gentile Bellini, 1480.

Ancient bridge on the approach to Bursa, shown in
the left foreground, at the foot of Ulu Dağ,
the Mount Olympus of Bithynia, by Charles Allom, 1838.

Prince Jem and his father Mehmet II, by Gentile Bellini, 1480.

Prince Jem, detail of the above painting by Gentile Bellini.

OPPOSITE Beyazit defeating
Jem at the battle of Yenişehir,
20 June 1481.

RIGHT Sultan Beyazit II,
c.1482.

BELOW Bab-üs Saadet, 'The
Gate of Felicity', entrance to
the Inner Palace of Topkapı
Sarayı, by Charles Allom, 1838.

Silver coin *(akçe)* minted by Jem Sultan at
Bursa in 1481.

OPPOSITE Sultan Beyazit II holding court in
the Palace of Topkapı Sarayı, Istanbul.

Jem's arrival on Rhodes, a painting by Tahirzade Hüseyin Behzad, 1955.

to Innocent, Caoursin reminded the pope of the heroic role that d'Aubusson and his knights had played in the defence of Rhodes against the Turks in 1480, adding their wishes for the future: 'The Rhodians hope, most blessed father, to see the Turkish tyranny extinguished under your most fortunate pontificate!'

A few days later Caoursin and his associates were received by the pope in a private audience to discuss the affairs of the order. Innocent expressed his strong desire to have Jem brought from France and held in a fortress of the papacy, but still to remain in the custody of the knights. Caoursin and his companions demurred, saying that they had no authority to deal with this request, whereupon the pope asked them to discuss the matter with d'Aubusson when they returned to Rhodes. The envoys proposed that Pierre d'Aubusson's brother Guiscard, Bishop of Carcassonne, should be made a cardinal, and Innocent responded by saying that he would do what he could to secure this, provided that the grand master would cooperate in having Jem brought back from France to the papal states.

Caoursin and the English Turcopolier John Kendal then went on to Naples, where they were received by King Ferrante. The king explained that he too was anxious to obtain custody of Jem, whom he wanted to use in a war against the Turks. The envoys, however, gave him the same answer that they had given the pope. Ferrante added that his son Alfonso, Duke of Calabria, had already written to d'Aubusson on this matter, and that he would now write to the grand master himself.

The Mamluk sultan Kaitbey had also started negotiations with the Knights of St John for custody of Jem. Kaitbey knew of Beyazit's intention to march against Kasim Bey of Karamania to punish him for helping Jem in the civil war, and he feared that the sultan would continue on into the Egyptian provinces. Therefore, in May, Kaitbey sent a diplomatic mission to meet with Pierre d'Aubusson in Rhodes. The Egyptian envoy explained the purpose of his visit and asked d'Aubusson to send a representative to Cairo to conclude an agreement with Kaitbey concerning Jem. D'Aubusson said that he would give the matter some consideration, although secretly he had no intention of giving Jem to the Mamluks.

Whilst at Bois-Lamy it emerged that Jem had been secretly corresponding with his mother, still in Kaitbey's care, in Cairo. This correspondence came to light early in 1484 when the Venetian *bailo* at Methoni in the Peloponnesus arrested one Nicolas de Nicosie, who was found to be carrying their letters. The *bailo* sent news of this to Beyazit who immediately demanded that Kaitbey send Jem's family back from Cairo to Istanbul. Kaitbey's refusal to comply would be used by Beyazit as a pretext to declare war on Egypt – a conflict that would go on intermittently for seven years.

D'Aubusson had heard that Kaitbey had been trying to use Jem's mother to gain control of Jem, and so he decided to turn the situation to his own personal advantage. He accepted 20,000 gold sovereigns from Kaitbey, in return agreeing to outfit a 'giant ship' to bring Jem back to Egypt, although he had no intention of doing this and simply pocketed the money. D'Aubusson also accepted money from Jem's mother for the same purpose. Both of these deceits were uncovered a decade later, to the grand master's great humiliation.

On 21 July 1485 Caoursin and John Kendal returned to Rhodes and reported to d'Aubusson, giving him King Ferrante's letter requesting custody of Jem. At the same time d'Aubusson put

Kaitbey's request before the Council of the Knights, who agreed to form a commission, comprising Caoursin, Kendal and Galceran de Luge, to consider the issue. D'Aubusson argued that because of the international situation they should delay in taking action on Jem's future as long as possible: Italy was racked by internal disputes, and, left to their own resources, the Christian princes could not resist the Ottomans. The Council agreed. They would tell Kaitbey that Jem could not be handed over without the pope's approval, and they concluded that it would be better to leave Jem in France until the situation was more conducive to the pope organizing a crusade.

Meanwhile, Beyazit, at the instigation of Venice, had been preparing a fleet to attack King Ferrante of Naples, who was in alliance with the Duke of Ferrara and the pope against the Serenissima. When d'Aubusson learned of this he sent Mosco Perpiano as envoy to Istanbul in March 1485. Perpiano was to tell Beyazit that if he took his ships past Gallipoli in the Dardanelles it would be the equivalent of a declaration of war, and that this would unite the princes of Europe in a crusade against the Turks with his brother Jem as the figurehead. Perpiano's words had a great impact on Beyazit who remained silent for a long while after the envoy finished speaking. The sultan then turned to Perpiano and made him swear to secrecy about what he was about to hear. Beyazit called for Ishak Pasha and two other vezirs. He told them that the Ottoman fleet must not pass Gallipoli that year. He then wrote to d'Aubusson notifying him that he had called off the expedition against Naples.

This extraordinarily successful negotiation, d'Aubusson reminded the princes of Europe, was another reason why they should be grateful to the grand master, adding that it was their possession of Jem that had given them the power to hold off Beyazit. D'Aubusson now concluded that it would be in Europe's best interest to use Jem as a talisman to repel the Turks, rather than to give him to one of the Christian princes to use in a crusade, which, he believed, would have little chance of success anyway. Beyazit for his part thanked d'Aubusson by sending him a Byzantine reliquary – the supposed right hand of St John the Baptist, with which Jesus had been baptized, along with a written statement attesting to its validity. The reliquary was taken with all due solemnity to the Church of St John on Rhodes, where it was placed in a golden tabernacle set with precious stones.

With the expedition against Naples abandoned, for the time being at least, Ottoman forces rampaged into other territories. Early in April 1485 Beyazit ordered the Ottoman governor of Karamania to reconquer several provinces that had been taken by the Mamluks from the Ramazanoğlu Türkmen, Jem's former allies. The sultan also began preparing a powerful fleet and army for an invasion of Egypt. Ottoman forces at the same time embarked on a new wave of conquest in central Europe sparking alarm through Christendom. Beyazit's peace treaty with Mathias Corvinus had left him free to invade Moldavia and Wallachia, and the following summer Beyazit personally led his army across the Danube, capturing Kilia in July and Akkerman in August. Moldavia and Wallachia thus became trans-Danubian provinces of the Ottoman Empire, remaining under Turkish rule for nearly four centuries. Beyazit himself is said to have remarked that he had 'won the key of the door to all Moldavia and Hungary, the whole region of the Danube, Poland and Tartary, and the entire coast of the Black Sea'.

Corvinus now feared that Beyazit would not keep to their peace treaty, and so he secretly continued his efforts to obtain Jem, hoping that he could use him in a pre-emptive attack on the Turks. The pope was deeply concerned about the Turkish conquests on the Danube, as well as the news that Beyazit was arming another fleet, possibly to attack Italy. On 21 November 1484 Innocent addressed an encyclical to all the Christian princes of Europe, warning them of the danger that the Turks posed to the Church and Western civilization in general. He urged them to send ambassadors to Rome as soon as possible, with full powers to decide on the measures to be adopted, as the situation was so critical that they could not delay. He also wrote to Ferdinand and Isabella of Spain, urging them to exert all their strength against the Grand Turk, 'the Enemy of the Faith', particularly in the defence of Sicily. And on 2 February 1485, the pope wrote to King Ferrante of Naples telling him that Beyazit was preparing forces that might well attack Italy, and proposing a detailed plan for the protection of the Italian coast. He also proposed measures for the defence of Rhodes, and though d'Aubusson welcomed these suggestions he was wary of committing himself to a crusade.

But Innocent's hopes for European stability, and in turn a crusade, were dashed by his disputes with Naples. Both King Ferrante and his son Alfonso, Duke of Calabria, seemed to be constantly at odds with the papacy. This came to a climax in 1485 when the barons of the Kingdom of Naples rebelled against Ferrante, and the papacy took the side of the barons. On 14 October Innocent issued a bull declaring war on Naples.

Ferrante was supported by his son-in-law Mathias Corvinus as well as by the Dukes of Milan and Florence, while the pope concluded an alliance with Genoa and enlisted the services of the Venetian commander Roberto Sanseverino. The war raged right up to the walls of Rome, and the city was saved only by the last-minute arrival of Sanseverino's troops on 28 December.

The situation deteriorated again when the *condottiere*, Boccolino Guzzoni, took advantage of the war and rebelled against the papacy. He set out to seize control of the papal town of Osimo, in the Marche de Ancona, where he hoped to rule independently of the pope, with the aid of the Turks if necessary. At the same time news reached Rome that Corvinus was sending an army to invest Ancona, and that Turkish ships had been sighted on the Adriatic. The papacy was on the verge of collapse when France and Spain intervened, arranging a peace treaty that was signed in Rome on 10 August 1486. The treaty had the effect of ending Guzzoni's rebellion, at least temporarily. But Ferrante almost immediately violated the terms of the treaty and instigated disturbances in the papal states, while Guzzoni renewed his assault and laid siege to Osimo. Innocent had been forced to defer his dream of a crusade once more, as well as his plan to gain custody of Jem.

During the autumn of 1485 two of Jem's companions who had been taken away to Rhodes were allowed to rejoin him in Bois-Lamy; these were Ayas Bey, his taster, and Sinan Bey, his chief doorkeeper. They told Jem of the secret negotiations between d'Aubusson and King Ferrante, which might result in him being transferred to Naples. Ferrante had been represented in these negotiations by his son Cardinal Giovanni d'Aragona, who had also been negotiating a peace treaty between Naples and Rome. But on 17 October 1485 the cardinal died in the plague in Rome. When hostilities were renewed between the papacy and Naples the discussions concerning Jem's custody were abandoned.

Secret bargaining between d'Aubusson and the pope concerning Jem began the following February, the pope being represented by cardinals Marco Barbo and Giuliano della Rovere, the future Pope Julius II, and the knights by Caoursin and Philippe de Cluys. The first part of their draft agreement stated that in the interests of Christianity, Jem would be placed in the custody of the pope in the Marche de Ancona, and its cities and fortresses would be placed under the cardinal legate Jean de la Balu. Jem would be guarded by knights, officers and mercenaries nominated by d'Aubusson or his delegates. Cardinal Balue would swear to guard Jem and not dispose of him to anyone without the agreement of the pope and d'Aubusson. D'Aubusson would still retain legal rights to Jem along with 10,000 ducats of the yearly payment of 45,000 ducats from Beyazit. The second part of the draft agreement stated that the pope would appoint d'Aubusson as a cardinal because of his heroism in withstanding the Turkish siege of 1480. D'Aubusson was to have the advantages of being a cardinal without losing any of the privileges he enjoyed as grand master. The pope also united the Order of St John with those of the Holy Sepulchre, Bethlehem, Nazareth, St Lazare and Montmorillon, with all their benefices and revenues, giving d'Aubusson the privilege of opening commanderies even in Rome, and in addition granting the knights the right to trade with Syria and Egypt. It was also finally agreed that the grand master's brother, Guiscard d'Aubusson, would be made a cardinal. The agreement was contained in a papal bull drafted on 13 February 1486, signed by the three cardinals and the two Rhodian envoys. Another bull, concerning Pierre d'Aubusson's appointment as cardinal, dated that same day, was given to Balu to be activated when Jem was brought to Italy. The pope expressed his delight at having concluded this agreement with the knights. But it remained to be seen whether the transfer of Jem to the papacy could actually be carried out since none of the provisions in the agreement could come into effect and be made public without the approval of the King of France, a process that would be fraught with politicking and delays beyond anyone's wildest imaginings.

Innocent also concluded a peace treaty with Naples, announced in a papal bull in St Peter's on 2 June 1486. Cardinal Balu declared that he was unhappy with the treaty and protested, whereupon he was opposed by Cardinal Rodrigo Borgia, the future Pope Alexander VI, who called him a drunkard. Balue responded by calling Borgia a 'Marrano', or converted Jew, and the son of a whore, whereupon a brawl erupted between the two cardinals and their respective supporters. Nevertheless the peace treaty was finally signed on 11 August, and was proclaimed in a more cordial atmosphere at St Peter's a month later.

Innocent's optimism that he was moving close toward uniting Europe in a crusade against the Turks was shortlived. Mathias Corvinus declared in a letter to the Duke of Ferrara that since the pope had denied him custody of Jem he would interfere with all efforts of other Christian princes to use the Turkish pretender as a figurehead in a crusade. Meanwhile the German emperor Frederick and King Casimer of Poland asked the Venetian Senate to call a halt to its war with the papacy, requesting at the same time that Venice help them against Hungary, but this request was refused, since the Venetians were on good terms with Mathias Corvinus. The Venetians sent Giovanni Dario to Istanbul to negotiate a peace treaty between the Germans and Poles on one hand and between the Ottomans and the two European states on the other. But if Beyazit showed any signs of displeasure at this, then Dario should stop immediately and beg the sultan to excuse the Venetian Senate for having taken this initiative.

Ferrante also wanted a peace treaty with the Turks and sent his envoy Francesco de Parez, Bishop of Teramo, to Rhodes. The envoy asked d'Aubusson to use his influence to persuade Beyazit not to send his fleet against Sicily and Naples, and if the sultan persisted he was to be warned that Jem would be put at the head of a Christian army which would invade the Ottoman Empire. The envoy said that Ferrante wanted a permanent peace with the Porte, but if Beyazit would not agree to this the king would be satisfied if the sultan would at least agree not to attack the Kingdom of Naples. Ferrante also asked d'Aubusson to give him custody of Jem, so that he could use him in a crusade. If d'Aubusson refused this proposal, then Ferrante threatened to end the peaceful relationship that existed between Naples and Rhodes.

Meanwhile there was news that Beyazit and Kaitbey had pulled back their forces from the marchlands in south-eastern Anatolia, indicating that a peace or at least an armistice had been agreed upon between the Ottomans and the Egyptians. Beyazit was still building up both his army and navy, and there were renewed fears that he might invade Italy, possibly with the help of Kaitbey. Venice urged the pope to obtain custody of Jem as quickly as possible in order to repel Beyazit. The pope took the advice and pressed d'Aubusson to urgently implement the terms of their agreement, so that Jem could be transferred from France to the papacy.

ဘ၁

During Jem's confinement at Bois-Lamy the nobles of France rebelled against the crown in the so-called *guerre folle,* or 'Fool's War'. One of the leaders of the rebellion was the Duke of Bourbon, Jean II, Constable of France, whose younger brother Pierre was Anne de Beaujeu's husband. After the revolt was put down Bourbon retired to his estate at Moulins, north of Clermont, a bitter old man alienated from his brother Pierre and Anne de Beaujeu.

Jem, who was now in the second year of his confinement at Bois-Lamy, decided to seek Bourbon's help in escaping from the knights. He thought that the duke might be willing to do this to embarrass Madame de Beaujeu, who had now become aware of the great value of the Turkish prince being held in France by the Knights of St John. Jem relied principally on two of his companions for this plan: his former chief treasurer, Hüseyin Bey and his officer, Jelal Bey – the latter having recovered from his illness and been brought to Bois-Lamy. The two men escaped from the commandery and made their way to Moulins, where Hüseyin found employment on the duke's estate, while Jelal remained in a hostel in the town so that he could act as a courier to keep in contact with Jem. Hüseyin then waited for an opportunity to get the duke's ear and ask for his help.

As the weeks passed Jelal travelled back and forth between Bois-Lamy and Moulins carrying messages for Jem. Then in the

late summer of 1486 Jem learned that he and his companions
would soon be moved back to Bourganeuf. Jelal learned of this
and informed Hüseyin, who bided his time at Moulins, trying to
gain the confidence of the Duke of Bourbon.

According to local tradition, while Jem was at Bois-Lamy he
had an affair with a daughter of the *chatelain* of the Chateau de
Boussac. The incident is not mentioned by Sadüddin, and other
sources confuse it with the affair between Jem and Philippine. At
the time the Lord of Boussac was Duke Jean IV le Veste, a former
councillor in Parlement, who in 1484 became a member of the
King's Council. He married Genevieve de Nanterre, who bore
him three daughters – Claude, Jeanne and Genevieve – all three
of whom were living in the chateau during the time of Jem's stay
in Bois-Lamy. Claude later married, but her sisters remained
single. It is claimed that Jeanne became Jem's mistress, and that
after he left Bois-Lamy she never married because of her love for
him. She is also supposed to have given birth to Jem's son, who
was secretly baptized in Limoges and raised as a Christian.

The rumour of Jem's illegitimate son reached Rome around
1500, and the then pope, Alexander VI, sent an agent named
Zorzi Paxi to France to follow up the story. Zorzi went so far as
to request an audience with Louis XII, who told him that to his
knowledge Jem had not established any liaison with a woman
during his years in France. In the early 1840s the French novelist,
George Sand, visited the Chateau de Boussac and reported that
she had seen a remarkable tapestry there with a series of images
of a beautiful young blonde maiden. The tapestry consisted of
six pieces, the first five symbolizing the five senses and the
sixth desire; the central figure in each panel is a blonde maiden
flanked by a lion and a unicorn. The most striking of the images,

symbolizing sight, shows the maiden holding a mirror so that the unicorn can see its own image, to which it reacts with a smile. The maiden herself came to be known as La Dame à la Licorne, the Lady with the Unicorn. The tapestry is known to have been woven in the southern Netherlands prior to 1500 for Jean IV le Veste. The arms of the le Veste family, which in each of the scenes appear on lances and banners held aloft by the lion and unicorn, contain three silver crescents on an azure band. There were several theories as to the identity of the maiden, one being that she was Marguerite d'York, third wife of Charles le Téméraire, Duke of Burgundy (r. 1433–77). But many believed that she was Jeanne le Veste, and that it was a present from her father, who would have given it to her about the time that Jem was staying in Bois-Lamy. The crescent, in the form of a sickle moon with a star (actually the planet Venus) between its horns, is the symbol of Islam, and the romantic orientalism of France fastened upon this to revive the local tradition of the Turkish prince Zizim and his romance with Jeanne le Veste.

George Sand was convinced that the maiden in the tapestry was Jeanne le Veste, who became the inspiration for her novel *Jeanne*, published in 1844. (She returned to the subject in 1847 in an article about the tapestry written for *l'Illustration*.) In 1853 the tapestry was purchased by the Cluny Museum in Paris, where it remains today, perpetuating the story of Prince Zizim and La Dame à la Licorne.

But one wonders whether the story has any basis in fact, or if it is part of the nimbus of legend that began to surround the exotic persona of Jem, the likes of whom had never been seen before in the West, a Turkish prince caged like a bird of paradise.

9

The Tower at Bourganeuf

J EM BEGAN his second stay at Bourganeuf in mid-August 1486,
after an absence of twenty-eight months. The fourth tower that
Guy de Blanchefort had added to his chateau – at a final cost
of 3,500 gold crowns – was now complete: it would be in this
vast structure, later known as the Tour de Zizim, that Jem and
his companions would live for most of the rest of their time in
France. The tower looked out on to the conventual church of
St John, whose campanile rose higher than any of the towers.
And surrounding the chateau itself were grounds and a high wall
with machicolations on both sides and a barbican, making it a
virtual fortress. Apart from an entrance via a gallery from the
older Tour de Lastic, the only door to the exterior of the Tour
de Zizim was thirty feet above the ground, accessible via a ladder.

The new tower was of particularly grand construction with the
interior divided into seven floors and a deep cellar all connected
by a spiral staircase. Sadüddin's chronicle describes the functions
of its various levels: the basement served as a *hamam*, or Turkish
bath; the first floor was for the wine and the steward who served
it; the second contained the kitchen and food stores; the third
housed Jem's companions; Jem's own apartments were on the

fourth and fifth floors; the knights guarding Jem lived on the sixth floor and stood watch on the seventh, which was fortified with machicolations. Local tradition differs from that of Sadüd-din's account in one detail, in that it has Jem's mistress, the slave girl Alméida, living on the fifth floor, an area referred to sarcastically by Blanchefort as 'Zizim's harem'.

In the main part of the chateau lived Guy de Blanchefort and his family, including his mother, the Marquise Souveraine d'Aubusson, and his sister Marie. Whereas Blanchefort's mother refused to have anything to do with the Turkish prince, his sister, Marie, was very much drawn to Jem, and would take the opportunity to meet him during his daily walks in the grounds of the chateau. Some French accounts claim that their friendship quickly developed into a passionate affair, which became apparent to everyone in the chateau. This aroused insane jealousy in Alméida, who was forced to wait on Marie when she came to visit Jem in the Tour de Zizim. On one of these occasions it is claimed that Alméida put poison in Marie's drink, and soon afterwards Marie died in agony. When Alméida confessed to Jem what she had done, Jem threw her out, telling one of his companions that he could have her as his mistress. Distraught, Alméida returned to her quarters and hung herself from a window, which thereafter was known as the 'window of the foreign woman'.

Not long after this double tragedy Jem was observed at the chateau in Bourganeuf by one of Beyazit's secret agents, a young Ottoman naval officer named Barak Reis (*Reis* meaning captain). Beyazit had sent Barak to see if his brother was still alive and well, for there had been a dearth of news about Jem after he left Savoy. Barak had made his first enquiries at Turin when he met the Duke of Savoy, who arranged for him to engage a guide named Talabot to help him find Jem. They followed a trail that led them from Savoy to La Marche, where they finally learned that there was a party of Turks nearby. Barak, in the account of his mission that he wrote for Beyazit, tells of the moment he finally caught sight of Jem, as Talabot led him into the church in Bourganeuf:

> On entering the church we saw a lot of Knights, each reading from a book in his hand. I stood in a secluded corner. The man conducting me came up and pulled me by the shoulder, and we went out of the church. We saw a number of men in turbans outside the castle by the moat. I saw six men in turbans. He himself [Jem] was wearing a garment of black velvet and was chatting with a man with a full beard – he looked like a civilian. He himself had his beard cut short and had let his mustaches grow long, but his face was pale: I asked Talabot about this, and it appears that at that time he [Jem] had just recovered from illness.

Having seen that Jem was alive and reasonably well Barak started back for Istanbul. While passing through Turin Barak met with Gaspare Grimaldi, Beyazit's Genoese agent, who gave him a letter for the sultan and told him that he was not to speak to anyone about it. Grimaldi's report to Beyazit, now preserved in the archives at Topkapı Sarayı, stated that he had met Barak and learned of Jem's existence in Bourganeuf. The Genoese agent then requested that Beyazit send him 'a first-class man for the business in hand' – most likely the assassination of Jem. The following spring, 1487, two Ottoman agents were arrested in Ancona, possibly assassins sent by Beyazit, although there is no record of what became of them.

Although the Tour de Zizim seemed impregnable, three

attempts were made to free Jem during this, his second stay in Bourganeuf. The first was made late in the autumn of 1486 by Ercole d'Este, Duke of Ferrara, who planned to free Jem so that the prince could escape to Hungary, to the court of Mathias Corvinus. The duke had hired two Genoese agents who had orders to kidnap Jem from Bourganeuf and hand him over to the Hungarian envoy Cesar Valentin, who would then conduct the prince to Buda. But the plot unravelled at the last moment, and the conspirators fled to escape arrest by the French authorities.

The second attempt was made by René, Duke of Lorraine, who had conspired with Charles I, Duke of Savoy, to free Jem when he was at les Echelles. This time Lorraine plotted on his own to capture Jem, hoping, like everyone else, to use him as a figurehead in a crusade. Lorraine had an extravagant claim on the Neapolitan throne, which he thought would be advanced by his proclamation of a crusade headed by the Turkish pretender, a dream that would seem to have had no hope of realization, if only because of the totally inadequate military force he mustered in his attempt to kidnap Jem.

On 10 March 1487 the duke met at his palace in Nancy, the capital of Lorraine, with two of his officers, Geoffroy de Bassompierre and Jacob de Germiny, who were in command of only twenty-eight armed men. After receiving their instructions from the duke, Bassompierre and Germiny headed for Bourganeuf with their men. However they were soon stopped and disarmed by a detachment of the king's troops, commanded by Bernard Ordoux. They were then brought before Charles VIII and confessed their plot, but Charles seems not to have taken the matter seriously, for he dismissed them without penalty. The Duke of Lorraine made no further effort to capture Jem, but because of his attempt the knights now guarded the prince even more closely than before.

By this time Hüseyin Bey had gained the confidence of the Duke of Bourbon and persuaded him to make an attempt to free Jem. Hüseyin set up an escape route with relays of horses, supplies and money, communicating the details to Jelal Bey so that he could inform Jem. Ayas Bey and Sinan Bey managed to make copies of the keys of the Tour de Zizim, and they organized the details of the escape plan from within the chateau. The conspirators agreed that the attempt would be made a month hence, when they would assemble at an appointed meeting place after breaking out of the chateau. On the scheduled day Jem and his officers would go for their daily walk in the grounds of the chateau, accompanied as usual by their twelve guards, whom they would overpower and kill. They would then unlock the outer gates of the chateau and make their way to the meeting place, where horses and a guide would be waiting for them.

But shortly before the day of escape, one of Jem's officers drunkenly revealed the plot to a guard, who told his captain. It was ordered that all of Jem's officers would be executed, but the king heard of this and forbade the executions, fearing it would draw attention to the fact that the Turkish prince was being held in France as a prisoner. Instead it was suggested that Jem's officers should be killed off over time, their deaths attributed to other causes. This was never carried out, but Jem and his officers were thereon guarded more closely and their freedom of movement severely restricted.

The failure of the escape attempts depressed Jem, but he refused to let his sadness show and tried to remain as calm and dignified as possible in front of others. He sought refuge in study and writing, and some of his writings touch on his melancholy, such as in one fragmentary *gazel* written during his imprisonment in the Tour de Zizim.

> *Lo, how the torrents smite their breasts with stones as on they go!*
> *Lo, how the realm of Space and Being pitieth my woe! . . .*
> *The clouds of heaven, weeping, wander o'er the mountain-peaks;*
> *Lo, how the burning thunder yonder moaneth deep and low!*

During this period an anonymous artist made a pen-and-ink drawing of Jem, which is now preserved in the public library of Arras. This is a particularly romantic image of Jem, showing him in left profile as a strikingly handsome young man with an aquiline nose, large eyes, and a closely-trimmed moustache and beard, wearing earrings and a bejewelled peaked cap with turned-up sides. This drawing was used as a model by the painter Hans Memling in his portrait of the *Martyrdom of St Ursula* (1489), which now hangs in the museum in Bruges. Ursula had refused to marry Attila the Hun, who thereupon ordered one of his archers to shoot her. The archer, who is shown as he is about to fire an arrow into Ursula's heart, is immediately recognizable as Jem from his handsome profile and distinctive cap, as portrayed in the Arras drawing. The nineteenth-century French historian Jules Michelet describes Jem's appearance in this drawing, noting: 'He has the air of a Christian knight, a very noble figure, sad and pale, the nose of a falcon, the eyes of a poet and mystic.' But Memling has changed the expression on Jem's face, for while in the Arras drawing he is smiling faintly, in the portrait of St Ursula's martyrdom he has a look of cruelty, for he is meant to characterize the Terrible Turk.

The Venetians learned from their envoy in Rome of the conditional agreement that had been made between the pope and Charles VIII to have Jem brought to the papal states. The Signoria instructed their envoy in Rome to urge Innocent to conclude this agreement as soon as possible, and to say publicly that Jem was being transferred of his own accord. D'Aubusson sent a message to the pope on 4 March 1487 with the same advice, and in the letter he warned that Mathias Corvinus was manoeuvring to buy Jem from the French.

D'Aubusson and the Venetian envoy stressed to Innocent that the international situation was now critical. Boccolino Guzzoni had once again rebelled, capturing Osimo in the Marche de Ancona. The pope's forces could not dislodge Boccolino, who had sent an envoy to Beyazit asking for help. Boccolino offered Beyazit Osimo and all of the Marche de Ancona if he sent troops, supplies and money right away. The envoy, a relative of Boccolino named Angelo Guzzoni, was to tell Beyazit of the agreement between d'Aubusson and the pope which would transfer Jem to the Marche de Ancona, where a crusader army would gather to make war on the Ottomans. But Angelo Guzzoni was stopped in Lecce by Ferrante's troops and the letter was taken from him. Innocent was outraged and condemned that 'son of iniquity and alumnus of perdition Boccolino Guzzoni' for his unholy alliance with the Turks.

On 25 February 1487 Ferrante sent a message to the pope via his envoy Vincenzo di Nola, enclosing the letter that had been taken from Guzzoni. The envoy, speaking for Ferrante, presented the letter as evidence of the danger facing Italy, saying there was no time to lose as Beyazit might have decided to accept Boccolino's offer. King Ferrante would thus seem to have been doing his duty as a Christian, but his perfidy and duplicity were such that at the same time he sent his envoy Francesco de Monti to the sultan to tell him of the military preparations being made by the pope and the Venetians, which he said were intended for an attack on the Turks. Ferrante assured Beyazit that of course he was not going to help the pope and his allies, reminding the sultan that they intended to use Jem in a crusade against him. That same day Ferrante sent instructions via an envoy to confirm the peace agreement between Naples and the Porte, in which they were to assist one another against their mutual enemies.

Venice was keen to maintain good relations with the Porte too, so on 3 April the Signoria sent Giovanni Dario as envoy to Istanbul. Dario was instructed to give the sultan news about his brother even before Beyazit asked about Jem. He was to say that the prince was in good health, and that he was in a fortified village under the control of Madame Beaujeu. He was also to tell Beyazit that Mathias Corvinus and the pope were each trying to gain custody of Jem and were both petitioning Charles VIII to this end. But Dario was to say nothing more than this, and if the sultan enquired he was to say that he had to have instructions from Venice before answering. Dario was also to learn about the state of preparation of the Turkish fleet and its objective, and if an expedition was planned he should try to convince the sultan not to let his warships pass Gallipoli. And if Beyazit were to refuse, Dario was to ask him to command his admiral not to attack ships of the Venetian Republic, in which case they in turn would respect the Turkish fleet.

Thus the Venetians put the Ottomans on their guard, as had Ferrante, whilst at the same time advising the pope to take quick action in bribing the court of France to hand over Jem. They added that the pope had advantages in this regard, because he could give both money and benefices to obtain Jem. As the Venetians said, 'Jem in the hands of the Holy Father would be a marvellous way to rein in Beyazit, preventing him from threatening the coast of the Holy See.'

Mathias Corvinus, having failed to kidnap Jem, tried to obtain custody of him through diplomatic means, sending his chancellor, Jean de Pruisz, Bishop of Varadin, as an ambassador to the French court. Other Christian princes, most notably the pope, were also petitioning for Jem, as was the Mamluk sultan of Egypt Kaitbey. The pope's petition was supported by the grand master of the Knights of Rhodes, who had informed the King of France and the other Christian princes of Europe that Sultan Beyazit was preparing to attack them. D'Aubusson wrote to Charles VIII that if Jem was in the custody of the pope then there would be no danger of Beyazit attacking Italy. In another letter to Charles the grand master insisted that Jem be brought to a fortified place of the Holy See, 'to secure our states and that of Christendom'. If Jem is kept in France, he said, this will not deter the Grand Turk from attacking Christendom, whereas if the prince is held in Italy by the pope this will frighten Beyazit so that he will desist.

The Hungarian embassy passed through Venice on its way across Italy to France. On the day after they left the Signoria sent a letter to Hieronimo Zorzi, the Venetian ambassador at the French court, informing him that the Bishop of Varadin had passed through Venice and was on his way to see Charles VIII, his main intention being to obtain custody of Jem. The first draft of a letter sent by the Signoria to Zorzi instructed him to do what he could to stop Varadin's intrigues and make sure that custody of Jem was not given to Mathias Corvinus. The second and final

draft instructed Zorzi to influence the French king to give Jem to the pope. This final instruction came after much soul-searching, in which prayers were said in the churches of Venice, asking for divine guidance to make the right decision, for the Venetians were torn between their desire to defend Christianity and their fear of provoking the wrath of the sultan.

Varadin's itinerary took him from Venice to Milan. There, in the name of Prince John, illegitimate son of Mathias Corvinus, he was to ask for the hand in marriage of Bianca Sforza, daughter of the Duke of Milan. He would then go on to France to negotiate for Jem, as well as to seek an alliance with Charles VIII against the recently-elected 'King of the Romans', Archduke Maximilian of Austria, son of the Emperor Frederick III.

Varadin's entourage was so extraordinarily sumptuous that it drew crowds as it passed through Europe. The bishop was followed in procession by 300 beardless young Hungarian noblemen mounted on 'identical horses', the youths dressed in purple robes, some of them wearing necklaces, those who were blond adorned with crowns of pearls in their hair. Early in July 1487 the Hungarian diplomatic train arrived in Ancenis, between Angers and Nantes, where Charles VIII was holding court.

Representatives of the pope and of the grand master of Rhodes had just left Ancenis, and envoys of other states would follow, each of them presenting their case for custody of Jem. The magnificence of the Hungarian ambassador's suite was such that it far outshone those of the other envoys. As Varadin's friend and compatriot Binfinus remarked: 'The Bishop of Varadin was so pompous in the accomplishment of his mission, that nothing more splendid was to be seen at any time in any nation.' The gifts he presented to the French court included 25,000 gold coins, twenty-five Arabian race horses, a number of other horses clad in armour, as well as embroideries in gold adorned with precious stones, engraved cutlery, oriental fabrics, and bedroom furniture all in gold. Most of the gifts were intended for Madame Beaujeu, for the bishop knew that it would be she who would make the final decision concerning Jem's custody, and he was sure that the presents would influence her judgment in his favour. This is verified by Hieronimo Zorzi, the Venetian ambassador, who wrote about her to the Signoria on 13 September 1487 in very uncomplimentary terms. He had been told, he said, that Madame had made much money out of the negotiations for custody of the sultan's brother, and that Mathias Corvinus had promised her a rich present, besides what she already had, if he could have Zizim. As Zorzi wrote in conclusion:

> Madame de Beaujeu is very avaracious, and does anything for money, regardless of the honour of God and of the Crown. To thwart this negotiation, the Pope must promise her a considerable amount of money before Zizim be removed from France; otherwise, should the Pope take no further steps, Madame de Beaujeu may, for gain, consent to Zizim being surrendered to the King of Hungary.

The mediator between the pope and the French court was Duke Lorenzo de' Medici of Florence. Lorenzo hesitated to act as a mediator partly because he did not want to jeopardize his friendly relationship with the Turks, but he also felt that his efforts might be in vain, since when dealing with the French, diplomacy was secondary to money. 'Nothing is done in the French court without money,' he said, and his agent, Tommaso Spinelli, writing to him from Ancenis, agreed: 'Here if you offer the right price you can usually get what you want.' Many believed that Madame Beaujeu and the Royal Council were solely interested in extracting as much money as possible from parties interested in obtaining custody of Jem, though the French were mindful to stay on good terms with the King of Hungary until their problems with the new emperor Maximilian were solved, as Spinelli wrote to his master: 'As long as the envoy of Hungary is in France we can do nothing, but as soon as he leaves the deal will be done, I think.'

Although Innocent was deeply vexed by the Hungarian petition for Jem, he first had to deal with the more pressing matter of Boccolino Guzzoni who was still holding Osimo, all the while offering Beyazit a route in to Italy. Innocent commanded Giuliano della Rovere, papal legate of the Marche de Ancona, to besiege Osimo, but the pope's impoverished forces were able to achieve very little. King Ferrante offered to send some money to the pope to help him build up his army, and at the same time he strengthened the fortifications at Brindisi, urging Innocent to do the same with Ancona. These were the two places on the coast where the Turks were most likely to attack, and the loss of Ancona would spell the doom of Italy. Ferrante sent his envoy Troianoi de Bottunis to Rome, Florence and Milan, where he met with the Duke of Bari to try to formulate a common plan of defence. On 24 April 1487 Innocent issued a brief ordering the siege of Osimo to begin.

Innocent appealed to the Milanese, and in May they sent Gian Jacopo Trivulzio, one of their best generals, but he too was unable to unseat Guzzoni. In July Rovere asked to be recalled and was replaced by Cardinal Balu. By the time Balue arrived at Osimo, Trivulzio had reduced the city to the point where Guzzoni's forces were on the verge of surrendering. The Florentine ambassador had been negotiating with Guzzoni, who eventually, as Sigismondo de' Conti wrote, agreed 'on the payment of 8000 ducats, to give up the city and repair to Florence'.

Meanwhile the Bishop of Varadin was growing ever more confident that he would secure custody of Jem, even requesting a safe-conduct pass through Savoy for himself and Jem in anticipation of his triumphant return to Hungary. On 7 September Varadin went to the town of Laval expecting to have an audience with the king, but when he arrived he learned that Charles had left for Paris. While in Laval, Varadin met Hieronimo Zorzi, the Venetian ambassador, and in an unguarded moment expressed his frustration, saying that he had expected to have obtained custody of Jem within a fortnight, but now after four months in France he had nothing. Corvinus had told him to return to Hungary, he said, but he was going to see the king one more time and persuade him to hand over Jem. Varadin also sent a secretary to Bourganeuf to talk with Jem, because Corvinus wanted to be clear on the prince's intentions.

The Venetian envoy immediately took advantage of these confidences to influence King Charles, Madame de Beaujeu and Guillaume de Rochefort, grand chancellor of the Royal Council, so that they would give Jem to the pope rather than Corvinus. Zorzi charged a friend with this mission, someone who knew Anne de Beaujeu and responded with the comment:

> Madame de Beaujeu is a great miser and does everything for money, without respect for the honour of God or of the Crown. And if it is necessary, the pope will promise her a great sum of money and she will agree without any other considerations than her greediness.

Bishop Varadin had installed himself in Paris to await the outcome of the negotiations. He lived there in great state, with no thought of the expense, and his table was said to be the most splendid in Paris. Once, in preparation for a banquet, his chef bought all the fish in the Paris market so that the king's own maître d'hôtel had to come to him to obtain some fish for the royal table. Varadin was well received and met all the notables in the French court and government, but still he heard nothing more on the decision regarding Jem.

While Varadin was still in Paris, John Kendal arrived representing the pope, the grand master of the Knights of St John and the wishes of Henry VII of England. Kendal was carrying the brief that Innocent had written regarding the transfer of Jem to the Holy See, along with the conditional agreement relating to this between the papacy and France. At the same time Hieronimo Zorzi was instructed by the Signoria to do everything he could to influence Madame de Beaujeu in favour of giving Jem to the pope, but that this must be done in the utmost secrecy, so as not to provoke Beyazit against Venice. Zorzi was also told to stay in France until both Varadin and Kendal had departed.

Soon after Kendal's arrival he persuaded the king and his council not to give custody of Jem to Hungary, and Varadin was so informed. Varadin and his entourage left Paris on 15 October, with an escort provided by the king, headed by Tristan de Salazar, Archbishop of Sens, who was to conduct the party to Lyon. On 2 November, a downcast Varadin left Lyon for Milan to conclude the engagement of Bianca Sforza with Prince John of Hungary.

The Venetians immediately informed Innocent, through their envoy in Rome, that the pope had secured custody of Jem, and at the same time they instructed their *bailo* in Istanbul to inform

Beyazit. The sultan replied that two of his envoys were on their way to France to take presents to Jem. When they stopped en route in Venice the authorities informed the pope, for there were fears that they might be going to assassinate the prince. The Venetian spokesman asked Innocent not to reveal the source of his information, for if Beyazit learned that it came from Venice he might turn his wrath on the Republic. But there is no further record of the two Turkish envoys, who apparently never reached Bourganeuf.

The failure of the Hungarian mission to France delighted the pope, and he decided to send two nuncios to France as soon as possible to conclude the negotiations on Jem as well as to settle other matters in the papacy's interest. He chose for the mission two experienced diplomats: Leonello Chieragato, the Bishop of Trau, and Antonio Flores, the papal protonotary. The nuncios were to stop first in Florence to seek the advice of Lorenzo de' Medici, whose daughter Maddalena was engaged to marry the pope's son, Franceschetto Cibo. The two nuncios met with Lorenzo in Florence early in December 1487, noting in their report to Innocent that in their talks with the duke they discussed Jem.

At that time Lorenzo was also talking about Jem with an envoy from the Mamluk sultan Kaitbey. The Egyptian envoy arrived on 11 November, and on the following day he was received by the government of Florence. Several days later he was conducted to Lorenzo's palace, where they exchanged gifts. Among the presents sent by Kaitbey were a lion and a giraffe, the latter being a source of wonder, for it was the first of its kind to be seen in Europe. In one of their talks the envoy mentioned that Kaitbey would like to see Jem moved from France and brought to a place where he could be used to threaten Beyazit more effectively. He said that Kaitbey would be willing to pay a large sum of money for this if the pope, after obtaining custody of Jem, would give him to Hungary, Naples, Venice or any of the other states where he could be used against Beyazit, so as to prevent the Turks from attacking them. The agreements between these governments should be secret, he said; the pope would have to take the initiative, since he was not under the same pressure as the other sovereigns. Also the pope was the only one who could claim Jem from d'Aubusson or the King of France, because as their Holy Father they could not refuse him.

Lorenzo passed on Kaitbey's suggestion to the papal nuncios. He also gave them a letter that the Egyptian envoy had brought from the Islamic caliph in Cairo addressed to the pope. The letter said that since Jem had given himself into the hands of d'Aubusson with the promise of safe conduct, then it was the duty of the pope as the supreme head of Christendom to give him justice. If the pope was ready to give Kaitbey any assurance in that respect, the Egyptian envoy would go to Rome to deal directly with Innocent. When the nuncios informed Innocent of this he responded by saying that he was pleased with Kaitbey's offer to contribute financially to the negotiations concerning Jem that had opened in the French court. Innocent meanwhile told an agent of Lorenzo de' Medici in Rome, Lanfredini, that Charles VIII had led him to believe that he was willing to turn Jem over to the Holy See, and that he had written to d'Aubusson to prepare the necessary galleys for the prince's journey. Lanfredini remarked in a letter to Lorenzo, 'You should know that as soon as the pope has Jem, he will appoint d'Aubusson cardinal.'

On 5 January 1488 the pope's nuncios stayed in Moulin, en route to Paris, where they were met by the Duke of Bourbon,

Jean II, who despite suffering from a bad attack of gout, received them warmly. The next day they were joined on the last leg of their journey by the protonotary Orioli. As they approached Paris they were met by a deputation from the Bishop of Bordeaux, André d'Epinay, who greeted the nuncios and invited them to stay in one of the king's villas, where they could prepare for their solemn entry into Paris the following day. The nuncios were confident that they would be successful in their mission, although they had heard much of Madame de Beaujeu and realized that the negotiations could become difficult and convoluted.

Meanwhile Jem was waiting for news in the Tour de Zizim at Bourganeuf, aware of the negotiations that were being held to decide his fate. He passed the time with his companions. According to legend, when he was alone in his room he played chess with his chimpanzee or chatted with his white parrot, who each morning greeted him with the first *sura* of the Kuran, the declaration of the Islamic faith: 'Verily, we come from God, and to Him we shall return.' And whenever the prince entered or left the room the parrot would call out, 'God give victory to Jem Sultan!', or so says the Turkish chronicler Evliya Çelebi.

During these long days Jem was often to be seen gazing out from the easterly-facing window on the fourth floor of the tower at Bourganeuf, for that was the direction of Anatolia, the site of the lost empire that he envisioned in his dreams, and which with each passing year seemed ever farther away.

10

Sold to the Pope?

A T THE BEGINNING of 1488 Jem was midway through the sixth year of his captivity, the last eighteen months of which he had been confined to the Tour de Zizim at Bourganeuf. Frequent reports were reaching him about negotiations at the French court concerning his custody, particularly the rumour that he was going to be sold to the pope.

The pope's representatives, Leonello Chieragato and Antonio Flores, made their formal entry into Paris on 17 January 1488. They were first invited to a mass at Ste-Chapelle and then conducted to the palace. The next day André d'Epinay, Archbishop of Bordeaux, presented them to the king, who welcomed them warmly. After giving the king apostolic benediction, the nuncios read the pope's brief and expressed the love that Innocent felt for Charles. They said that Innocent had sent them to discuss in his name the most grave questions of equal interest to the Holy See, Christianity and France. The king, speaking through the Archbishop of Bordeaux, replied that such matters could be discussed at the plenary sessions of the court the following day, and the nuncios could present their case fully then.

On 20 January a plenary session was opened by the French

chancellor, Guillaume de Rochefort, who announced that the court was ready to hear the pope's nuncios. Leonello Chieragato then argued the pope's case, explaining that without Jem the heart of Christendom would be in peril. Certain Italians, he said, such as Boccolino Guzzoni, had been so disloyal to the Christian cause as to call in the Turks. 'You have a powerful weapon in the person of Jem', Chieragato continued, 'whom you must give to the papacy, for if the pope has possession of him the Turks will never invade the Holy See.' If the king agreed to the pope's wishes, Chieragato concluded, he would have eternal honour and merit.

The whole court received this address with great approval, and some were so moved that they wept. Chieragato then attempted to read out a papal brief about a dispute between the papacy and the bishops of France – who were in a state of virtual rebellion against the Holy See – but the chancellor interrupted and said that it would be enough for the written text to be submitted to the court. Charles told the nuncios that their proposals, including their petition for the pope to have custody of Jem, would have to be discussed by the court and that they would be notified of the decision in writing. The nuncios pressed for another audience with the king but were told that in fact no decision could be made until the return of Fra Baldassare de Spino from Rome. Brother de Spino had been sent to Rome to carefully explain to Innocent the French king's reluctance to grant him custody of Jem for fear that the pope would hand him over to Maximilian. Maximilian had invaded France a few weeks after having been elected King of the Romans, and the French did not want this title to be ratified by the papacy until he had made peace with France. When the nuncios heard this they knew that their mission had suddenly become many times more difficult.

On 30 March the nuncios were eventually granted another audience with the king. This time they explained that Beyazit was preparing both land and sea forces for an expedition. They said that the pope was busy outfitting a fleet, but that the Holy See could not resist such a powerful adversary alone, and that Innocent hoped that Charles would help by sending Jem to Italy, thus enabling the pope to go on the offensive. Jem was 'wilting in inactivity', they said, while the pope could use him in the interest of Christianity.

Chieragato and Flores then presented the pope's brief to Madame de Beaujeu. They asked her to take a favourable view of Innocent's request for Jem, as well as other petitions from the pope, who said that he counted on her support as in the past. Madame de Beaujeu seemed satisfied and answered with her usual goodwill, saying that she would help them as much as she could, and that she was sure things would work out as they wished.

The next day the nuncios were met by the chancellor, Rochefort, who announced that the king was now willing to allow Jem to go to Italy, on condition that neither the papacy nor the Knights of St John handed the prince over to anyone else without the approval of the King of France. Hoping to close the deal and conclude their mission as soon as possible, the nuncios sent a request to Innocent saying that in order to complete their mission it was necessary to have the goodwill of the man who was considered to be the most influential of the king's advisors, Admiral Louis Mallet de Graville. André d'Epinay was a relative of the admiral, and the nuncios suggested that if he were appointed cardinal it would greatly enhance their cause.

All the talk in the French court now centred on the Turks' preparations for war. Letters intercepted by Venice revealed that

King Ferrante had been in contact with Beyazit, and that he hoped to acquire Jem so that the sultan would direct his attack away from Naples and toward the Holy See and Venice. A month earlier the Moorish ruler Abu-abd-Allah had pleaded with Beyazit to help him against King Ferdinand of Spain, and the sultan had sent a favourite named Kemal to make a naval demonstration at Malta. Ferdinand immediately fortified the coast of Sicily and the isle of Gozo, but the pope lacked funds to take any defensive measures. Cities on the coast of Italy feared a Turkish attack and all maritime trade stopped, so that their resources were badly strained.

The nuncios addressed the king and his council about the need for urgent action. The sultan had agreed to an armistice with Hungary, Venice, Naples and Rhodes, they said, which left the Holy See as the only target for attack. Thus, the nuncios explained, the fate of the Church was in the hands of Charles, whose delivery of Jem to the pope would bring relief from this imminent danger. If Charles would make peace with Maximilian and the Duke of Brittany, whose realm the French had invaded in May the previous year, then Beyazit would see that there was unity in Christendom and would hold back from attacking Europe.

The king and his council listened intently to the nuncios' words, and were debating their reply when a councillor arrived with news that changed the focus of their discussions. Flanders had been invaded by Maximilian. King Charles had often criticized the pope for supporting Maximilian, and Innocent had responded with scathing remarks about the French king. Rochefort took the opportunity to remind the nuncios of this, and expressed his indignation at the pope's remarks. The nuncios were deeply disappointed, feeling that Innocent's loose tongue had undone all the progress they had made toward securing custody of Jem.

Still, the nuncios had one last card to play – the nomination of the Archbishop of Bordeaux, André d'Epinay, as cardinal. But just as they were about to approach the French with their suggestion they learned of two further developments. Lorenzo de' Medici's agent, Tommaso Spinelli, had visited Madame de Beaujeu in Moulin and offered her 100,000 ducats on behalf of the Mamluk sultan Kaitbey to have Jem taken to Cairo. Lorenzo was to be rewarded for his intercession by special trade privileges for Florence in Egypt. And on 15 June the knight Martin Dausa arrived at the French court in Angers as an emissary of Pierre d'Aubusson, accompanied by Antoine de Blanchefort, *seigneur* of Bois-Lamy. The envoys were immediately received by the king, to whom they communicated the news that Beyazit was preparing a naval expedition against the Mamluks of Egypt. The Knights of St John were in terrible danger, they said, for the Turkish sultan might attack Rhodes if he defeated the Egyptians.

Flores said to Rochefort that he too feared for Rhodes, and stressed that it was imperative that a final decision be made about Jem, adding: 'Hand over Jem and soon you will hear that the Archbishop of Bordeaux has been nominated as cardinal.' Rochefort promised that the French would intercede to help the Knights of St John against the Turks. He then arranged for the papal nuncios to have another audience with the king. The nuncios told Charles that they had received authority from the pope to give the required guarantees concerning the transfer of Jem's custody, and that the pope was aware that his nomination of the Archbishop of Bordeaux as cardinal was essential. Rochefort suggested that it might be more acceptable if Jem was handed over first and the nomination of d'Epinay as cardinal announced afterwards, but the King's Council refused, insisting that they would hand over Jem only after this.

∞

After Bishop Varadin's failure in France, Mathias Corvinus sought to apply pressure to acquire Jem from a different quarter. On 10 June 1488 a Hungarian envoy arrived on Rhodes with a letter from Corvinus giving him unlimited power to negotiate with the Knights of St John. The envoy told d'Aubusson and his council that he was in contact with high-ranking Turks who were willing to abandon Beyazit and join with Jem if he were in Hungary. D'Aubusson answered that he could not move Jem without the agreement of the pope, who wanted to use the prince in the interests of Christianity.

That same day an Egyptian envoy arrived on Rhodes, offering to form a league with the knights with Jem as its leader. The Knights' Council dismissed the Egyptian envoy with fine words but no commitment. Mathias Corvinus briefly saw this as an opportunity to launch an attack against the Ottomans in Europe, but he abandoned the idea when it became clear that the pope was again blocking his attempts to acquire Jem. When the Turks pressed Corvinus to renew their armistice, he readily agreed. At the same time the Hungarian king stayed on good terms with Kaitbey, to whom he sent envoys, trying to persuade him to renew the war against the Ottomans.

But by late June the Ottomans had taken the initiative. A Turkish fleet with eighty sail passed Gallipoli on the Dardanelles and was seen from Rhodes on 28 June, headed for Egypt. After meeting with the Council of Knights, d'Aubusson reinforced Rhodes and sent ammunition to the fortresses of the order at Halicarnassus and Kos. On 15 August Egyptian troops attacked the Ottoman army near Tarsus. After a day-long battle the Egyptians were victorious, leaving 30,000 Turks dead on the battlefield, with a loss of only 8,000 of their own men. Despite the loss of many of the ships of the Ottoman fleet in a storm, the Turks rallied and succeeded in stopping the Egyptian army from invading Anatolia, forcing the Mamluks to retreat. On 8 September the Turkish ships were seen again by the Knights of Rhodes on their way northward to Istanbul, the pasha in command sending a friendly greeting to d'Aubusson as his flagship passed.

Whilst events in the eastern Mediterranean moved ahead, the negotiations at the French court concerning Jem's custody faltered, with Innocent continuing to insist that he would only nominate André d'Epinay as cardinal after Jem was transferred to his custody. Guy de Blanchefort informed the pope that he and John Kendal were waiting for authorization from the French court for Jem's transfer to Italy. As soon as they received this, Jem would be brought to a commandery of the order near the coast, and they would keep him there until galleys arrived to bring him to the Holy See.

Flores and Chieragato informed the pope that Rochefort had promised Jem to them, and asked that Innocent send ships to transport the prince to the Holy See without delay. The chancellor gave the nuncios assurances and talked to them in a friendly manner, but he expressed doubts that handing over Jem would enable the pope to organize a crusade that would push back the Turks. The nuncios answered that the crusade was uppermost in the pope's mind, and time was therefore of the essence. The chancellor added that he thought the Christian princes should meet in Italy under the leadership of the pope to decide on how to unify Europe so that they could organize an expedition against the Ottomans, saying, in reference to Jem, 'You'll take your Turk with you!'

However, Innocent was not prepared to give in over the issue of the timing of d'Epinay's nomination as cardinal, so the nuncios obtained an audience with the king and asked that royal commissioners be appointed in order to discuss the matter. Charles responded favourably and appointed two commissioners: the general of Languedoc, Guillaume Briçonnet, and the chancellor Guillaume de Rochefort. The commissioners took the opportunity to discuss with the nuncios other unresolved issues, including that of the papal tithe, which the French were no longer willing to pay. Rochefort advised the nuncios to put aside the matter of the tithe, as it would cause difficulties in the far more important matter of Jem's custody. But the nuncios, constrained by strict orders from the pope, insisted that the tithe and Jem's release were inextricably linked, in the manner of 'a bride and her dowry'. The commissioners gave in and agreed to Innocent's terms for the transfer of Jem's custody, and wrote to the king recommending that the prince be taken from France to the Holy See, with the requisite guarantees. Madame de Beaujeu approved the report of the commissioners and complimented them on their good work. The nuncios were told that everything would be arranged to their satisfaction; they would be given a galley and 100 royal archers to bring Jem to a port where he could embark for Italy, and Madame would do everything she could to help them.

News reached the French court around this time that Jem had

fallen seriously ill, though the sources were vague about the specific nature of his illness. Alarmed, the nuncios urged the French court to approve the draft agreement for the prince's immediate transfer, requesting that Rochefort deal with this before departing on a trip to Rome. The chancellor declared that the king would agree as soon as the draft was in his hands and would write the necessary documents for Jem's transfer.

According to the final agreement, a representative of the Knights of St John would sign a guarantee that d'Epinay would be appointed cardinal as soon as Jem was handed over to the Holy See, otherwise the guarantor would forfeit all of his possessions. The guarantor was Antoine de Blanchefort, who agreed to forfeit his chateau at Bois-Lamy along with all of his other possessions if d'Epinay was not appointed cardinal. Antoine de Blanchefort would hand over Jem to the grand master of Rhodes, who would bring the prince to the Holy See under strict conditions. The grand master was to ratify the conditions in the next six months, at which time Antoine de Blanchefort would be relieved of his responsibility. The agreement was signed on 5 October 1488 at the residence of the Archbishop of Bordeaux in La Fleche, north-east of Angers, in the presence of d'Epinay as well as Fra Baldassare de Spino and Jean de Zannochi, priest of the diocese of Bresse.

The terms of the agreement included significant concessions on the part of the papacy. Pierre d'Aubusson was to be nominated as a cardinal along with d'Epinay and named others, and the Knights of St John were to be given further important rights and immunities. The king obtained a promise that Innocent would grant dispensations to allow him to marry Anne of Brittany, since both of them had contracted marriages to others. Charles, while still Dauphin, had agreed to marry Margaret of Austria, daughter of the Archduke Maximilian. Anne on her part had been married by proxy to Maximilian. Apparently neither of these marriages had been consummated, making it a great deal easier for Innocent to annul them.

A separate treaty concluded between Innocent and the Knights of St John, with Charles VIII's approval, provided for the custody of Jem in the Holy See. According to this agreement, Jem would continue to have a bodyguard of the Knights of Rhodes, while the pope would receive the pension of 45,000 ducats hitherto paid to the Order of St John for the prince's maintenance. But the pope pledged himself to pay 10,000 ducats to the French if he handed over his charge to any other monarch without the King of France's consent.

Two days later the king left La Fleche for Baugé, with the pope's nuncios following behind. On 13 October Charles commanded that letters of transport and safe conduct be prepared for Jem and those accompanying him from France to the Holy See, including 400 armed knights of the Order of St John. However Charles withheld his signature on these letters pending settlement of another dispute, the interdict that the pope had placed on the city of Bruges in Flanders when Maximilian was imprisoned there. Charles had asked Innocent to lift the interdict as part of the original negotiations over the transfer of Jem. The nuncios complained to Innocent about the delay, saying that the Flanders situation was holding up a final agreement. But with victory in the negotiations so close, the pope gave in on this matter, and on 3 November lifted the interdict. Charles expressed his delight at the news and told the nuncios that he would do everything he could to please the pope.

And so in mid-November 1488 the knights prepared to move Jem from the Tour de Zizim at Bourganeuf, where he had been confined for two years and three months, and bring him down to the Mediterranean coast. Jem had recovered from his recent illness, and he was buoyed up by the prospect of leaving France, though he knew that he would merely be moving from one prison to another, and that he would soon be in the custody of the pope.

There was one final royal decree required before Jem could be taken from France, and Charles held back on signing this, probably on the advice of his sister Madame de Beaujeu, who was annoyed that the pope had not yet nominated d'Epinay cardinal. On 5 December the nuncios wrote to Innocent explaining the latest twist, writing: 'It is incredible to see how much the nomination of d'Epinay as cardinal means to the French, and how they don't want to see it delayed under any pretext.'

The king returned to Paris on 20 January 1489, with the nuncios accompanying his entourage. That same day two other envoys arrived in Paris, one of them, Camillo Pandone, representing King Ferrante of Naples, the other, Antonio Rerichio, sent by Sultan Beyazit. The papal nuncios were shocked by the presence of the two other envoys, and immediately did what they could to discredit them, saying that King Ferrante was in league with Beyazit, who was most afraid of his brother being given to the pope.

Pandone spoke first and put the case for Jem being transferred to Naples to deter Beyazit from attacking his kingdom. The Turkish envoy, Rerichio, then addressed the king saying, 'Don't think that Beyazit is frightened of his brother, but Jem is clever and if he left France he would campaign against the sultan, and that's why he must remain here.' Rerichio said that the sultan would give Charles the Church of the Holy Sepulchre as soon as

Jerusalem was captured by the Ottomans. Besides this, Beyazit would give the king two of the most sacred Christian relics in Turkey: the tip of the lance that had pierced Christ's side (the shaft of which was already enshrined at Ste-Chapelle in Paris), and the canopy under which Mary had lain when she gave birth to Jesus. Beyazit promised that he would search the Ottoman Empire for other relics to send to Charles, to whom he also offered an annual subsidy of 40,000 ducats to keep Jem and not turn him over to the pope. Moreover, Beyazit offered a military alliance, promising to aid Charles against his enemies in Europe. If Charles did not accept the offer, Beyazit threatened to make peace with Kaitbey and join with the Mamluk sultan to destroy Christendom. Rerichio then spoke privately to the king, arranging for him to be given what the papal envoys presumed to be a huge cash payment. Charles concluded the audience saying that he would deliberate with his council before giving Rerichio an answer. Before Rerichio departed he distributed 100,000 ducats in bribes to various influential members of the council.

The Royal Council was divided over Beyazit's proposal. The papal nuncios addressed the council and ridiculed the sultan's offer, saying that the Turks were not likely to capture Jerusalem or make an alliance with Kaitbey, since they had recently suffered a catastrophic defeat at the hands of the Mamluks at Tarsus. They emphasized that Jem no longer wanted to live as a captive in France, citing the prince's recent illness as being a consequence of his long confinement. The envoys also reminded Charles that he had given his word that Jem would be transferred to the Holy See, and it would be scandalous if he changed his mind.

Hearing of these new negotiations, Queen Beatrice of Hungary, wife of Mathias Corvinus, and daughter of Ferrante I of Naples, sent a servant as an envoy to the French court to make yet another appeal for Jem to be given to her husband, promising a larger annual subsidy than had been offered by the Turks. When the envoy was told that Jem would be given to the papacy he complained bitterly, saying that Innocent intended to hand over the prince to Venice, gaining the support of several in the council when he pointed out that Hungary could stop the German princes from attacking Flanders. The papal nuncios responded by saying that the pope only wanted to use Jem in the interests of Christianity, and that he would not hand over Jem to Venice or any other state.

At the conclusion of the meeting the council sent a message to Guy de Blanchefort, telling him not to proceed with the transfer of Jem until they decided upon the new proposals that had been made to them. The messenger was Baron Jacques de Sassenage, father of the fair Philippine, and she may have taken this last opportunity to send a note to Jem. But when the baron arrived at Bourganeuf he found that the Tour de Zizim was empty, for the knights had already left with Jem.

11

From Bourganeuf to Rome

T HE KNIGHTS, commanded by Guy de Blanchefort, left
Bourganeuf with their captives on 10 November 1488,
moving them surreptitiously by stages to the Mediterranean
coast, afraid that King Charles would change his mind once and
for all about allowing Jem to be moved to the Holy See.

According to Sadüddin, they travelled first eastward, to Felletin,
due south of Aubusson. There they stayed at a commandery,
another chateau of the Blanchefort family. Then, after passing
south of Monteferrand they approached the town of Courpière,
where they learned from their scouts that Anne de Beaujeu was
staying. And so, since they were afraid that she might take Jem
from them, they bypassed the town, crossing the River Dore and
then the Loire. This brought them to another Blanchefort chateau
at Chazelles, where they passed the night before moving on to Lyon.

The party stayed in Lyon for a few weeks until, on 5 December,
they were able to find a river boat to take them down the Rhône.
Their next stopping place was Valence, at the confluence of the
Rhône and the Isère, where they went ashore to eat and spend
the night before going on to Ponte-de-Sorgues, a short way north
of Avignon. The knights and their captives spent several weeks

in Ponte-de-Sorgues, waiting for a caique to take them on the remainder of their journey down to the Mediterranean coast. When they did embark it was not on a caique but on a much larger sea-going vessel, which took them down the last stretch of the Rhône to the Mediterranean and then eastward along the coast to Marseilles. After two days they sailed to Toulon, where the *Grande Nef du Tresor* and two other Rhodian galleys were waiting for them.

As Jem and his companions boarded the *Tresor*, and the crew took aboard supplies, Guy de Blanchefort and the knights awaited news of the pope's negotiations. On the fifth day in Toulon a courier arrived with a message from Charles Allemand, commander of the Knights of St John in Avignon, saying that the king had changed his mind about letting Jem leave for Italy, and that a royal courier had been sent with instructions that the prince remain in France.

On hearing this Guy de Blanchefort gave orders for the Rhodian ships to get underway as soon as possible, to sail for Civitavecchia, the port for Rome. After six days waiting for a favourable wind the *Tresor* and its companion galleys set sail, leaving the port just as the royal courier arrived in Toulon, too late to stop them. The date was 21 February 1489, six years, four months and six days since the *Tresor* had first brought Jem to France.

Charles and the Royal Council were furious when they learned of this. They accused Leonello Chieragato and Antonio Flores of having tipped off the knights, of letting them know that the council had been deliberating over other offers, but the nuncios denied this. Several members of the court accused André d'Epinay of having relayed information to the nuncios, but he had not. The truth was that the knights had been informed by their own spies in the French court: when it looked as though the king was seriously considering offers from other quarters they simply took matters into their own hands.

Aboard the *Tresor* was a French deputation headed by the *maréchal* Antoine de Gimel, who had been appointed by Charles VIII to accompany Jem to Rome. Gimel was at first unaware that the king had changed his mind about letting Jem leave. But at some stage, as the *Tresor* headed across the Ligurian Sea toward Italy, he learned of this, though there was little he could do about it. During the voyage Gimel developed a close friendship with Jem, whose warm personality and good manners, according to Sadüddin, he greatly appreciated.

The voyage went smoothly until the small Rhodian fleet reached the strait between Elba and the Italian mainland at Piombino, when a violent storm arose, 'dousing the galleys like a water-mill'. During the storm the *Tresor* was separated from the other galleys, and was forced to take refuge in the lee of an island. At midnight a mast broke and the anchor rope parted, and all aboard prepared to jump into the sea and swim ashore, but then 'God restored his favour' and the storm abated.

At that moment six galleons arrived and surrounded the *Tresor*. The galleons proved to be under the command of the infamous pirate captain Villemarin, whose flotilla had also taken refuge in the lee of the island. As soon as Villemarin saw the flag of the Knights of St John he immediately signalled that he was a friend and willing to help. The knights transferred some of their company from the damaged *Tresor* to a pirate galleon. The other two Rhodian galleys rejoined the *Tresor,* and they sailed together with the pirate to the port of Sentisare, where the *Tresor* was repaired and Villemarin's galleon was returned to him.

On 6 March 1489 the *Tresor* anchored at Civitavecchia. The pope was informed immediately and he sent commissioners to the port, headed by his nephew Niccolo Cibo-Bocciardi, Archbishop of Arles, and the French legate Cardinal Balu, with orders to expedite the transfer of Jem and his companions to Rome. The commissioners arrived in Civitavecchia the following day, when Guy de Blanchefort formally transferred custody of Jem to Cardinal Balue, acting in the name of the pope.

Within days Innocent had convened a consistory in which he created five new cardinals: the archbishops André d'Epinay and Lorenzo Cibo, Innocent's nephew, the bishops Ardicino della Porta and Antioniotto Pallavicini, and the grand master of the Knights of St John, Pierre d'Aubusson. The pope also created three other cardinals *in petto*, or secretly, one of whom was the second son of Lorenzo de' Medici, the fourteen-year-old Giovanni, the future Pope Clement VII. D'Aubusson was not present at the time, and so Innocent sent his red hat to Rhodes, where the grand master received it in a solemn ceremony in the Church of St John on 29 June, the feast of St Peter and Paul. The pope also sent two briefs to the nuncios in France, one of them to be passed on to André d'Epinay to tell him of his appointment as cardinal, and the other to be given to the chancellor Guillaume de Rochefort to confirm the appointment of two French cardinals, one being Pierre d'Aubusson. These appointments served to mollify the anger felt by the king and his council toward the Knights of St John and the pope for their abrupt removal of Jem from France. Charles expressed his satisfaction to the nuncios, who promptly reported this to the pope.

The elevation of Pierre d'Aubusson to the rank of cardinal was applauded throughout Europe as a fitting reward to a great warrior and champion of Christianity. There is no record of anyone overtly suggesting the grand master was being rewarded for having delivered Jem to the pope, or any accusations that he had violated the agreement of safe conduct that he had given to the prince when he first came to Rhodes. In fact, all of the Christian states of Europe sent d'Aubusson their congratulations, beginning with Venice.

On 13 March, Jem and his companions were taken by the knights on a ship that sailed down the coast from Civitavecchia to Ostia, at the mouth of the Tiber. There Jem was welcomed by Franceschetto Cibo, son of the pope, who held the fortress at Ostia. Just two months before Franceschetto had been married in Rome to Maddalena de' Medici, daughter of Lorenzo de' Medici, the first time that the son of a pope had been publicly recognized. According to the nineteenth-century German historian Anton von Reumont, Franceschetto was mean and avaracious, and led a disorderly life 'which was doubly unbecoming in the son of a Pope. He paraded the streets at night ... forced his way into the houses of citizens for evil purposes, and was often driven out with shame.' Such was the man who was to be placed in charge of Jem during the rest of the papacy of Innocent VIII.

Later that same day Franceschetto Cibo left with Guy de Blanchefort and the knights who were guarding Jem, and together they sailed up the Tiber to Rome. At this time Rome had a population of less than 50,000, and only small areas of the ancient imperial capital enclosed by the walls of Marcus Aurelius were still occupied, though the new Renaissance city was beginning to take form. The knights and their entourage prepared to enter the city through Porta Portese in Trastevere. Jem was mounted on a mare from the papal stables, flanked by Franceschetto Cibo and Guy de Blanchefort. Waiting outside the gate to welcome them were officials of the pope's household, along with the houses of the cardinals and other high-ranking clerics, groups of lay dignitaries, and several foreign ambassadors. Among the officials was Johann Burchard, the pope's master of ceremonies, whose diary provides a detailed record of all public events in the papal court during the years 1483–1506, including Jem's formal entry into Rome.

After describing the notables assembled to meet Jem, Burchard wrote that the first to approach Jem was an envoy of Kaitbey, who had been sent to Rome to speak to the pope about the prince's future. Burchard described how the Egyptian approached Jem with his escort, stopping to dismount forty paces from the prince, then walking to within fifteen paces, whereupon he prostrated himself and touched the ground with his head. He walked closer and now touched the ground with his left hand, kissing it, after which he knelt down and kissed Jem's right leg, his right hand, and then his sleeve, bursting into tears as he did so. Jem stayed impassive and made no motion other than touching the envoy's neck, after which he dismissed him with a single word, whereupon the Egyptian remounted and rode back to join his escort. Meanwhile one of Jem's officers advanced and exchanged kisses on both cheeks with all of the Egyptian delegation. Each of the Egyptians touched the ground in front of Jem, and he responded by inclining his head slightly.

The heads of the papal household and of each of the cardinal's houses then came forward and greeted Jem, welcoming him to Rome and presenting gifts to him, which he hardly appeared to notice. Burchard, who rode next to Jem's interpreter, described the ensuing procession, which got under way only after a dispute between Guy de Blanchefort and Count Emilio Parisiano d'Ascoli, as well as between the envoys of Naples and Venice over the order in which they should ride. Blanchefort eventually gave way to d'Ascoli, but he was given precedence over the Neapolitan and Venetian envoys, who thereupon refused to join the procession. Only then did the procession begin, riding through Porta Portese, the contingents described by Burchard passing in turn.

They were led by a detachment of cavalry under Domenico Doria, followed by the houses of the cardinals; the 'French chevaliers and seigneurs accompanying Jem'; the prince's companions, 'a dozen in number'; the equerries of the pope, the senators of Rome, together with Count d'Ascoli 'and several gentlemen'; the servants at arms, the herald of the King of France, Rossillon; 'the clerk of ceremonies and his master, Johann Burchard', who was to the right of Jem's interpreter. Then came Jem himself, haughtily ignoring the crowd that flanked the line of march, as Burchard notes: 'The son of Mahomet disdained to vouchsafe them a single glance. With his head enveloped in a turban and his gloomy countenance veiled, he sat almost motionless on the white palfrey of the Pope.'

On Jem's right rode Franceschetto Cibo, 'son of the Pope', and on his left Guy de Blanchefort, 'Prior of Auvergne and nephew of the Grand Master Pierre d'Aubusson'. Next followed the French ambassador Seigneur de Faucon and his entourage; Antoine d'Aubusson, 'brother of the Grand Master of the knights of St John of Jerusalem'; the 'turcopolier John Kendal and several officers of Prince Jem', who rode ahead of and to the right of the ambassador of the Sultan of Egypt and his entourage; 'the cubiculaires of the Pope and the Rhodians'; and finally the 'pontifical cavalry who rode at the rear of the procession'.

After passing Porta Portese, the procession made its way through Trastevere to cross the Tiber on Ponte Bartolomeo. It then turned to pass through the Pescheria, the 'place of the Jews', and Campo dei Fiore, before crossing the Tiber again on Ponte Sant' Angelo, to arrive at the Castel Sant' Angelo, the papal fortress that had been built in AD 139 as the Emperor Hadrian's mausoleum. There they turned left to approach the Vatican, where they passed though Porta Viridaria to enter the Apostolic Palace, immediately to the north of the old church of St Peter's, which would be replaced by the present basilica beginning in 1506.

The entire population of Rome, it seemed, had turned out to line the route, everyone straining to catch a glimpse of the son of Mehmet the Conqueror, the Grand Turk, who had terrorized the Christian world for nearly three decades. Jem's appearance at that time is described in a letter from Matteo Bosso to the Abbe de Fiesole, where the writer overestimates the prince's age by ten years.

> The aspect of the barbarian is fierce, his body stocky and robust. His head is large, his chest well developed and prominent. His height is above average. One of his eyes is closed and half crossed, his nose aquiline. His expression is worried and he looks everywhere in a threatening way. He is about forty years old, and looks very much like his father, whose engraved medallion I have seen often at the abbey, and he is much like his father in character and in his inflexible harshness and cruelty.

On the same day that Jem entered Rome Charles, the young Duke of Savoy, died. Jem's sense of sadness and unease at this news was deepened when he heard that it was rumoured that the duke to whom he had become so attached during the previous six years had been poisoned.

Innocent had been waiting anxiously to meet Jem, for he had great plans for the prince. He was confident that he could win Jem around to his dream of mounting a crusade by using the charm that had eased his rise to the papacy. The day after his arrival in Rome Jem was invited by Innocent to a public consistory. The pope opened the meeting by greeting the new cardinals who were in attendance, and by presenting those who had not yet received them their red hats. Innocent then ordered Franceschetto Cibo and Guy de Blanchefort to go to Jem's apartment and conduct him to the meeting hall, along with his companions. Jem entered the hall and approached the pope, preceded by an armed guard and flanked by Cibo and Blanchefort, with his officers and servants following him.

Jem had been told by the master of ceremonies that he should greet the pope in the Turkish manner, touching the ground with his right hand and kissing it. But Jem refused to do this, nor would he genuflect in front of the pope. Instead he paused in front of the papal throne and inclined his head slightly, so imperceptibly that observers hardly noticed it, according to Burchard.

Jem then ascended the steps of the throne and stood in front of the pope with his turban on, bending to kiss Innocent on the right shoulder. Through his interpreter he thanked the pope for the warm welcome he had been given and said that he was happy to be in his presence, after which he requested a private audience as soon as possible. The pope answered him favourably and replied that Jem could trust him. Innocent went on to say that Jem had been brought to Rome for his own good, and that he was not to doubt this but to live in the Vatican without fear, for everything had been arranged so that his affairs would have a happy outcome. Jem expressed his confidence in what Innocent had said and thanked him. He then descended from the dais and kissed each of the cardinals present on their right shoulder. The Turkish officers then knelt in turn before the pope and kissed his feet, after which they fell in line behind Jem as he was conducted back to his apartment.

Three days later Jem was given a private audience with the pope, the only other person present being the prince's interpreter. Innocent began by asking him why he had fled to a country with a religion different from that of his own. Jem answered that he had never intended to go to France, but to Hungary, and that he had originally taken refuge on Rhodes because of the promise of safe conduct he had been offered there, but, despite the word of Pierre d'Aubusson, he had been detained as a prisoner until now. He asked the pope to release him immediately so that he could go to Egypt to be with his mother, wife and children, from whom he had been separated for so long. His emotion was so great that he had tears in his eyes, and Innocent was so moved that it was said that his eyes filled with tears also.

According to Sadüddin's account, after a silence the pope tried to give Jem some hope for the future. He said that if Jem gave up thoughts of empire he could go to Egypt and retire with his family, but that if he wanted to regain his throne then it would be best for him to ally himself to Mathias Corvinus of Hungary. Jem was noncommittal, and Innocent told him to take his time and think the matter over. And when an envoy arrived from Corvinus, Innocent apparently summoned Jem to another private audience at which he insisted that the time had come for Jem to make a decision, strongly advising him to go to Hungary with the envoy. But Jem refused, saying: 'If I do as you advise, then after I arrive in Hungary I will have to march with a Christian army against Muslims, and then the *ulema* [Muslim authorities] of my country will condemn me as a traitor. I will not give up my religion on any account, not even to regain my empire.' When Innocent heard this he was angered, and turning aside he cursed Jem in Italian, apparently calling him 'a dog and a bastard'. Jem, who had learned some Italian from his guards, understood the gist of what the pope had said and responded calmly: 'If one who comes to see you is as unhappy as a mongrel dog, then what can he do?' When Innocent heard this he felt ashamed, apologized to Jem for his remark and had him returned to his apartment.

Sadüddin's version of this meeting is highly suspect, first of all because Jem had always expressed a desire to join Mathias Corvinus in leading an expedition against Beyazit. Sadüddin, writing for a Turkish audience, was doubtless trying to show Jem in the best light, and thus may have changed the story to portray the prince as a loyal Muslim. Besides, after going to such lengths in order to get Jem, Innocent had no intention of giving up his captive to Corvinus. And Innocent would never have given Jem to be used in a political cause at the expense of the long-cherished dream of a crusade.

Indeed, on 8 May 1489 Innocent issued a brief requesting representatives of the Christian powers to meet in Rome to make plans for united action against the Turks. His nuncios explained to the various princes of Christendom that the pope's possession of Jem offered an extraordinary opportunity, for the prince had promised, if he regained his father's throne through the help of the Christian princes, that he would withdraw the Ottoman forces from Europe and even give up Constantinople. Innocent pleaded once more for harmony:

> And while we wait for your confidences, we have com-
> manded that Prince Jem be guarded in our palace in the
> Vatican, for his security and prestige. And when it comes
> to us, we will do whatever we can to make war against the
> Turks.

The pope's plea for a united front against the common enemy was met with applause by the Venetians, but they asked the pope not to take action against the Turks for the time being, for their security and commercial interests required that they stay on good terms with the Porte. The Signoria sent a letter to the pope warning him that Beyazit was making preparations for war, and urging him to guard Jem vigilantly against attempts to kidnap or assassinate him. They said that the attempt might be made by Beyazit, by Mathias Corvinus, or by King Ferrante of Naples who, according to the Venetian secret service, had an agent operating in the Vatican, although they would not identify the person so as not to compromise the source of their information.

King Ferrante had been enraged when he learned that Jem had been taken from France by the Knights of St John, and he considered several plans to seize the prince. He had offered d'Aubusson a large sum of money to have Jem taken to Naples, undoubtedly on Corvinus's behalf, and had even contemplated abducting the prince as he was being transferred from France to Rome.

Several days later the Signoria informed the Turkish grand vezir that the pope was not considering a crusade and only wanted Jem to protect the interests of Christianity. In another message, sent on 10 May 1489, the Signoria ordered the *bailo* in Istanbul to tell Beyazit that Jem was installed in the Vatican and was being treated with all the respect due to his rank. They also recommended that the Turkish ambassador in Rome keep a close watch on the envoy from Naples and try to counter every manoeuvre made by King Ferrante.

The Mamluk sultan Kaitbey had not given up his attempts to obtain custody of Jem either. He still hoped to use the prince to gain support in Anatolia for a war against Beyazit. It was reported at the Hungarian court that the Egyptian envoy had offered Innocent a huge sum for the possession of Jem, and that the pope was willing to accept the offer, his justification being that he would spend this money to equip a fleet for the crusade against the Ottomans. A rumour also spread that the pope was planning to sell Jem to the Venetians, who would then lend their fleet to Innocent for his crusade. A French Carmelite monk had heard this rumour in Rome, and when he returned to France he reported it to King Charles. The French court was appalled by this; the pope's nuncios vehemently denied it was true and wrote to the pope advising him to quell the rumour.

Meanwhile the papal nuncio at the Hungarian court, Bishop Angelo of Orte, had been working hard trying to arrange a truce between Mathias Corvinus and the Emperor Frederick III, part of the pope's effort to achieve European unity in preparation for a crusade against the Turks. Corvinus feared that Innocent's plans for a crusade meant only that he would send Jem along with a Venetian fleet to attack Istanbul. Corvinus told the nuncio that he did not believe that the Venetians for their part had any intention of going to war against the Turks, for that would run counter to their commercial interests, and their previous conflicts with the Ottomans had given them good reason to fear the sultan's military might. Corvinus pledged that if the pope sent Jem with a Venetian fleet against the Turks he himself would immediately seek terms with the sultan.

Angelo responded by assuring Corvinus that the pope would never make such a decision, to which the king replied sceptically: 'I tell you, my lord legate, the pope can do nothing with the Turk [Jem] except what the King of France decides. He received [Jem] with this understanding. The whole matter rests in the hands of [Cardinal] Balue. He manages everything, although the king of France was perfectly willing that [Jem] should come into my hands.'

Angelo tried to placate Corvinus: 'Most serene king, these details are unknown to me ... I think our lord [the pope] has the free disposition of the Turk, but his holiness wants to hear the desires of the Christian princes to order the better and more wisely to consider the declaration of war.'

Corvinus responded by telling Angelo that he had good reason for his suspicion, saying 'You may not believe, my lord legate, the things I say. They do not come from the persons you are thinking of. I have my information from elsewhere and from a good source.' He then showed the nuncio two letters from the Egyptian sultan Kaitbey, one written in Arabic and the other in Turkish, but when Angelo politely asked him what the two messages said the king seemed to have second thoughts about the matter and abruptly changed the subject.

A few days after Jem was settled in his apartment in the Vatican a Turk arrived in Rome, saying that he was a refugee from the sultan and had come to share the captivity of Beyazit's brother. When he was introduced to Jem the Turk kissed the ground and embraced the prince, calling him his *padişah*, or sultan. Jem was instantly repelled by the man, certain that he was an assassin sent by Beyazit, and he said as much to Franceschetto Cibo, who was present at the time. Cibo had the Turk arrested and taken to Castel Sant' Angelo, where after being tortured he admitted that he had been hired by King Ferrante of Naples to kill Jem. This caused a great commotion in the Vatican, where stricter security was brought in to prevent any outsiders from getting near Jem, and precautions were taken to prevent anyone from poisoning him.

The only visitor who was allowed to see Jem in the days immediately after this incident was Antoine de Gimel, the French *maréchal* who had accompanied him aboard the *Tresor* from France to Italy. According to Sadüddin, Gimel had come to say goodbye to Jem before returning to France. At one point Gimel said to Jem, 'How strange it is that during your stay in France you never went to see the King in Paris, which is like no other city in the world, a veritable paradise.' Jem answered, 'How could I go there when the King of France said that he could not suffer the sight of a turban in his capital. Anyway, I was a prisoner, a foreigner, abandoned by everyone, at the mercy of my enemies; how could I have met the king?' Gimel answered, 'God forbid that our king ever said that he did not want to see you. On the contrary, he would have sent for you himself and made you come if he hadn't been told that you didn't want to see him at all, for I know myself that he was very interested in your majesty and would have welcomed you in his court.' Gimel went on to say that when he returned to France he would go to see the king and tell him of the shameful way in which the Knights of St John had behaved, preventing Jem from visiting the royal court in Paris and lying to both him and Charles about their attitude toward one another.

When they parted Jem gave Gimel 'an admirable and very swift horse' from among the mounts allocated to him from the papal stables. While back in France Gimel met King Charles on a royal hunt. The king admired the horse that Gimel was riding and asked where he had obtained it. Gimel said that it had been given to him by Jem, and told him how the Turkish prince had tried to see the king, only to be told by the knights that he would not be welcome in the French court. Charles was angered when he heard this and said that he would punish those involved, for he much regretted that he had not met Prince Jem.

Meanwhile fighting broke out again between the Mamluks and the Turks. Pierre d'Aubusson wrote to the pope saying that Jem was the cause of the war between the two Muslim powers, both of whom had recently sent envoys to Rhodes. He said that Kaitbey was particularly anxious to join a Western alliance against the Turks and to have Jem sent to Egypt, while Beyazit feared that his brother might be handed to his enemies, particularly the Mamluk sultan and the Hungarian king. Beyazit protested to d'Aubusson, complaining that his brother's transfer to Rome was a violation of the peace treaty between the Porte and the Order of St John, and that he knew the pope intended to use Jem in a crusade against him. D'Aubusson sought to reassure the sultan, saying that the pope had no forces of his own and was completely dependent on the Christian princes. The King of France was very powerful, he said, and in his hands Jem might be dangerous to Beyazit, and so it was to the sultan's benefit that his brother was in Rome. He concluded by advising that the best way for Beyazit to have peace, which he said he desired, was to keep the Ottoman fleet from passing beyond Gallipoli, for the appearance of Turkish galleys in the Mediterranean was the surest way to unite the Christian princes.

Thus as Jem adjusted to life in the Vatican he found himself at the centre of the ongoing struggle between Christian West and Islamic East. The move to Rome had renewed his hopes that he might one day regain his freedom and his throne, but as weeks and months passed he realized that, despite the luxurious surroundings of his apartment in the Apostolic Palace, he was no more than a prisoner, vulnerable to assassination attempts by his brother. The German historian Ferdinand Gregorovius captured Jem's mood at this time:

> There Djem made his dwelling in the rooms set apart for the reception of monarchs . . . , where he bestowed not the slightest attention on the carpets, clothes, hangings and ornaments sent him by the Pope. The Sultan's son henceforth passed his joyless days in the Vatican, guarded by some Rhodians and treated like an imprisoned monarch; fear of treachery made his lonely existence yet more pitiable. He amused himself with hunting, music and banquets, or with Turkish apathy slept through the day.

12

A Prisoner in the Vatican

THE APOSTOLIC PALACE in the Vatican was much less extensive in Jem's time than it is today, comprising only the building that forms the south-east corner of the present complex, its central courtyard known as the Cortile del Pappagallo. The courtyard was already partially enclosed by buildings when Nicholas V became pope in 1447, and during the eight years of his papacy the remaining structures around the court were erected. Jem's apartment was on the upper floor on the north side of the palace, which looks out over what later came to be known as the Cortile del Belvedere, a sixteenth-century extension of the complex.

The work carried out by Nicholas V was resumed with great enthusiasm by Sixtus IV, who in the years 1477–80 built the Sistine Chapel immediately to the south-west of the Apostolic Palace. The original paintings in the chapel were begun in 1481 and completed on 15 August 1483, when Sixtus dedicated it to the Virgin Mary. The frescoes on the south wall of the chapel are scenes from the Life of Moses, with the Crossing of the Red Sea in the panel just to the right of centre, a work of Cosimo Rosselli. The scene showing the drowning of Pharaoh and the Egyptians commemorates the failure of the Ottoman siege of Rhodes in 1480 and the Christian recapture of Otranto the following year. Jem would have seen this painting when he moved into the Apostolic Palace, but probably its significance would not have been explained to him.

Jem's apartment was one of those reserved for royal guests. Sigismondo de' Conti says that the rooms were sumptuously furnished and adorned with gold and silver, and looked out on a vineyard and pleasant gardens. He goes on to say that Jem's maintenance was provided with the greatest liberality, costing 15,000 ducats a year, and that Innocent stood this expenditure because of the advantages which the whole of Christendom derived from the papacy having custody of the prince. During the first few days in Rome Jem's morale was higher than it had been at any point at Bourganeuf, where he had become deeply depressed, feeling that he would end his days as a prisoner in the Tour de Zizim. But it was not long before Jem slipped again into despair. Sometimes, despite his earlier disapproval of drunkenness, he would try to forget his misfortunes with alcohol, but when he regained his reason his hopeless situation weighed heavily upon him, and he became extremely irritable, making life difficult for his servants, companions and guardians, his once vigorous constitution degenerating with the never-ceasing pain of his lost throne and freedom.

The effect of Jem's imprisonment on his character and body is commented on in many contemporary writings, for he was an object of fascination in Rome: the brother of the mighty Grand Turk, now caged in the Vatican. The most colourful of these is by the celebrated painter Mantegna, who was working in the Vatican at the time. Mantegna described Jem in a letter to the Marquis Francesco Gonzaga of Mantua, dated 15 June 1489:

> The brother of the Turk lives here in the Palace, carefully guarded. The Pope provides him with pastimes of all sorts, such as hunting, music, banquets, and other amusements. Sometimes he comes to dine in the new palace, where I am painting, and behaves very well for a barbarian. His manners are proud and dignified; even for the Pope he never uncovers his head, nor is it the custom to uncover in his presence. He has five meals in the day, and sleeps awhile after each; before meals he drinks sugared water. He walks like an elephant, with a measured step like the beat of a Venetian chorus. His people speak highly of him, but as yet I have had no opportunity of seeing whether this is true. He often keeps his eyes half-closed. His nature is cruel, and they say he has killed four people; today he has severely maltreated an interpreter. He is credited with great devotion to Bacchus. His people are afraid of him. He takes little notice of what passes, as if he did not understand. He sleeps completely dressed, and gives audiences sitting cross-legged, like a Parthian. On his head he wears thirty thousand yards of linen; his trowsers are so wide he can bury himself in them. The expression of his face is ferocious, especially when Bacchus has been with him.

With Jem securely in his custody, Innocent began pushing ahead with his plans for a crusade including opening negotiations with Sultan Kaitbey and making contact with representatives from all the Christian powers in Rome regarding a crusade. Beyazit learned of the pope's plans and sought to head them off by having Jem assassinated. For this he hired a renegade Italian nobleman named Cristoforo Castracano, also known as Macrino, a cousin of the infamous Boccolino Guzzoni. Two years earlier Innocent had removed Macrino from his fief in the Marche de Ancona. Macrino fled to Istanbul and into the arms of Beyazit. The sultan now gave him money and presents, and promised him the city of Negroponte and the command of 200 galleys if he would assassinate Jem. The story is told by Stefano Infessura, the Roman historian, who says that Macrino's plan was to put poison in the reservoir that fed the fountain in the Cortile del Belvedere, which supplied drinking water for the pope and his household, including Jem. The Venetians learned of the plot and apprehended Macrino when he arrived in Venice from Istanbul. They then turned him over to Innocent, who imprisoned him in the Castel Sant' Angelo, where he was tortured until he confessed. Macrino claimed that the sultan had recruited other assassins to perform the task if he failed, 'so that the pope and the others [that is, those who drank from the fountain, including Jem] could hardly escape'. Infessura does not give the names of the other conspirators, but one of them was said to be a Dominican friar. Infessura records that Macrino was executed on 7 May 1490 by being drawn and quartered, after which the four parts of his corpse were put on display at four of the gates of Rome. Infessura concludes his account of this incident by noting that four or five days afterwards Rome and its environs were enveloped in black clouds and swept by torrential rains, which were attributed by some to divine wrath at the barbarous execution of Macrino, so contrary to Christ's example 'of mercy, restraint and humility'.

Meanwhile Innocent had been busy corresponding with the Christian princes of Europe, inviting them to a congress that would convene in Rome on 25 March 1490, to deal with the task of organizing an expedition *contra Turcum*. Burchard noted in his diary the hope that the expedition would be greatly expedited 'by means of the Turk [Jem], who dwells with his Holiness, true heir of his late father [Mehmet II], much beloved by his subjects, and the bitter enemy of his brother who now rules the Turkish empire'.

The pope's personal emissary, Raymond Peraudi, who had spent years promoting Innocent's cause in Europe, wrote to King Casimer of Poland telling him of the pope's unremitting efforts to organize a crusade, saying that the time was now ripe. He said that Jem had promised, if the Christians helped him to regain his throne, that he would return to them all of the lands in Europe that had been conquered by the Turks, and even to give up Constantinople. With this in view, he wrote, the pope was calling all of the princes in Europe to a congress so as to organize a crusade against the Turks.

The congress opened as scheduled on 25 March, the Feast of the Annunciation, when the college of cardinals and the foreign diplomatic corps attended a solemn high mass in a chapel of the Vatican before beginning deliberations. The congress itself began with a stirring address delivered by Pietro Mansi, Bishop of Cesena, who pleaded with the delegates to put aside their internal disputes and embark on the glorious crusade in the manner of their illustrious forebears: 'Remember what your ancestors did! Rewin yourselves that holy city of Jerusalem, the sacred sepulchre of our Saviour . . . Leave to posterity deeds worthy of all praise and imitation!'

All of the European states sent representatives to the congress except Venice, which stayed away, not wishing to upset its relationship with the sultan. The delegates had already prepared detailed plans for the military and naval campaigns required for the

crusade, as well as the organization of the various national contingents involved. But early in April the activities of the congress
were brought to an abrupt halt by the news of the death of
Mathias Corvinus, who had died of a stroke, aged forty-seven. A
public mass was held in the Sistine Chapel on 29 April for the
repose of Corvinus's soul, and despite the strained relations
between the pope and the Hungarian king, Innocent praised and
honoured Corvinus as the 'faithful defender of Christianity
against the oppressions of the Turks'.

The death of Corvinus greatly upset the balance of power in
central Europe, destroying the stability that Innocent needed
to promote his crusade. At the request of Frederick III and
Maximilian, the congress was adjourned for a while, and business
did not recommence until after Pentecost. On 3 June all of the
envoys, together with the college of cardinals, met in the Apostolic
Palace. Innocent opened the congress with a lengthy address in
which he summarized the efforts he had made to mount an
expedition against the Turks. He said that he had worked tirelessly
and had personally made large financial sacrifices to obtain custody of Jem, whom he believed to be of crucial importance in
their enterprise. He told the delegates that Sultan Beyazit was
very much afraid of his brother, and that a faction among the
Janissaries had gained popular support for a revolt to overthrow
the sultan in favour of Jem. It was thus the bounden duty of the
delegates not to let this heaven-sent opportunity pass.

Innocent urged the delegates to consider the details of their
expedition, the number of soldiers and ships involved and their
commanders, armaments, finances, provisions, and operational
plans, including the proposed duration of the campaign. He also
suggested that he might follow the example of Sixtus IV, and 'by

his Apostolic authority impose a truce between all Christian Princes for the time being'. The delegates conferred at great length about the details of the expedition, which they finally agreed upon and reported to the pope and the college of cardinals. They thanked the pope for his exertions in the matter of Jem, 'who was most valuable as a standing menace to the sultan, and a means of breaking up his empire'. 'He should,' they said, 'be carefully guarded in Rome for the time being, and, later on, counsel should be taken as to how he would be most advantageously employed in the campaign.'

As regards the composition and organization of the crusading army, the delegates thought that it should number about 95,000 men in three divisions: a papal and Italian contingent; a German corps, including the Hungarians, Bohemians and Poles; and a third unit made up of the French, Spanish, Portuguese, Navarrese, Scots and English. Each of the three divisions would have its own commander who would take orders from a commander-in-chief, whom the Germans thought should be the aged Emperor Frederick III, or failing that his son Maximilian, the King of the Romans; other delegates felt that the 'captain general' should be elected by the princes and the pope. The delegates were unanimous in suggesting that each prince should levy a toll on his subjects to pay for the expenses of the war, which they believed might be of three years' duration.

Their plan was that German troops would march south through Hungary and Wallachia; the allied fleet would attack the Peloponnesus and the island of Euboea in the Aegean; the French and Spanish with Italian cavalry would land in Valona and march through Albania and northern Greece, while a simultaneous assault would be made against the Moors in Spain. The delegates emphasized that prior to the campaign the pope should endeavour to put an end to the disputes between the Christian princes, or at least arrange for an armistice for the duration of the crusade. They also felt that, if possible, the pope himself should accompany the expedition, principally to settle 'differences and discords if (which God forbid) some should arise in the expeditionary force'. The delegates concluded by saying that they could not commit themselves to any definite course of action, for they would first have to consult with their respective governments.

The pope agreed with all the essentials of the delegates' conclusions, adding a few points of his own. He thanked the delegates for their approval of his plan of fighting the Turks with Jem at the head of the crusade. The question as to whether Jem should accompany the expedition in a captive or active capacity, he would leave to those who were best acquainted with the enemy and their country; but stressed that the decision on this point should not be long delayed. Innocent declared that he was prepared to lead the crusade personally. The war must be counted to last five rather than three years, and should begin in the following year, when the Mamluk sultan of Egypt was expected to make an attack on the Turks. Innocent insisted on the great importance of immediate action. In conclusion, he expressed his surprise that the envoys declared themselves unable to come to any definite decision without consulting their superiors, seeing that he had expressly requested that they should be provided with full power for this very purpose. He hoped, at any rate, that they would lose no time in coming to a decision, lest the moment was lost. The congress was officially closed by the pope on 30 July 1490, to be reconvened when the delegates had received the requisite full powers to make binding agreements on the part of their governments.

But the congress never reconvened, leaving Innocent's dream of a crusade against the Turks in tatters. Sigismondo de' Conti was of the opinion that the crusade would have been carried through had it not been for the death of Mathias Corvinus. The Hungarian king had endured years of land warfare against the Turks, experience that would have been invaluable in Innocent's crusade, and Corvinus stood to gain more than any other European ruler from a Christian victory over the Ottomans. With Corvinus's death Eastern Europe had lost its strongest figure, and, with the accession of the weak Ladislas II of Bohemia to the Hungarian throne, the Magyar nobles took control and the kingdom reverted to medieval anarchy, destroying the principal bulwark that had protected central Europe from the Turks. Maximilian took the opportunity to recover his hereditary possessions in Hungary, though Innocent eventually persuaded him to agree to a peace with Ladislas. The final blow to Innocent's dreams for a crusade came with a renewed quarrel between Maximilian and Charles VIII. This broke out with greater violence than ever when final arrangements were made for the marriage of Charles and Anne of Brittany, destroying the internal peace of Europe.

All of this weighed heavily on Innocent, and in late August of 1490 he became gravely ill. This aroused serious concerns in Venice, for the Signoria had received reports of further plots to assassinate Jem, and that the pope's illness had led to decreased vigilance in protecting the prince. The Signoria also feared that if the pope died Jem might be endangered by the anarchy of a papal interregnum. Indeed, Infessura notes that on 27 September a riot broke out in Rome, leading workers in the countryside to flee to their homes and townsmen to take up arms, 'because it was everywhere declared for certain that Pope Innocent was dead'. There were rumours that on that day the pope's son, Franceschetto Cibo, had tried to seize the papal treasury, but the cardinals had stopped him. That same day Cibo tried to gain possession of Jem, in order to sell him to King Ferrante of Naples, it was said, but once again he was thwarted by the cardinals.

The morning after the disturbances the cardinals went to the papal apartment in the Apostolic Palace, where Innocent lay in a coma. Infessura reports that they made an inventory of the pope's belongings 'although a good part of them had been taken and shipped to Florence by the said Franceschetto'. The pope's remaining possessions were placed in the custody of Cardinal Savelli, who stayed in the palace to keep watch over them until the situation stabilized. Rumour had it that the cardinals had found 800,000 gold florins in a chest in the pope's apartment, as well as another 300,000 in a box in Castel Sant' Angelo. But, against all expectations, Innocent recovered, furious at all of those who had so rudely anticipated his death, saying: 'I hope one day to fall heir to all these lord cardinals.'

By mid-November 1490 Innocent had regained his strength to the point that he could leave Rome for a holiday, which he passed in Ostia and Porto. He returned to the Holy See on 30 November, the feast of St Andrew, when an Ottoman envoy, Mustafa Pasha, made his formal entry into the city, welcomed by the families of the pope and cardinals as well as a number of foreign ambassadors and throngs of curious Romans. Mustafa had arrived in Ancona on a Rhodian galley in the company of Guy de Blanchefort, who escorted him to Rome. The following day he was received by the pope in a formal audience, attended by the college of cardinals, officials of the Curia and the foreign diplomatic corps.

Mustafa had begun his career as one of Beyazit's palace pages and had risen to the rank of *kapıcıbaşı* which entitled him to be called a pasha. The Turkish chronicler Idris, writing around 1510, says that Beyazit sent Mustafa to Rome to report on his brother Jem and 'to bring news of great kings and rulers of the infidel'. Sadüddin says that Mustafa's mission was the result of a secret exchange of letters between the sultan and the pope.

Mustafa presented the pope with a letter from 'Sultan Beyazit II, greatest king of kings and emperor of two continents . . . to the supreme father and lord of all Christians'. The letter, written in Greek and dated 'Istanbul, 17 May 1490', was translated into Latin and read aloud by an interpreter. The letter stated that Beyazit had learned from the grand master Pierre d'Aubusson that his brother Jem had been brought to Rome, 'a fact in which we can take great pleasure' – the sultan obviously having taken on board d'Aubusson's words of advice. Beyazit said he hoped his brother might be maintained in the Vatican on the same terms as those agreed upon by the grand master Pierre d'Aubusson eight years before, 'according to a convention of peace entered into between us, which has been kept by both sides up to now, and has been the cause of our friendship'. Beyazit went on to say that to obtain the pope's approval of the conditions of Jem's maintenance

we have sent our faithful slave, the *kapıcıbaşı* Mustafa Pasha, with one of the officials of the cardinal [grand] master in order that we may be assured by him that you also have confirmed this agreement so that our friendship may increase: whatever therefore our envoy, the most faithful slave Mustafa, shall say in the presence of your Magnificence, receive as though they were our own words.

Mustafa told the pope that his master fully intended to abide by the agreement previously made with the grand master, the terms of which were then reviewed. If Jem were well guarded in Rome, he said, the sultan would be willing to live at peace with all Christians. Innocent replied that he was pleased with the sultan's attitude, and that he would discuss the matter with the cardinals, and would give the envoy an answer at a subsequent audience. Before withdrawing, Mustafa presented the pope with rich gifts from the sultan, including tapestries, gold-embroidered fabrics, and furs of sable, ermine and vair (squirrel).

Mustafa's next audience with the pope occurred a week later, in the presence of an interpreter, the cardinals and Franceschetto Cibo. The pope now asked the envoy how much the sultan had paid the grand master for Jem's maintenance. Mustafa's answer revealed to the pope that d'Aubusson had been receiving considerably more than the 45,000 ducats a year specified in the initial agreement. Innocent did not question the envoy further on this occasion, dismissing him with the statement that he would have an answer within a few days, so as not to delay his departure.

The new agreement called for the sultan to pay 40,000 ducats a year to the pope for keeping Jem in custody, Mustafa having brought 120,000 ducats with him as an advance payment for three years. (By way of comparison, the annual budget of the Venetian Republic at that time was 1,115,000 ducats.) Before paying over the money Mustafa insisted on seeing Jem in the flesh, for he had been instructed to find out for certain if the sultan's brother was alive and well, and if he was, to determine whether he was securely guarded. Despite the objections of the knights, most notably Guy de Blanchefort and John Kendal, Mustafa was allowed to request an audience with the prince. Jem agreed to meet the pasha but only in an appropriately regal setting. Jem's apartment on the upper floor of the Apostolic Palace was immediately refurnished in a more luxurious manner and hung with tapestries and precious fabrics, with a richly adorned throne brought from the pope's rooms for his use.

Jem received the envoy seated in the throne *ala Turcesa*, flanked by his officers and with two of the pope's nephews – Cardinal Antoniotto Gentile Bellini and Archbishop Niccolo Cibo-Bocciardi – among those present. One of Jem's officers met Mustafa at the doorway, but before admitting him he took a piece of linen cloth and brushed him off from head to foot 'just as if he had been covered with flour or dust', according to Infessura. The envoy was then told to kiss the cloth and only then was he allowed to approach the throne, prostrating himself three times as he did so, the third time remaining on his knees in silence.

Jem gestured to one of his officers, who told Mustafa to speak only in response to questions. Speaking in Turkish, Jem asked Mustafa if he had any letters, whereupon the envoy held up a large envelope, closed with a seal, which he licked to demonstrate that it was not poisoned. Two of Jem's officers took the envelope and examined the seal to see if it had been opened. They then handed the envelope back to Mustafa, who opened the letter, which he licked on both sides before handing it to one of Jem's officers. The officer then read the letter in a soft voice into the prince's ear so that only he could hear. According to Infessura, in the letter Beyazit chided Jem for his poor judgement and lack of trust. He said that Jem would have been wiser to trust his brother rather than infidels, but that in any event Beyazit could only be concerned 'as a brother for a brother's safety'.

Mustafa then pointed toward the presents that Beyazit had

sent for his brother, including jewels and brocades, which Jem indicated should be distributed among his officers. He then dismissed the envoy with a wave of his hand, after which the others in attendance left Jem alone with his officers. Infessura, in ending his account of this singular audience, noted that 'when all those present had been dismissed, [the Turks] had a good deal to say among themselves, which our people neither heard nor understood'.

Mustafa was subsequently questioned at another audience with the pope, in the presence of Guy de Blanchefort, about the sultan's dealings with Pierre d'Aubusson. Innocent suggested that the grand master had received considerably more money than stipulated in the agreement between the sultan and the Hospitallers. Blanchefort denied this, saying that, anyway, there was no written agreement about the money to be paid for Jem's maintenance, only a verbal one. The pope regarded this as a blatant lie and demanded a copy of the original protocol between the Knights of St John and the Porte. Another controversy arose when Mustafa said that Beyazit had never requested that his brother should be guarded in the Vatican by the knights, as they themselves had always claimed. Innocent criticized the knights for their deceptions, and he told the Turkish envoy that he could not give him a final answer to be delivered to Beyazit until he had discovered the truth about the agreement that had been made between the sultan and the grand master.

On 3 January 1491 Innocent informed the college of cardinals and the diplomatic corps of his intended reply to Sultan Beyazit. At an earlier audience the knights had given the pope a Latin translation of the remarks that the Turkish envoy had made at their first meeting. Innocent called attention to the envoy's statement that if Jem was well guarded in Rome the sultan was willing to live at peace with all Christians. Mustafa said that this was his own interpretation, and that his actual brief from Beyazit stated that, if Jem were securely guarded in Rome, the sultan was willing to keep peace with the pope, the Knights Hospitallers of Rhodes and the Venetians, and the latter only at sea, but that he had not mentioned any other Christians. Innocent responded that in view of this ambiguity, the Turkish envoy and representatives of the Knights of St John, undoubtedly Guy de Blanchefort and John Kendal, should be admitted to the audience chamber in order to testify.

Innocent wanted to interrogate Mustafa in person so he called in his nephew, Niccolo Cibo-Bocciardi, Archbishop of Arles, who could speak Turkish. Mustafa was asked about Beyazit's remarks concerning peace with Christianity. The envoy replied that he had never said that Beyazit was prepared to live at peace with all Christians, and reiterated that his remark to that effect had only applied to the pope, the grand master of Rhodes and the Venetians. He said he regretted the misunderstanding, and had not intended that his comments would be otherwise interpreted. Innocent then turned to the knights, criticizing them for having misrepresented the sultan's intentions. They replied that when they departed from Rhodes, on 4 August 1490, Mustafa had led them to believe that his mission was to establish peaceful relations with all Christian princes, and that they could not account for his subsequent limitation of that policy to the pope, Rhodes and Venice. They assured the pope of their sincerity and that of their grand master, and they hoped that His Holiness would take this into account in giving his answer to the sultan's envoy. Innocent then informed Mustafa that he could leave when he wished; the answer to the sultan had already been prepared and would be read to him, and he would receive the text in a Turkish translation before his departure.

Innocent's letter to Beyazit is dated 3 January 1491, the same day as the extraordinary audience at which he had confronted the Turkish envoy and the knights with their apparent duplicity. The letter stated that Mustafa had been given an honourable reception before the college of cardinals and the foreign diplomatic corps, and that his words, 'which we believe have come from your own heart, betokened peace'. Since the sultan's letter and the remarks of his envoy were so important, concerning all Christians, the pope believed that they must be shared with all of the princes in Christendom. This was why the pope had invited the foreign diplomatic corps to hear Mustafa Pasha, so that they could report to their respective governments and have them consult with the papacy. When the pope received their advice he would be able to give the sultan his response, but since he did not wish to delay the Turkish envoy he would write to him in Istanbul. Innocent closed the letter by saying that Mustafa Pasha had been given the opportunity to see that Jem was in good health and honourably treated in the Apostolic Palace.

Before the Turkish envoy left Rome, according to Infessura, Jem entertained him and his entourage at a banquet in the prince's apartment. Aside from his officers and servants, Jem had been deprived of Turkish companionship during his years of exile, and so he took this opportunity to meet with Mustafa and his associates, to talk with them about old friends and familiar places. This meeting is recorded by the Turkish chronicler Idris, relying largely on Mustafa's own testimony. According to Idris, the pope permitted Mustafa to see Jem, 'in the place where he was kept confined. He heard from Jem's mouth his complaints of home-sickness and his request of forgiveness from his elder brother, the Sultan of Islam.'

Idris goes on to say that Mustafa had one last private meeting with Innocent before he departed for Istanbul, at which time 'he consolidated with the pope by documents and oaths which are acceptable according to the Christian practice of agreement and compact'. According to Idris, the most important point on which both sides agreed was to keep Jem closely guarded in the Vatican and 'not let him fall upon Islamic territories' as long as the pope and sultan lived.

After Mustafa and his retinue left, Jem felt even more isolated than before, descending into the melancholy which had begun to draw a veil between himself and even his closest companions. Although he would not have known of the secret agreement between the pope and Beyazit, if indeed the account by Idris is to be wholly relied upon, Jem must have felt by now that he would never regain his freedom, that he was doomed to spend the rest of his days as a prisoner in the Vatican.

13

A New Pope

WHILE MUSTAFA was still in Rome another Muslim envoy presented his credentials in the Vatican, bringing a message to Pope Innocent from Sultan Kaitbey.

According to Infessura, Kaitbey offered the pope 200,000 ducats if he would send Jem to Cairo, so that the prince could join him in a war against Beyazit. In return Kaitbey promised to give Jerusalem and its environs to the Christians, who would also have freedom to go to and from the Holy Land without interference or payment; he would also return all lands that formerly belonged to Christian princes, including Constantinople, when he and Jem took the city from Beyazit. The pope seems to have politely declined Kaitbey's offer, partly because he was already receiving 40,000 ducats a year from Beyazit, whom he did not wish to offend whilst he continued with his plans to gather together a crusade.

By September, Venetian intelligence from Istanbul indicated that Beyazit was plotting afresh to have his brother assassinated. On 25 September 1491 the Council of Ten, which served as the doge's cabinet, directed the Venetian ambassador in Rome, Girolamo Donato, to inform the pope of rumours that the sultan was trying to bribe certain members of the papal court to murder Jem 'by poison or by any other means'. Letters from the Council to Donato identified two of the plotters as the merchant Giovanni Battista Gentile and the Dominican Fra Leonardo of Chiavari, both of whom were Genoese living in Pera, the European quarter of Istanbul. The Venetians were unaware that both Gentile and Leonardo were secret agents of the pope, representing Innocent in the clandestine discussions with Beyazit that led the sultan to send his *kapıcıbaşı*, Mustafa, as an envoy to Rome to discuss the status of his brother Jem. The Venetians believed that the person inside the papal court whom the sultan was trying to bribe was the pope's nephew, Niccolo Cibo-Bocciardi. Niccolo had easy access to the prince, spoke fluent Turkish and had become a close friend of Jem. He had also acted as interpreter during Innocent's talks with the sultan's envoy, and referred to him as 'my beloved Mustafa Bey' in a letter to Beyazit in 1494. That same year Beyazit actually recommended to Pope Alexander VI, Innocent's successor, that he make Niccolo a cardinal. However no strong evidence exists to indicate that Niccolo ever accepted a bribe from the sultan, or that he was directly or indirectly connected with any plot against Jem's life.

ဆ

Early in 1492 the Muslims lost their last possession in Spain when Granada fell to the troops of King Ferdinand on 2 January, ending almost eight centuries of Islamic settlement on the Iberian peninsula. Ferdinand's campaign against the Muslims in Spain, the climax of the *Reconquista*, was seen as a crusade that would end with the recapture of Jerusalem. As early as 1486 the Marquis of Cadiz had predicted that Ferdinand would 'not only . . . gain the Kingdom of Granada, but he will subdue all of Africa . . . and he will take the Holy House of Jerusalem . . . and with his hands he will put the banner of Aragon on Mount Calvary'.

The news reached Rome about an hour past midnight on the morning of 1 February and was celebrated in a three-day festival, which is described by Gregorovius:

> The Spanish envoys who had brought the news caused the taking of Granada to be represented with a wooden imitation fortress and gave bull-fights on the piazza. Cardinal Borgia also gave the people bull fights according to the Spanish mode. It was February and the Carnival season, and seldom had Rome beheld diversions of such rare and pagan splendour.

According to Sigismondo de' Conti, the last scene in the festival was a float in which the victorious figures of Ferdinand and Isabella were conveyed in a high carriage, holding a golden palm, while at their feet the defeated Moorish king, Abu-abd-Allah, was dragged in chains, with weapons and armour suspended on wooden frames, 'such as are shown in the trophies of the ancients and on the monuments of the Caesars'. Jem is known to have witnessed at least part of this festival, a scene which must have depressed him – Christendom celebrating the downfall of the last Muslim kingdom in Spain.

Ferdinand, in a letter to Pope Innocent, complained that King Ferrante of Naples, his cousin, had secretly aided the Moors in their final struggle. Ferrante was aware that his cousin knew of his treachery, and realized that he should seek the pope's protection. Thus even before Ferdinand's final victory, late in the autumn of 1491, King Ferrante had decided to complete the rapprochement with the Holy See that had been begun by the papal–Neapolitan treaty signed in Rome on 11 August 1486. That treaty had been negotiated by the Neapolitan humanist Giovanni Pontano, who served as Ferrante's secretary. Pontano, who had the deep respect of Pope Innocent, returned to Rome in November 1491, and, according to Burchard, 'on January 27 [1492] in a secret consistory . . . peace was concluded between our most holy lord, the pope, and the most illustrious Ferrante, king of Naples'.

Ferrante, who had never given up hope of acquiring Jem, took advantage of the reconciliation to ask Innocent once again for custody of the prince, but Innocent refused. The papacy then notified the Venetians, who in reply instructed Girolamo Donato to convey to the pope their 'great and reverent thanks' for informing them of Ferrante's renewed attempt to obtain custody of Jem. Donato also congratulated Innocent on his steadfastness in retaining control of Jem, 'on whose life and safety, as we have often said before, depend most surely the peace, quiet, and tranquility of the entire Christian commonwealth'.

On 7 May 1492 the Venetian Senate directed Donato to seek an audience with the pope to warn him about the Turks' latest military preparations. Beyazit had mustered a powerful army at Edirne and assembled a fleet of 'eighty sail, including thirty galleys' in the Sea of Marmara and the Dardanelles. Donato also reminded Innocent that he had, with Jem in his custody, 'that instrument which is most suited to restraining the appetite and ambition of the said Turk [Beyazit]'.

On 19 May King Ferrante sent his secretary Giovanni Pontano

to Rome to inform the pope that the Turkish fleet had entered the Aegean, and that the sultan was also about to send his army into the field. Pontano reminded the pope that he had a special responsibility for the common safety of Christendom, and in the person of Jem he had 'an instrument of exceptional utility' to use against the sultan. However, Innocent had already received a letter from the Venetian Senate on 7 May, that 'thanks to God with the possession of Jem we have been able to make the sultan refrain'. The letter went on to say that Beyazit's threatening behaviour had been triggered by rumours that Innocent intended to sell Jem to Naples, but that the Venetian *bailo* in Istanbul had convinced the sultan that this was not true and he had therefore drawn back his forces.

Meanwhile Beyazit, disturbed by the rapprochement between Ferrante and the pope, sent new envoys to Naples and Rome bearing a most precious relic: the tip of the spear with which Longinus had pierced the side of Christ which had been enshrined in Constantinople and acquired by Mehmet II when he conquered the city. This was the same relic that Beyazit offered the King of France three years earlier in an attempt to stop Jem from falling into the pope's hands.

The pope sent a delegation of cardinals to meet the Turkish envoys at Ancona where they placed the sacred spearhead in a crystal reliquary set in gold, and brought it to Rome. When the envoys and the cardinals reached Rome on 31 May the pope went to meet them outside the Porta del Popolo, took the reliquary in his hands with the greatest reverence, and delivered a short address on the Passion of Christ. He then carried it in solemn procession to St Peter's, the route to the church having been richly decorated in its honour. After a service in St Peter's, Innocent had the reliquary conveyed to his private apartments, where it was enshrined.

Beyazit's chief envoy presented two letters to the pope; the contents of one were recorded by Sigismondo de' Conti. The letter said that the sultan was sending to Rome the spearhead that pierced the side of the great prophet Jesus Christ, and that the sultan requests that his envoy be permitted to see Jem, so that he can quickly bring back to Istanbul reassuring news of the prince's good health as well as that of the pope himself. There is no record of the pope's reply to this request, but he probably allowed the Turkish envoy to see Jem, who would certainly have been glad to meet him, for he rarely received the chance to hear news from his homeland.

On Sunday, 3 June 1492, the pope's granddaughter Battistina was married to Luigi of Aragon, Marquis of Gerace and uncle of Ferrante II, Prince of Capua. The ceremony took place in the garden of the Apostolic Palace, which was lavishly decorated for the occasion. Jem would have been able to watch the ceremony, for his apartment overlooked the garden from the top floor of the palace.

On the following day there was a secret consistory at which the Prince of Capua, known familiarly as Ferrantino, was invested with the Kingdom of Naples, effective with the deaths of his father Alfonso II, Duke of Calabria, and his grandfather King Ferrante. Ferrantino's investiture had been necessitated by Innocent's declaration, in a public consistory three years before, that the House of Aragon was dispossessed, and that the Kingdom of Naples had thus reverted to the Holy See. Ferrantino was received with the highest honours by the pope, who hosted the prince and his party in the Apostolic Palace. But Innocent had reason to regret his hospitality to the rapacious Neapolitans, as Gregorovius writes in describing Ferrantino's stay in Rome: 'The prince [Ferrantino] dwelt in the Vatican, and his numerous retinue – he had come with an escort of 900 horse and a train of 260 mules – thanked the Pope for the hospitality received by carrying off the furniture of their rooms, even to the very carpets.'

Innocent gave a final audience to Beyazit's envoys on 14 June, just prior to their departure for Istanbul. He told the chief envoy to inform the sultan that in the event of an Ottoman attack on Hungary or any Christian country he would retaliate by using Jem. The pope also sent a private courier of his own to Istanbul with the same message. Beyazit nevertheless continued to build up his forces, as the Venetians warned King Ferrante, who in the summer of 1492 fully expected a Turkish attack upon Italy.

∞

Sigismondo de' Conti wrote that the reception of the sacred spear-head 'was almost Innocent's last act'. Innocent had been ill for two years, suffering from what his secretary describes as a urinary disorder and a quartan fever, so called because it recurred every four days. At the beginning of July 1492, Innocent took a turn for the worse and it was evident to those around him that he was slowly dying. As the Florentine envoy, Filippo Valori, wrote on the nineteenth of that month, 'All hope is abandoned; the pope's strength is so entirely exhausted that the spirit is all that is left to him; but he retains his full consciousness.' Sigismondo tells of how the pope summoned the cardinals to his bedside and asked them to forgive him for having been inadequate for the task he had undertaken, exhorting them to choose a worthier successor. He asked them to take an inventory of the valuables in his apartment, ordering that the sacred spearhead should be taken to St Peter's.

During the last days of Innocent's life the cardinals gathered in the palace, to look after the affairs of the Holy See in the absence of other authority. On 17 July they took the sacred spearhead from the pope's bedroom to St Peter's, and in the two days that followed distributed 48,000 ducats that he had asked be given to various of the pope's relatives. On the morning of 20 July they appointed Niccolo Orsini, Count of Pitigliano, to muster 100 archers to police the streets of Rome and 200 infantry to guard the city's gates and bridges. Three days later they assigned another 100 men to Orsini's force, as well as 1,000 more as a special guard for Jem. On 24 July another 400 were assigned to Orsini to protect the Vatican and the Borgo, the quarter between St Peter's and Castel Sant' Angelo, while the Abbot of St Denis was made governor of Rome with another force of 400 men. The next morning the Vatican and several other places were fortified and artillery was set up in strategic positions. The Florentine envoy Valori noted that Jem was moved into a tower above the Sistine Chapel, 'a very strong place, where he will be as secure as he would be in the Castel Sant' Angelo'.

That same morning, Friday, 25 July 1492, Innocent received the last sacrament of extreme unction, and at nine o'clock that evening he died, aged about sixty, having served as pope for nearly eight years. The cardinals declared that a period of mourning would begin on Saturday and last for nine days, after which a conclave would be held to elect a new pope.

Innocent was buried in St Peter's, opposite the tomb of Pius II, 'whom', as Sigismondo wrote of his master, 'he tried to emulate as a good and laudable pontiff'. Years later Innocent's body was transferred to the splendid bronze tomb in St Peter's created by Antonio del Pollaiuolo. The cost of the monument is estimated to have been about 4,000 ducats, just a tenth of the annual subsidy paid by Sultan Beyazit for his brother Jem's maintenance in the Vatican. This is the only papal monument from the ancient basilica that is preserved in the new St Peter's, to which it was transferred in 1621, placed high against the second pier on the right in the left aisle. There Innocent is shown in two scenes, in one of which he is seated on his throne, holding a model of the sacred spearhead, in the other laid out on his deathbed – the actual reliquary containing the spearhead built into one of the piers that support the dome. The inscription on the monument, added at a later date, suggests that Innocent's fellow Genoese Christopher Columbus set sail to discover the New World on the very day that the pope died, but his departure actually took place on 3 August 1492, nine days after Innocent passed away.

Innocent's passing also roughly coincided with another momentous historic event, the expulsion of the Jews from Spain by Ferdinand and Isabella. The order of expulsion was signed by them on 31 March 1492, and all the Jews were gone from Spain by 31 July of that year. Many of the expelled Jews found refuge in the Ottoman Empire at the invitation of Sultan Beyazit, while a number of them came to Rome, settling principally in the ancient Jewish quarter around the Piazza della Ebrei, through which Jem passed on the day that he first entered the city.

Rome had remained surprisingly calm during Innocent's final illness and the period of mourning that followed, although an envoy from Mantua reported on 7 August that 'it is true that a few were killed and others wounded, especially during the time that the Pope was *in extremis,* but afterwards things went better'.

Meanwhile negotiations went on behind the scenes in preparation for the conclave to elect a new pope. Valori informed the government in Florence that the favoured candidates were Cardinals Oliviero Caraffa of Naples and George Costa of Lisbon. Giuliano della Rovere had the support of his native Genoa as well as that of Charles VIII of France and Ferrante of Naples, while others variously favoured Ardicino della Porta, Ascanio Sforza, and Rodrigo Sforza, although the odds were against the latter as a Spaniard (he was actually a Catalan), for many of the Italian cardinals were determined not to elect a foreigner. As Riario wrote of the various alliances and negotiations, including large-scale bribery, that took place prior to and during the conclave: 'In regard to these intrigues I will not attempt to enter into details which would only serve to bewilder you and myself, for they are innumerable and change every hour.'

The conclave began on 6 August in the Sistine Chapel, with twenty-three cardinals in attendance. On 10 August the Florentine ambassador, who was one of the guards of the conclave, wrote that there had been three scrutinies, or votes, and no one had received the necessary two-thirds majority, with Caraffa and Costa seeming to have the best chance. But then there was a sudden realignment of support, and early in the morning of 11 August the window of the conclave chamber was opened and a voice shouted out *'Papam habemus!',* 'We have a Pope!' Rodrigo Borgia had been elected as pope, taking the name of Alexander VI. 'The bell of the Capitol was rung,' Gregorovius wrote:

the people here rushed to sack the house of the elected candidate; then ran to St Peter's, where the new Pope descended to receive his first oaths of homage. Cardinal Sanseverino, a man of gigantic strength, lifted Borgia in his arms and placed him on the throne above the high altar, introducing him as pope to the applauding crowd.

ဢ

Rodrigo Borgia was born in 1431, the son of Don Jofré de Borja, a Catalan nobleman of moderate means. His mother, Donna Isabella, was the sister of Pope Calixtus III, Alonso de Borja, whose family claimed royal descent from the ancient kings of Aragon. Rodrigo first came to Rome in 1449 or soon after, when his uncle Alonso, then a cardinal, arranged for him to study under the humanist Gaspare da Verona, who kept a school for young relatives of prelates. Gaspare described young Rodrigo thus in his biography of Pope Paul II:

> He is handsome; with a most cheerful countenance and genial bearing. He is gifted with a honeyed and choice eloquence. Beautiful women are attracted to love him and are excited by him in a quite remarkable way, more powerful than iron is attracted to a magnet.

Alonso de Borja had been elected to the papacy in 1455 as Calixtus III, and the following March he made Rodrigo Borgia and his cousin Luis Juan de Mila cardinals in a secret conclave. Two years later Calixtus made Rodrigo commander of the papal army and vice chancellor of the Church, posts which he held with great distinction for thirty-five years under five popes. Pius II, who succeeded Calixtus III in 1458, wrote of the young vice chancellor appreciatively: 'Rodrigo Borgia is now in charge of the Chancellery; he is young in age, assuredly, but he is old in judgement.' He was sent by Sixtus IV as papal legate to Spain in 1472, remaining for more than a year before returning to Rome, where during the next two decades he became one of the principal figures in the papal court. As Sigismondo de' Conti wrote of him at the time of his election as pope:

> It is now thirty-seven years since his uncle Calixtus III made him a Cardinal, and during that time he never missed a single consistory unless prevented by illness from attending, which very seldom happened . . . He was tall and powerfully built; though he had blinking eyes, they were penetrating and lively; in conversation he was extremely affable; he understands money matters thoroughly.

The Spanish bishop Bernaldino Lopez de Carvajal, writing in 1493, extolled the physical beauty and strength of the new pope, and Hieronimus Porcius, writing that same year, remarked on his eloquence and good breeding:

> He is tall, in complexion neither fair nor dark; his eyes are black, his mouth somewhat full. His health is splendid, and he has a marvellous power of enduring all sorts of fatigue. He is singularly eloquent in speech, and is gifted with an innate good breeding, which never forsakes him.

By the time of Alexander's election he had fathered six children, and he was credited with having sired two or three more during the years of his papacy, despite the fact that he was over sixty when he became pope – although such conduct was not particularly unusual or frowned upon for an ecclesiastic of his high station. But there was indignation at what the historian Ludwig Pastor called 'the shameless bribery by means of which he had secured his election'. But examination of the records of the 1492 conclave have led modern historians to take a more lenient view. According to Michael Mallett, 'Promises and simony there may have been, but it seems more likely that they were not out of proportion to practices at previous conclaves, and that they did not greatly affect the outcome of the election.'

Another charge against Rodrigo Borgia was that of nepotism, of which Mallett remarks that 'Alexander VI was certainly the greatest nepotist of all, but as one of only three foreign popes of the period he had the greatest need of the support of his family.' The extended Borgia family were extremely numerous, some of them having made their way into the papal hierarchy during the papacy of Calixtus III, and now added to these were the new pope's own children.

Rodrigo's children, of whom there were certainly eight and possibly nine, can be divided into three groups: those born before he departed for Spain as papal legate in 1472, those born to his mistress Vanozza de' Cataneis between 1475 and 1481, and those born after he became Pope Alexander VI. The mothers of his first three children, Pedro Luis, Isabella and Girolama (all born before 1472), are unknown. With his mistress, Vanozza, Rodrigo had Cesare, Juan, Lucrezia and Jofré. Those born after his election as pope were Giovanni, Laura Orsini, daughter of the pope's younger mistress Giulia Farnese (although current opinion doubts that Alexander VI was actually the father), and Rodrigo, who was born in 1503, the last of Rodrigo Borgia's children, sired over four decades.

The pope's first son, Pedro Luis, purchased the estates of Gandia in 1485 and was given the title of Duke. He died in Rome in 1488, having made a will bequeathing his duchy to his younger brother Juan, who thus became the second Duke of Gandia. Alexander VI, like his uncle Calixtus III, then used his Catalan relatives to counteract the military threat of the two most powerful of the Roman aristocratic families, the Orsini and Colonna. Two days after Calixtus was elected in 1455, Leonardo Vernacci wrote to Piero de' Medici to say that 'The Catalans are in command.' During the papacy of Calixtus one in five posts in the hierarchy of the Vatican was held by Catalans. This became even more pronounced under Alexander VI, who had only three Italians in his household, all of the others being Catalans, who when alone with the pope and his family spoke their native Catalan.

The coronation of Pope Alexander VI was held on Sunday, 26 August, celebrated, as the ambassador of Mantua wrote, 'with more pomp and with more fanfare than any pope has ever been crowned in our lifetime'. Another observer remarked that 'Antony was not received with as much splendour by Cleopatra as Alexander by the Romans.'

The papal procession began at St Peter's and wound across Rome to the Lateran, where the popes had lived until 1309 in the Palazzo Lateranense. The procession was headed by thirteen squadrons of papal cavalry, followed by the pope's household, the foreign ambassadors, and the college of cardinals, all mounted on splendidly caparisoned horses, each cardinal attended by twelve retainers. The pope, riding in a gilt carriage under a canopy to protect him from the blazing sun, was preceded by Count Pitigliano, whose sword was drawn to symbolize his role as Captain General and Protector of the Church. Behind the pope followed the captain of the papal guard with his troops, while the rear of the parade was brought up by the protonotaries and senior officials of the Curia.

Gregorovius wrote that 'The coronation festival ... was celebrated with a splendour hitherto unknown. Artistic taste and servility vied with one another in glorifying the Spaniard Borgia as a divinity.' Remarking on the 'statues and pictures, triumphal arches and altars that stood in the streets', the German historian remarked:

> Perhaps some Christian may have looked in grief on this pagan pomp, on these mythological figures of gods and on the noisy procession, in the midst of which the successor of the apostles was carried like an idol on a gilded car, while the air was filled with the shouts of the populace, the braying of trumpets and the thunder of cannon.

Alexander fainted twice from exhaustion and the extreme heat during the festival, first when the procession reached the Lateran, and again in a chapel of the basilica of San Giovanni in Laterano. After the conclusion of the service the procession reformed and made its way back to the Vatican, arriving just two hours before midnight, when Alexander took to his bed in the papal apartment of the Apostolic Palace. Floramonte Brognola, the Mantuan envoy in Rome, wrote to Francesco Gonzaga, the Marquis of Mantua, describing the procession, remarking that the papal court was 'dead tired', their fatigue aggravated by the heat and dust and the crowds of noisy spectators. 'Your Highness can imagine,' he wrote in conclusion, 'what it was to have to ride from eight to ten miles at a stretch in such a crowd.'

Meanwhile Jem had been brought back to his rooms in the Apostolic Palace, on the floor above the pope's apartment, after having been confined for three weeks in the tower above the Sistine Chapel. There is no record of what Jem saw or heard during the month and a day that passed between the death of Innocent VIII and the coronation of Alexander VI, but there is no doubt that he was aware of every detail of the interregnum, and that he wondered what changes the new pope might bring, for his confinement, starting from the moment he set foot on Rhodes, had now lasted for more than ten years.

14

In the Court of the Borgias

J EM'S CLOSE CONFINEMENT during the interregnum had made him extremely restive. This mood continued even after he was returned to his own apartment on the top floor of the Apostolic Palace, directly above the suite occupied by Pope Alexander, who would soon be made aware that his Turkish prince was dangerously unhappy with his plight.

Alexander held his first consistory on 31 August 1492, five days after his coronation. His first order of business was to divest himself publicly of his numerous and rich benefices, which were distributed among the cardinals, six of whom were appointed as papal legates. He gave the bishopric of Valencia to his son Cesare, although Innocent VIII had already bestowed on him that of Pampeluna, and then he made his nephew Juan Borgia-Lanzol, the Archbishop of Monreale, Cardinal of Santa Susanna. Juan was the first of five Borgias whom Alexander VI made cardinal, including his son Cesare, who was appointed the following year, along with Alessandro Farnese, brother of Giulia Farnese, the pope's mistress, who was immediately dubbed the 'petticoat' cardinal. Gianandrea Boccaccio, writing to the Duke of Ferrara about Alexander's outrageous nepotism, declared that 'ten papacies would not have sufficed to provide for all these cousins'.

Cesare Borgia was regarded as the most brilliant of the pope's children: 'Cesare possesses distinguished talents and a noble nature,' wrote the Ferrarese envoy Giacomo Trotti in 1493, 'his bearing is that of the son of a prince; he is singularly cheerful and merry and seems always in high spirits.' Cesare's formidable reputation appears to have been well founded, as Ludwig Pastor wrote: 'He combined unusual military and administrative talents with an iron will. Like most of the princes of the day his one aim was to obtain power, and no means was too bad for him provided they would serve his end.'

Alexander's favourite among his children was his daughter Lucrezia, who, unlike her brother Cesare, did not live up to her lurid reputation, as Reumont wrote in 1883:

> chroniclers and historians have conspired with the writers of epigrams, romances, and plays to represent Lucrezia Borgia as one of the most abandoned of her sex, a heroine of the dagger and poisoned cup . . .
>
> The most serious accusations against her rest on stories, which in their foulness and extravagance, surpass the grounds of credibility and even of possibility . . . Numbers of well attested facts prove them to be calumnies . . . Lucrezia must be acquitted of the great majority of the charges brought against her.

Lucrezia's contemporaries regarded her as extremely attractive, charming and joyous. Niccolo Cagnolo of Parma gives an account of Lucrezia as she was in 1502, at the age of twenty-one:

> She is of medium height, delicate of appearance, her face rather long as also is her finely cut nose; her hair golden,

her eyes greyish, the mouth rather large with brilliantly
white teeth; the throat smooth and white, yet becomingly
full. Her whole being breathes laughing good humour and
gaiety.

This physical description of Lucrezia lends weight to the theory
that she was Pintoricchio's model for St Catherine of Alexandria
in his fresco, the *Disputation of St Catherine*, painted in the years
1492–95 for Pope Alexander in the Hall of the Saints of the Borgia
Apartments. The scene shows St Catherine disputing a theological
question with the enthroned Roman emperor Maximinius, who
it is claimed was modelled on Cesare. A man with drooping
moustaches to the left of the throne is Andreas Palaeologus, of
the imperial Byzantine family, who was in Rome at the time. But
it is the two prominent turbaned figures in the fresco that draw
the eye: one has a moustache, and stands to the right of the
emperor; the other, in the right corner of the lunette, is bearded
and mounted on a horse. The latter is Jem, for there is no mistak-
ing the Turkish prince's majestic appearance, his strong resem-
blance to Mehmet II, looking very much the sultan as he gazes
imperiously toward the beautiful young saint disputing with the
emperor. Jem was well known to Lucrezia and the pope's other
children, particularly his sons Cesare and Juan, and he was in
the palace when Pintoricchio was decorating the Borgia Apartments in the early years of Alexander's papacy. So there is every
reason to believe that the Turkish prince served as the model for
the turbaned figure on horseback in the Hall of the Saints.

It has been suggested that another image of Jem appears in a
manuscript in the Vatican Museum. This is a watercolour miniature of a turbaned, and this time mustachioed, figure, which
appears in the upper left-hand corner of a musical score in one

of the choir books of the Sistine Chapel (*Capella Sistina Ms 41*), dating from the end of the fifteenth century. The manuscript is the oldest known copy of the *Missa La sol fa re mi* by Josquin Desprez, a Flemish composer who at the time was in the service of Cardinal Ascanio Sforza, and who may well have known Jem in the Vatican.

ৡৢ

During the first days of his papacy Alexander received envoys and messengers from leaders across Christendom congratulating him on his coronation. One of the messages was from King Ferrante of Naples, who is said to have wept in frustration when he heard that Rodrigo Borgia was elected rather than his own favourite, Giuliano della Rovere, but now he wrote to assure the pope of his devotion 'as a good and obedient son'. A more sincere message was sent by Pierre d'Aubusson, who wrote to say that he and the Knights Hospitallers 'were moved with no small pleasure' to learn of the election of Alexander VI, who as cardinal had been protector of their order, and that under his wise leadership they might see the East freed from Turkish tyranny, adding that Alexander was fortunate 'in having next to him the illustrious Jem Sultan, the terror, the exterminator of the Turks'.

Messages of congratulation also arrived with embassies from England and Scotland. Records in the Venetian archives note in summary that 'King Henry VII has charged the Bishop of Durham, and John Giglis, his ambassador at Rome, whom he confirms in their office, to yield canonical obedience to his Holiness,' and 'James IV, King of Scotland, has sent the Bishop of

LEFT Pierre d'Aubusson, Grand Master of the Knights of St John at Rhodes.
ABOVE Pope Innocent VIII, copy of the original by Mantegna.

LEFT Pope Alexander VI, detail of a fresco by Pintoricchio in the Borgia Apartments in the Vatican.
ABOVE King Charles VIII of France, terracotta bust by an unknown Florentine sculptor of the late fifteenth century, in the Bargello, Florence.

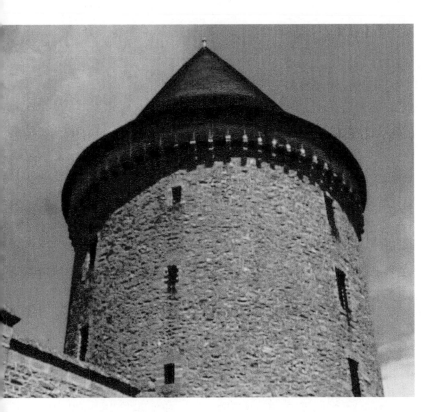

The Tour de Zizim at Bourganeuf.

La Dame à la Licorne, detail of one of the tapestries at Aubusson.

Jem Sultan, pen-and-ink drawing by an anonymous artist, *c*.1488.

<small>OPPOSITE</small> The Martyrdom of St Ursala, by Hans Memling, 1489.
The archer about to shoot Ursala was modelled on Jem.

LEFT Jem Sultan being presented to Pope Innocent VIII by Guy de Blanchefort, the Prior of Auvergne.

BELOW Castel Sant' Angelo, Rome, mid-nineteenth century.

OPPOSITE Jem Sultan, detail of *The Disputation of St Catherine*, by Pintoricchio, Hall of the Saints in the Borgia Apartments, the Vatican.

The Muradiye and
its imperial tombs,
Bursa.

RIGHT Interior of
Jem's tomb, Bursa.

Aberdeen and other ambassadors to tender his obedience to the Apostolic See.'

Alexander began his reign with an attempt to restore law and order in Rome, for during the interregnum there had been 'more than two hundred and twenty murders', according to Infessura. The new pope also imposed a strict economy on the papal household, whose costs he is said to have reduced to 700 ducats a month, besides the 300 ducats monthly that he allotted to Jem's maintenance from Beyazit's annual subsidy of 40,000 ducats.

On 13 October 1492 the Council of Ten sent a message to Andrea Capello, the Venetian envoy to the Holy See, warning that they had heard that the Turkish prince was very unhappy with his continued confinement in the Vatican and had plans to escape. Two days later the Council wrote again to Capello, instructing him to advise Jem, through an intermediary, to be patient and not to risk his bright prospects for the future by an attempt to escape that would cost him the goodwill of the pope, the King of France, and the Knights Hospitallers. The prince must be content to wait for the 'time of his proper glory', which would soon come, and have confidence in the goodwill of the Venetians and their support for him and his cause.

When the pope learned of this he summoned Capello, demanding the name of the person who informed the Venetians of Jem's plans to escape. Alexander also wanted to know the details of the plot, so that counter measures could be taken. Capello answered that Jem himself had plotted the escape and had sent a secret agent to tell the Venetian Senate of his plan, and to ask them for a trireme or even a simple barge that might take him down the Tiber. The Senate had refused to help Jem and tried to dissuade him from his escape attempt, which, they said, would expose him to multiple dangers. Jem's agent understood these concerns and reported them to his master. Capello was permitted to tell all of this to the pope but not to reveal the name of Jem's agent, because the Senate had given him their word that they would not expose him. The Council of Ten instructed Capello to tell the pope that he should convince Jem that the Holy See was trying to protect him, and to remind the prince that Beyazit would do anything to eliminate his dangerous brother.

The pope responded to this warning by moving Jem to the Castel Sant' Angelo, and to justify this he planted rumours that attempts were afoot to assassinate the prince. The conditions under which Jem was kept remained relatively liberal, and before long Alexander restored the prince to his original apartment in the Apostolic Palace. Jem was also allowed to take occasional outings in Rome, and was invited to social events in the Vatican. Many observers in Rome at this time noted that the pope's son Juan Borgia, the Duke of Gandia, would often accompany Jem on these excursions, each of them wearing a turban and an imperial Ottoman robe. The diarist Burchard wrote:

> Djem was not allowed to leave Rome, yet Alexander VI and his sons treated the prince in a very friendly and courteous fashion. He moved about the city with an escort and was accorded an honourable place in all ceremonial functions. Don Juan Borgia in particular appeared to cultivate him and frequently dressed in the style of a Turk when accompanying Djem on his journeys through Rome.

One Sunday in May 1493, Burchard witnessed a papal procession through Rome. Jem rode between Count Pitigliano and Juan Borgia; the crowd were startled by the appearance of Juan, who wore a turban and an imperial Ottoman robe. Behind Jem followed the pope, and behind him a cross bearer, five cardinals and a number of attendants. The destination of the procession, which snaked clockwise around Rome, was the basilica of San Giovanni in Laterano. There they dismounted and Alexander went with his attendants to examine the roof of the church, which was in need of repairs, while Jem accompanied Juan Borgia to see the tomb of Pope Martin V and other sites of interest in the basilica. The return route of the procession took them north-westward to the Piazza Santa Maria del Popolo, says Burchard, 'and from here turning to the left along the road by the river, past the house of the cardinal of Parma, by the bridge of Sant' Angelo, they returned to the Apostolic Palace'.

Jem would have been present a month later when Lucrezia Borgia was married to Giovanni Sforza in the Vatican, watching the events from the balcony of his apartment overlooking the Belvedere. 'When the banquet was over,' says Giacomo Trotti in a letter to Duke Ercole of Ferrara:

> the ladies danced, and as an interlude, we had an excellent play with much singing and music. The pope and all the others were there. What more can I say? My letter would never end were I to describe it all; thus we spent the whole night, whether well or ill, I will leave to your highness to determine.

Meanwhile Alexander had been working to create a triple alliance of the Holy See with Milan and Venice, which, by excluding King Ferrante of Naples, would upset the balance of power in Italy to the benefit of the allies. The new league, in which Siena, Ferrara and Mantua were also included, was announced in Rome on 25 April 1493, and was celebrated by a special service in the Church of San Marco, to which the pope rode on horseback. Two weeks earlier the Venetians had instructed Andrea Capello to ask the pope to include specific mention of Jem in the articles of their proposed alliance. Innocent concurred, and an article was included in the final treaty in which the pope agreed to turn over Jem to the Venetians if they were attacked by the Turks, so that they could use the prince against Beyazit. The Turks learned of the new league and expelled the Venetian *bailo* in Istanbul 'when some of his letters in cypher' were intercepted. Fearing Beyazit's reaction, the Venetians sent Domenico Trevisan as an envoy to Istanbul, hoping that he could persuade the sultan that the league was purely defensive.

Beyazit's three-year payment for Jem's maintenance at the Vatican expired on 20 May 1493. Prior to that date the pope had sent an envoy to Istanbul to ask the sultan to pay 40,000 ducats for his brother's 'pension' for the coming year. The envoy was the Genoese Giorgio Bocciardi, brother of Niccolo Cibo-Bocciardi, Archbishop of Arles, who on his return reported that the sultan was no longer willing to pay for Jem, and was in fact preparing to build ships for a naval expedition, and that he had been provoked into doing so by the formation of the new league.

ಬಿ

On 12 October 1492 Europe's horizons shifted far westward, when Christopher Columbus, 'Admiral of the Ocean', landed on an island that he called San Salvador, which he claimed for Castile and Leon. He returned to Palos, via the Azores and Lisbon, on

15 March 1493, convinced that he had discovered a route to the [East] 'Indies'. Later that same year, after being petitioned by Spain and Portugal, Pope Alexander agreed to set a boundary between their respective spheres of influence in the New World. All new land discovered to the west of a meridian lying 100 leagues beyond the Azores was to belong to Spain, everything to the east of that line was the dominion of Portugal (a demarcation that is still in evidence today in South America, where Portuguese is spoken in Brazil and Spanish in the rest of the continent).

One would suppose that Jem, living in such close proximity to the pope, would have heard of the discovery of the New World by Columbus and it would have set him poring over the *Geographia* that Francesco Berlinghieri had sent to him a decade before in Bois-Lamy, where the map of the world came to an abrupt end just westward of the coast from which Columbus had set sail. New worlds to be discovered and conquered, while Jem remained a prisoner in the Vatican, which could surely only have deepened his depression.

ဆာ

Ferrante now made an effort to improve relations with the Holy See, suggesting that a marriage be arranged between an illegitimate daughter of his and the pope's son Cesare, who, though recently appointed Archbishop of Valencia, was thinking of returning to civilian life. Ferrante also encouraged another dynastic match, one that would have wed Cesare's younger brother Jofré and a princess of the House of Aragon. But both proposals fell through, leading Ferrante to complain bitterly about

Alexander in a letter to Antonio d'Alessandro, his envoy at the court of Spain:

> Alexander VI has no respect for the holy chair which he
> occupies, and leads such a life that everyone turns away
> from him in horror; he cares for nothing but the aggrandize-
> ment of his children by fair means or foul. All his thoughts
> and all his actions are directed to this one end. What he
> wants is war; from the first moment of his reign till now,
> he has never ceased persecuting me.

Alexander responded calmly to King Ferrante's various attacks and aggressive schemes in the hope that he could end the long estrangement between Naples and the papacy. Ferrante tried to take advantage of the atmosphere of goodwill, as he had tried to do with Pope Innocent, and request that the pope send Jem to Naples, where the king would be able to use the prince more effectively against his brother. Ferrante even went so far as to send a message to Istanbul boasting of the warm relations that now existed between him and the pope, who had given him 'total custody and governatoral dominion over Jem Sultan'. The Porte immediately sent an agent to Venice to determine if Ferrante's claim was true. The Council of Ten responded on 1 April 1493, informing the agent that Jem was still in Rome, that he was more carefully guarded than ever, and that the pope and the King of Naples were not on good terms but were actually involved in a serious dispute with one another.

On 3 April, Andrea Capello, the Venetian envoy in Rome, wrote to the Council of Ten to inform them of a communication that had been received from Hadım (meaning 'the eunuch') Ali Pasha, the new Ottoman grand vezir. Ali Pasha had sent one of his relatives as an envoy to Rome with instructions to make certain proposals to the pope, 'which will be to the convenience and satisfaction of his Holiness and to the great benefit of Christendom'. After seeing the pope, the Turkish envoy departed for Apulia, where he had left two of his sons whom he would bring back to Rome to leave as hostages with the pope as evidence of the sincerity of the sultan's offer. The pope called in Capello and asked him to talk with the Turkish envoy when he returned, so that he could inform the Signoria of the issues involved. Capello was instructed by his government to thank the pope for having sought his help on this matter, but he was told to avoid dealing directly with the Turkish envoy when and if he returned. He was also told to ask the pope to keep the Signoria informed of everything the envoy had to say, and also not to allow the Turk to see Jem, for the Venetians believed that his intentions were sinister. The envoy never returned, and the Venetians concluded that their suspicions were justified, which led them to warn the pope from further contacts of this sort.

The Venetians soon had occasion to notify the pope of another such attempt. The Council of Ten wrote to Capello to tell him that an unsavoury character named Lactantino Benzio had arrived in Istanbul in September 1492, and had identified himself at the Porte as a nephew of Cardinal Piccolomini and as a member of the household of Cardinal Ascanio Sforza. The Porte had apparently hired Benzio to carry out a mission in Rome, which the Venetians suspected was an attempt to assassinate Jem. The Council of Ten had accordingly sent instructions to all Venetian *bailos* and captains in the Aegean to arrest Benzio on sight. Meanwhile they instructed Capello to make secret enquiries to see if Benzio had arrived in Rome, and also to determine whether he had any connection with the households of either of the two cardinals. Capello was to warn the pope to guard Jem as closely as possible, but he was not to reveal the source of his information regarding Benzio, so as not to compromise the agent in Istanbul who had discovered the plot. Nothing came of this plot, and Benzio was never heard of again. Such were the intrigues that swirled around Jem during his years as a prisoner in the Vatican.

Jem's communications with his mother in Cairo continued throughout his confinement in the Vatican, his mother using desperate measures to keep in touch with her son, including bribing Sultan Kaitbey and others. The Venetians took every opportunity to inform Beyazit of Kaitbey's actions, and tried to use them to provoke another war between the Ottomans and Egypt. While Beyazit was not pleased that Jem was in contact with his family, he found their letters useful in keeping track of his brother. One of the sultan's agents reported that Jem's mother sent a white horse to her son (though there is no record of whether it ever arrived in Rome). One undated letter from Jem to his mother says that a friend of his, a relative of the pope, intended to visit Jerusalem, and he asked that the man be well looked after. A second letter, sent to Cairo in 1493, is a short note to Kaitbey thanking him for taking care of Jem's family. A third note, also dated 1493, is written by Jem to his mother, asking her to send him one of the women in his harem in the care of some of his officers. It is not clear which woman he was referring to, or whether she was the mother of one of his children. There is no record of whether the woman ever arrived in Rome, though it seems unlikely that she did, for the presence of a Turkish woman in the Vatican would hardly have escaped comment, particularly among the pope's enemies, who would have publicized it as yet another example of the depravity of life in the court of the Borgias.

Burchard reports the arrival in Rome on Sunday, 9 June 1493, of a Turkish envoy whom he calls Chasimpueg, a corruption of Kasim Bey, who was conveying several letters from Sultan Beyazit to Pope Alexander. According to Burchard, 'The purpose of the ambassador's visit was to pay the final instalment currently owing in the annuity to the pope under the terms of the agreement made about the detention of Prince Djem.' The pope sent a deputation under Count Pitigliano to meet the envoy and his entourage a mile outside the city, which they then entered through the Porta del Popolo and proceeded to the Palazzo San Martinello, where the Turks were to be housed. En route they were joined by the foreign diplomatic corps and other dignitaries, including Jem, who was accompanied by two of his guards from the Order of St John.

Three days later Kasim Bey was invited to an audience with the pope, which took place at the beginning of a secret consistory at the Vatican. Burchard describes the Turkish envoy's entry into the meeting hall, to which he was escorted by the captain general and the Vicar of Pesaro as far as the end of the assemblage of cardinals, who were drawn up in two ranks rather than in the traditional circle.

> The ambassador advanced toward the pope with only Don Giorgio and myself to accompany him. Neither at the edge of the consistory nor immediately in front of the pope did Chasimpueg genuflect or bow his head to His Holiness, but

throughout marched steadily forward, erect and with his head covered, to come to kiss the pope's hand and robe. Then, standing before His Holiness, he declared that Sultan Bajazet, the Emperor and Ruler of Europe and Asia, sent his greetings.

Chasimpueg handed over his letters to the pope and stepped back behind the cardinals' benches, where he looked for a seat to sit down on. When I told him that this was not a customary procedure, even for an ambassador of the emperor, Chasimpueg squatted on the floor, Turkish fashion, or like one of our tailors.

Beyazit's messages were handed to a cleric named Demetrio Guaselli, who, according to Burchard, 'knelt outside the consistory to read the letters, and he first recited their contents in the original Greek and then read the Latin translation provided with them'. When the letters and their translation had been read, the pope questioned Kasim Bey, asking if there was anything he wished to say. 'The ambassador, still squatting as I have described,' wrote Burchard,

> replied through his interpreter, Don Giorgio, who knelt beside him, that the sultan, his emperor and master, was well, that he was very happy at the pope's elevation to his office, and committed his beloved brother Djem to the pontiff's care so that his detention should be pleasant and he should lack nothing for his comfort ... The sultan requested that he, Chasimpueg, should be allowed to visit his brother to present him with gifts, and then to return as quickly as possible to Turkey to take back news of the pope's well being. All these points the ambassador explained in a disjointed fashion rather than in a single speech, and he spoke only one sentence at a time through an interpreter.

The pope agreed that Kasim Bey could visit Jem, and then said that he wished to talk with him further in private. In the meantime, six slaves from Kasim Bey's retinue entered the meeting hall, each accompanied by a papal groom. According to Burchard, each of the slaves 'carried in his hands and over his arms pieces of brocaded cloth and of camlet and silk in vividly different colours, totalling some twenty strips in all'. When the pope saw these articles,

> he concluded that the ambassador had brought them as gifts to him, particularly as a token to bury past disputes, and he therefore thanked Chasimpueg for the present. The ambassador then arose, and when the chamberlains had taken the gifts from their bearers, he departed with all his household.

After meeting with Jem, the details of which are not recorded, Kasim Bey had a private audience with the pope. In his diary, Infessura repeated the rumour that the Turkish envoy had given the pope 80,000 ducats for Jem's maintenance for the past two years, as well as another 10,000 ducats for the prince himself, since he 'wished to be supported at his own expense . . . all marvelled that the Grand Turk should have sent tribute to the pope and the church of God'. Alexander conveyed his thanks to Beyazit, and said that the sultan could show his friendship for Christianity by refraining from the attacks he had been making on Christians in the Balkans and the Aegean. He said that Kasim Bey could also tell Beyazit that his brother was well and in good hands, which he hoped would influence the sultan to embark on a more peaceful policy toward Christendom.

But Beyazit persisted in his attacks, launching an invasion of

Croatia in the autumn of 1493. Alexander wrote a circular letter to the Christian princes of Europe, on 2 October 1493, appealing to them to take common action for 'Italy and the Christian religion are in peril', warning that 'this business brooks of no delay, but requires immediate preparation'. Alexander sent an envoy to Beyazit, warning him to cease his invasion of Croatia, otherwise his brother Jem would be turned over to the Christian princes. The pope also planned to send another letter to the Christian leaders, reminding them of the perilous state of Christendom, 'and to urge them on to an expedition against the Turks, showing how great a victory may be expected by means of the Turk's brother, who is here'.

Before long, however, Pope Alexander faced a threat from a wholly different and unexpected quarter. King Charles VIII of France had become set upon the idea of pursuing his extravagant claim to the Neapolitan throne, which would lead him to invade Italy in the first stage in a crusade to recapture Constantinople and Jerusalem. After Madame de Beaujeu's retirement from high politics the young king had fallen under the sway of his court favourites, Etiennne de Vesc and Guillaume Briçonnet, who, according to John S. C. Bridge:

> egged Charles on to the siren voices that called to him from Italy; they dangled before his fascinated eyes the crown of Naples and the sceptre of the East. They told him that along with the throne of France he had inherited the just pretensions of the House of Anjou to its ancient Italian possessions. Let him, then, assert his claim, and dispossess the Aragonese usurper.

Charles was also heavily influenced by the writings of a four-teenth-century seer, Telesphorus of Cosenza, who said that a

French king would defeat the Antichrist, receive the ancient imperial crown of Byzantium, and lead 'the seventh and final crusade for the Holy Land, which they will recover'. Charles began to be convinced that he was the 'second Charlemagne' long predicted in French tradition, and references to this are frequent in his Italian campaign. The Venetian ambassador Zaccaria Contarini, on a visit to convey his congratulations to Charles on his wedding to Anne of Brittany in 1491, leaves us with an unflattering description of the young king:

> His Majesty, the King of France, is twenty-two years old, small and ill-formed in person, with an ugly face, large lustreless eyes, which seem to be short-sighted, an enormous aquiline nose, and thick lips, which are continuously parted; he stutters, and has a nervous twitching of the hands which is unpleasant to watch. In my opinion – it may well be wrong – he is not of much account either physically or mentally.

Contarini then tried to balance his report with some positive comments he had heard about the French king:

> He is well spoken of in Paris as being a good hand at tennis, hunting, and tilting – pursuits to which, whether for good or ill, he devotes much time. He is praised also in that he now desires himself to debate and decide questions which in the past he would leave to certain members of his Secret Council, and it is said that in this respect he acquits himself quite creditably.

As the first stage of his campaign Charles negotiated a series of treaties, buying off potential enemies who might attack France while he was abroad. The first, the Treaty of Etaples, signed on

3 November 1492, saw Henry VII of England agree to give up the foothold that his army had established at Calais, and withdraw his troops on promise of 745,000 gold crowns payable in fifteen years. Next came the Treaty of Narbonne, on 23 May 1493, in which Charles ceded the French districts of Franche-Comté and Charolais to the Archduke Maximilian. In the Treaty of Barcelona, signed in January 1494, Charles agreed to restore the Catalan counties of Roussillon and Cerdagne to King Ferdinand of Spain. Anne of Beaujeu was distressed by these treaties and warned her brother about their consequences, telling him: 'You will pay dearly by a long repentance.'

Charles's dynastic claims most directly challenged King Ferrante. Ferrante for his part had long felt angered by the cosy relationship between the papacy and the French king, and on 18 December 1493 Ferrante wrote of his displeasure in a letter to the Neapolitan envoy in Rome:

> We and our father have always been obedient to the popes, and yet, one and all, they have invariably done us as much mischief as they could; and now although this pope is a countryman of ours, it is impossible to live with him a single day in peace and quietude. We know not why he persists in quarrelling with us; it must be the will of Heaven, for it seems to be our fate to be harassed by all the popes.

Ferrante believed there was no chance of stopping the French, and that the kingdom which he had built up at the cost of so much bloodshed was doomed. But he was at least spared the sight of its downfall, for he passed away in Naples on 25 January 1494, after a tumultuous reign of thirty-five years, to be succeeded by his son, the Duke of Calabria, who came to the throne as

Alfonso II. Gregorovius wrote of Ferrante's passing as a great loss to Italy:

> . . . for he alone had averted foreign invasion and had kept a watchful eye over the movement of the Turks. He alone had set a limit to the policy of the Papacy. In him died the last statesman among the princes of the time in Italy. His son Alfonso now succeeded him to the insecure throne, a man devoid of courage and intellect, proud, without moderation, cruel, false and vicious.

Charles was greatly encouraged in his ambitions by the news of Ferrante's death and determined that Alfonso would not remain for long on the Neapolitan throne. The pope sought to dissuade Charles from his Neapolitan venture, which would not only wreck the pope's own plans for a crusade but would place all of Italy in peril. As Alexander wrote to Charles on 20 March 1494:

> We are again compelled to urge and pray your serenity to give up this war against Naples, for the common defence of Christianity; and turn with us to the expedition we have planned which without question this war would obstruct completely. Let your majesty consider how you are at odds with yourself, for while you say you are arming against the infidels, you are undertaking a war with Naples.

On 18 April the pope called a secret consistory that authorized the investiture of Alfonso II as King of Naples. Alexander's nephew, Cardinal Juan Borgia-Lanzol, was nominated as papal legate to go to Naples to perform the actual investiture and coronation, which took place on 8 May. Among those who attended the ceremony was an envoy from the Porte, with a retinue of twelve Turkish attendants. Burchard noted in his diary that the Turkish envoy attended the coronation ceremony at the cathedral, but when the cardinal legate began to say Mass the Turk was excused by the master of ceremonies.

The French were furious at Alfonso's investiture, and Charles declared that he would withdraw his obedience from the pope, warning that all French benefices would be taken away from the cardinals who sided with Alexander, and given to Cardinal Ascanio Sforza, brother of Lodovico il Moro, the king's Milanese ally. Charles won another ally in Cardinal Giuliano della Rovere, the papal legate to Avignon, who fled to the French court on 23 April. Giuliano abandoned the fort of Ostia at the mouth of the Tiber, which had been in his charge, claiming that he feared the pope was going to attack and kill him. He fled to Genoa, from whence Lodovico il Moro enabled him to proceed to France. There he went first to his episcopal palace at Avignon, and then to the camp of Charles VIII, who had already announced his intention of starting for Italy. Cardinal Giuliano's influence, added to that of Lodovico il Moro, spurred the young king to begin his expedition as soon as possible.

At this stage Charles's imperial ambitions were, as the German historian C. von Höfler described them, to

> possess himself of the Italian peninsula between the French state and the continent; to attain imperial dignity, whether in the East or the West, remained at the present undeter-mined; to make the Papacy again dependent on France, and himself the master of Europe.

But the young king's dreams of glory went even beyond this, to the destruction of the Ottoman Empire itself and the recapture of Jerusalem from the Muslims, which he believed he could accomplish by using Jem in a crusade against his brother. Such was the tempest that threatened to burst in the summer of 1494, and at the eye of the storm was Jem Sultan, isolated within his palatial prison in the court of the Borgias.

15

The French Invade Italy

On 29 August 1494, Charles VIII took leave of his queen, departing to lead the expedition that he believed would immortalize his name. Five days later he crossed the frontier between France and Savoy, and on 5 September he arrived in Turin. The townspeople welcomed him and his army with enthusiasm, strengthening his desire to reassert the claim of the House of Anjou to the Duchy of Savoy, which was as untenable as the claim on the Neapolitan kingdom. As Charles wrote in a letter later that same day:

> At Turin I saw my cousins, the Duchess of Savoy and her sister, and upon my word I assure you that I seem still to be in France, so warmly am I welcomed. Never was I better received: the country is full of people eager to greet me, to hand over the keys of their towns, and to offer gifts of jewellery; and the streets are decorated. Indeed, everything is done for me that could be done.

The size of the forces which Charles had assembled to invade Italy has been variously estimated by contemporary sources and later historians to have been somewhere in the region of over

40,000 combat troops, 10,000 of whom were aboard the French fleet, commanded by the Duke of Orleans, while the rest marched across the Alps. According to a contemporary source there were 10,000 heavy cavalry, 6,200 archers, 8,000 arbalesters or cross-bowmen, 8,000 Breton pikemen, 8,000 gunners, 200 artillery officers, 1,200 guns, 8,000 artillery horses, as well as a large number of auxiliary personnel in the various technical services. There were also numerous non-combatants; according to John S. C. Bridge these included:

> gentlemen's servants and attendants on the men at arms, trumpeters and drummers, farriers and ammunition-makers, waggoners and muleteers; a complete household staff was in attendance upon the King; the baggage train was enormous; and at Fornovo, at the close of the campaign . . . the army was still accompanied by some ten thousand non-combatants.

The plan of defence against the French invasion had already been drawn up by the late King Ferrante, and his son Alfonso now put it into operation in alliance with the pope. To prevent the advance of the French, Alfonso sent his son Ferrantino with an army to the Romagna, whence he was to threaten Lombardy, while Piero de' Medici, the Florentine ruler, defended the frontiers of Tuscany. At the same time a Neapolitan fleet assembled at Leghorn under Don Federigo, Alfonso's brother, to attack Genoa, which was under Milanese control. The pope was to protect the papal states with troops stationed in Tuscany.

Meanwhile Pope Alexander and King Alfonso of Naples were joined in an anti-French league by Florence, Siena, Bologna, Pesaro, Urbino and Imola, while Venice declined to join because of her fear of violating the terms of her peace treaty with the Turks. Beyazit had sent an envoy to Naples to offer Alfonso military aid against the French, conveying the message that the sultan 'did not want them in Italy'. In August the Venetians learned that Alfonso had sent an envoy to Istanbul to ask the Porte for aid, suggesting that the sultan attack Chios to divert the Genoese from cooperating with the French. It was rumoured that Alfonso offered to cede Brindisi and Otranto to Beyazit in return for his help, preferring to give them to the Turks rather than lose his kingdom to the French. By now Beyazit recognized the formidable power of the French army, and he declined to send aid to Alfonso, saying that he did not want to become involved in Christian affairs, since he was at peace with *all* of the princes of Western Europe.

Pope Alexander had no objection to Alfonso's attempt to obtain aid from the Turks against the French. In June Alexander had sent the Genoese envoy Giorgio Bocciardi to ask Beyazit to send the yearly payment of 40,000 ducats for his brother Jem's 'pension', since he needed the money to defend himself against Charles VIII. On Bocciardi's return journey he was accompanied by Kasim Bey, who had come as Beyazit's emissary to Rome the previous year. Kasim Bey carried letters from Beyazit to the pope, as well as the sultan's annual payment of 40,000 ducats for Jem's maintenance.

The two envoys landed in Ancona in mid-November 1494 and headed for Rome. But ten miles from the coast they were attacked by a band of 250 armed men led by the Lord of Senigallia, Giovanni della Rovere, Cardinal Giuliano's brother, who robbed them of their dispatch boxes. Kasim was able to escape by giving up the 40,000 ducats he was carrying, and took refuge in a nearby castle, but Bocciardi was taken prisoner to Senigallia, on the coast north-west of Ancona. Giovanni della Rovere immediately wrote to his brother, Cardinal Giuliano, telling him what had happened and informing him of the contents of the letters that the envoys had been carrying. Giuliano then passed on the letters to Charles VIII.

Meanwhile Kasim Bey was rescued by the people of Ancona, who feared that if the Turkish envoy were harmed they would suffer the sultan's wrath. The Marquis of Mantua promptly sent assistance to Kasim Bey and received him in his palace, as he wrote to Beyazit, 'for the love he bore the sultan'. He then sent Kasim Bey back to Istanbul, bearing a letter in which the marquis told Beyazit that his envoy has done everything possible to fulfil the mission with which he had been entrusted, but that he had been prevented from doing so by the perfidy of Giovanni della Rovere.

The letters seized by Giovanni della Rovere were published by the pope's enemies, most probably Cardinal Giuliano and others at the French court. One of the letters contained a copy of the pope's verbal instructions to his envoy, which Bocciardi had obviously been forced to write down by his captors at Senigallia. Giovanni, writing to his brother Giuliano, expressed his shock at the contents of this letter, 'which contained astounding and to Christianity most dangerous things, whence it was evident that the pope wished to sell Djem to the Grand Turk, whose aid he sought against France'.

According to the diarist Johann Burchard, the pope's letter of instruction to Bocciardi began:

> ... you will signify in our name that the King of France is pushing on towards Rome with the greatest land and sea forces, supported by the Milanese, Bretons, Portuguese, Normans and others in order to wrest from us Djem Sultan,

the brother of his Highness, and to seize the kingdom of
Naples and oust King Alfonso, to whom we are bound by
the closest ties of blood and friendship.

Bocciardi should tell Beyazit that the French king intended to
seize Jem, whom Charles wanted to set up on the throne in
Istanbul after he had conquered Naples. Bocciardi was also to ask
Beyazit to persuade the Venetians to join in the league against
the French, saying that it would pose no threat to the Ottoman
Empire because of the 'good and true friendship' which existed
between the pope and the sultan.

The other documents in Kasim Bey's dispatch case included
four letters dated from Istanbul on 15 and 18 September 1494, sent
by Beyazit to the pope as expressions of the sultan's friendship. One
of the letters praised Giorgio Bocciardi for his efforts in carrying
out his important diplomatic mission, and then went on to make
the astonishing request that the pope give a cardinal's hat to the
envoy's brother, Niccolo Cibo-Bocciardi, Archbishop of Arles.

Historians contemporary and modern generally accept the
authenticity of the four letters. But a fifth letter from Kasim Bey's
dispatch case has been the subject of controversy for more than
five centuries. Burchard recorded the letter, from Beyazit to the
pope, in full in his diary. After the usual extravagant greetings,
the sultan apparently wrote:

> amongst other things, Don Giorgio told us how the French
> king is eager to seize Djem, Our brother, at present in Your
> Highness's keeping, and this would be an act much against
> Our wish, bringing great harm to Your Highness and injury
> to all Your Christian peoples. We have therefore reached an
> agreement with Don Giorgio for the peace, aid and honour
> of Your Greatness and also for Our satisfaction.

Beyazit then elaborated on this agreement and the advantages it would bring:

> the execution of Our brother Djem, who is held in Your Highness's hands, should be carried out, for this would be a release into life for him, useful for Your authority and most convenient and gratifying to Our position. If Your Magnificence is agreeable to please Us in this matter, and indeed We trust that You will be prudent to be so, then for Your greater security and Our deeper satisfaction, You should execute the deed as quickly as possible.
>
> ... Thereby Your Highness will be the better pleased and Djem will more quickly be delivered from the straits of this world so that his soul shall have peace in the next. Furthermore, if Your Highness will undertake to fulfil this agreement, and will command that Djem's body will be delivered to Us at any point on our coasts, We, Sultan Bajazet Chan, promise to hand over three hundred thousand ducats at any place pleasing to Your Eminence, with which You may buy possessions for your sons.
>
> ... These three hundred thousand ducats We shall have consigned to any person Your Highness appoints before the body is handed over to Our servants. Moreover, We promise that during the lifetime of each of Us, We shall always maintain a deep and lasting friendship with Your Highness, aiding You as much as possible without any deceit.

Beyazit then pledged:

> Above all this and to give Your Highness still greater satisfaction, We promise that neither We Ourselves, nor Our subjects, nor any person from Our lands, shall hinder or harm Christians, whatever their rank or condition, by land or by sea, except where some seek to harm Us or Our subjects.

... To remove any doubt, We, Sultan Bajazet Chan, swear by God, the True One who created Heaven and Earth and everything that is in them, in whom We believe and whom We adore, to observe all that is contained in the agreement, and in nothing ever to act contrary to Your Highness. Written at Constantinople in Our Palace, September 14th, 1494, according to the coming of Christ.

Alexander certainly never received the 300,000 ducats from Beyazit, which would have amounted to more than the annual revenue of the Holy See, nor is there any strong evidence that the pope tried to have Jem murdered. Most historians agree that the fifth letter was a forgery, probably concocted by Cardinal Giuliano della Rovere and the French court to destroy the pope's reputation.

Giuliano had made other efforts in this direction, most notably his declaration of the need to call a council to proceed against Alexander VI in the cause of reforming the Church. This greatly alarmed the pope, who felt very vulnerable to the insistent demands for Church reform, particularly because of his blatant use of bribes in his election. Gregorovius wrote of Alexander's fears in this regard:

His simoniacal election was the secret terror of his whole life. He dreaded above all things the use that might be made of this blot in his title to the Papacy, by the Cardinals of the opposition and his other enemies to bring about his downfall, in view of the universal feeling of the crying need of reform in the Church.

Charles VIII arrived at Asti, thirty-five miles east of Turin in the Piedmont in late summer 1494. He was greeted by the Duke of Ferrara and Cardinal Giuliano della Rovere, and soon afterwards they were joined by Lodovico il Moro, the Regent of Milan, and by the Duke of Orleans. Orleans reported that on 5 September his naval force had defeated Don Federigo's Neapolitan fleet at Rapallo, twelve miles east of Genoa, which augured well for the campaign. But a week later Charles became ill with what seems to have been a mild form of smallpox, and was unable to leave his room for more than three weeks. The French campaign was halted and there were fears that it might not be resumed. However on 18 September Fabrizio Colonna's troops captured the fortress of Ostia, which had been abandoned by Cardinal Giuliano della Rovere, expelling the papal castellan, and raising his own ensign over the citadel, together with those of Charles VIII and Cardinal Giuliano. On 16 October Charles sent part of his fleet to the Tiber and landed troops to garrison the citadel at Ostia, after which the French sailed back northwards. The loss of Ostia was a severe blow to the pope, since the fortress controlled the mouth of the Tiber and the maritime approach to Rome, making it difficult and expensive to bring supplies into the city.

A letter from the Florentine envoy Filippo Valori, dated 9 October 1494, warned Alexander of a plot to assassinate both Jem and the pope, this time by the Colonna clan. When the pope learned of this he immediately had Jem protected by an additional force of heavily armed papal guards under the command of two of his nephews, Francisco and Galceran Borgia, the latter being a knight of Rhodes.

Before Charles left France, he had sent Guy de Blanchefort to Rhodes with letters asking Pierre d'Aubusson to come to Rome to discuss plans for a crusade against the Turks. Charles wrote again to d'Aubusson after his army entered northern Italy and repeated his request that they confer in Rome, saying that he had need of the grand master's knowledge of the Turks and their diplomatic and military affairs.

Around this time the pope began to have doubts about the loyalty of the Knights Hospitallers, who were predominantly French, and so he decided to dismiss the knights guarding Jem and send them back to Rhodes. Alexander informed d'Aubusson of his decision in writing, saying that ten knights would be returning to Rhodes, naming six Frenchmen, three Italians and one Spaniard, all of whom he commended to the grand master for their integrity and loyalty. The pope retained one Knight Hospitaller, a Catalan named Antonio de Santo Martino, who, he said, would remain with Jem.

Jem was sad to see the knights go and wrote Pierre d'Aubusson a letter of appreciation, praising the guards for their loyal service:

> Most kindly and faithfully have I been served by the said knights, without being able to testify my gratitude in the slightest degree by remunerating them in the manner I should most ardently have desired. With the warmest and most affectionate cordiality, I beg of your very reverend lordship, very kindly to look upon them as persons peculiarly commended to you by your love to me. I will think every favour and benefit which you bestow on them as conferred by your condescension on myself personally.

Meanwhile Charles had resumed his campaign. He entered Pavia in triumph on 14 October and four days later he was in Piacenza. There he learned of the death of Giangaleazzo, Duke of Milan, and of the succession to the ducal throne of Lodovico il

Moro, who was suspected of having poisoned his nephew. Shortly afterwards, he learned that Caterina Sforza, ruler of Forlì and Imola, had declared for France. The French troops crossed the Apennines, causing consternation in Rome, where the alarm was aggravated by the revolt of the Colonna and Savelli, instigated by Cardinal Ascanio Sforza. French galleys soon began to appear at the mouth of the Tiber, which made the occupation of Ostia still more serious for Alexander.

The French entered Tuscany and encountered little resistance. Piero de' Medici presented himself at the French camp on 26 October and surrendered Florence and all of the other cities under his control. The fearsome Dominican friar Savonarola, preaching from his pulpit in the cathedral of Florence, had predicted the invasion by Charles VIII's forces as the scourge of God to punish Italy for its sins, most notably the corruption of the Church. 'The sword has arrived,' he cried out on 1 November, 'the prophecies are on the eve of fulfilment, retribution is beginning; God is the leader of this host.' Eight days later the people of Florence rose in revolt, forcing Piero de' Medici to flee along with his brother, Cardinal Giovanni de' Medici, the future Pope Leo X, leaving their palace and its art treasures to be looted by the rebel mob.

Charles VIII entered Lucca on 8 November, and on the following day he was welcomed at Pisa by the townspeople, who hailed him as their liberator from Florentine tyranny. Cardinal Piccolomini had been sent by the pope as an envoy to try and come to terms with the French, but Charles refused to see him, saying he was coming to Rome to deal with Alexander himself. Piccolomini wrote to Alexander from Lucca on 4 November, telling him that the French authorities had proclaimed that their king was coming to Rome 'to reform the Church'. Charles responded by issuing a proclamation to all of Christendom explaining the lofty purpose of his expedition.

In this document, which was published in French and Latin and soon after translated into German, Charles declared that the object of his expedition was not conquest, but simply the overthrow of the Turks and the liberation of the Holy Land. He claimed that he only desired to recover possession of his Neapolitan kingdom in order to accomplish this. He asked nothing from the pope but a free passage through the 'States of the Church', and supplies for his troops on their march; if this were to be refused he would take it without leave. He took no responsibility for any ill consequences that might ensue, and if necessary he would renew his claims before all the princes of Christendom, whom he proposed to summon to join him in his expedition against the Turks.

Two attempts were made at this time to persuade the pope to support Charles. The first of these was by Cardinal Ascanio Sforza, who came to Rome on 2 November and asked Alexander to abandon Alfonso, pointing out the dangers that were to be feared from the French king if the pope did not at least remain neutral. But Alexander refused, telling Ascanio that he would rather sacrifice his papacy, his possessions, and even his life, than abandon Alfonso. At this point, it was claimed, Alexander felt so vulnerable that he considered fleeing Rome, and he conferred with the Venetian *bailo* about whether he might find a refuge in Venice. Marino Sanudo wrote that the French king, through the urgings of Cardinal Giuliano della Rovere, intended to summon a Church council that would depose Alexander, who, according to the Venetian diarist, lived in fear of being replaced by an anti-pope.

A few days later another attempt was made to bring the pope

over to the French side, this time by Pandolfo Collenuccio, who represented the Duke of Ferrara. Once again Alexander refused, saying that he would rather give up his crown and his life than become a slave of the French king, who, he said, was intent on conquering the whole of Italy.

When Alexander learned, on 14 November, that Charles had refused to receive Cardinal Piccolomini, he appointed the French Cardinal Peraudi as papal legate and sent him to see Charles. Peraudi was instructed to inform the king that Alexander would come to meet him in order to discuss the proposed crusade; but Charles declined the offer, saying that he wished to pay homage to the pope in the Vatican. At the same time Charles and his advisors succeeded in winning over Peraudi, who was a fervent supporter of the crusade, and Alexander found himself more isolated then ever. As a last resort he sent a third legate, Cardinal Federigo Sanseverino, but Charles informed him that he had resolved to spend Christmas with the pope in Rome, where he would deal with the Holy Father in person.

Soon afterwards the town of Viterbo surrendered to the French, whose advance was so rapid that Giulia Farnese, the pope's mistress, fell into their hands while travelling. However she was soon released at the pope's request, according to Giorgio Brognolo, the Mantuan envoy. Brognolo, in relating this incident, ends his report by saying that 'The French King will not meet with the smallest resistance in Rome.'

On 24 November, the pope summoned the Prince of Anhalt, ambassador to the Holy Roman Empire, telling him, according to Burchard, that Charles 'was seeking not only to create a kingdom for himself from the cities and lands of Italy that rightly belonged to the Holy Roman Empire, but also to usurp the title and authority of that Empire'. Alexander said that he would never submit to this, 'even if a naked sword were held to his throat', and he asked that His Highness the Emperor Maximilian 'as the only Advocate of the Holy Roman Church, should be informed of these things, and should be exhorted most earnestly to succour the Holy Roman Church, the Holy Roman Empire, and the whole of Italy with the aid essential for their honour and good'. The Prince of Anhalt humbly undertook to carry out this commission.

Rome was in a perilous situation, blockaded to seaward by the French-held fortress of Ostia and on land by the Colonna, and food was becoming increasingly scarce. The gates of Rome were chained and some were walled up. On 10 December, Ferrantino, the Duke of Calabria, led the Neapolitan army into the city, with 5,000 infantry and 1,000 cavalry. Their arrival seems to have given the pope courage to move boldly against his enemies, for he tried to enlist the help of the Germans and Spaniards resident in Rome, including innkeepers, merchants and artisans, but they explained that they were unable to do so, Burchard wrote, because 'they were bound to the regionary captains of the city, whose orders they had to obey in an emergency, and that they could not be released from these duties'.

Alexander was now desperate, not knowing whether to stay and defend the Holy See or flee. Burchard described how, as the French army approached, the pope moved all of his belongings to Castel Sant' Angelo, as he and the cardinals prepared for the worst.

On Thursday, December 18th, all the pope's possessions, including his bed and credence table, were assembled for removal by road from the Vatican Palace to Castel Sant' Angelo. The vestments from the Apostolic Chapel, all the money chests from the sacristy, the palace weapons and stores of food, and all the papal belongings were sent to the castle, while the cardinals also prepared to leave, loading packhorses and furnishing their mounts for the road.

The pope's most valuable possession, Jem, was also moved to the Castel Sant' Angelo. With the help of the architect Antonio da Sangallo the Elder, Alexander had had the defences of the castle greatly strengthened, erecting bastions at the four corners of its outer walls to protect his residence at the uppermost level of the fortress, and it was here that Jem would be kept, close by the pope and under heavy guard.

The port of Civitavecchia was taken by the French on 17 December, and the same day the Orsini went over to the French and admitted them to their fortress of Bracciano, north-west of Rome, where Charles set up his headquarters. French troops had already taken a number of castles along the roads leading into Rome, building wooden bridges over the Tiber, and by 19 December they had even reached the walls of Rome, where, according to Marino Sanudo, they challenged the Neapolitan troops to come out and do battle with them. Burchard reports that on that day the first French outposts appeared on Monte Mario, overlooking Rome on the north-west, and thereon their cavalry could be seen from the Vatican. During the next three days French troops broke into the city suburbs by Monte Mario and penetrated as far as the church of San Lazzaro and the fields close to the Castel Sant' Angelo, where they seemed poised for an attack on the fortress. Jem would have been able to see the French troops from the terrace of the papal apartments. Watching them he doubtless wondered how this new and dramatic turn of events would affect his fate, for he knew that Charles, the King of France, had come to get him.

16

A Captive of the French King

B Y THE END OF DECEMBER 1494 food supplies in Rome had just about run out, though Castel Sant' Angelo was still well stocked for a long siege. But the people of Rome had no intention of subjecting themselves to such a protracted war, and they made it known to the pope that if he did not come to terms with Charles within two days they would themselves admit the king into the city.

Ferrantino, the Duke of Calabria, urged the pope to excommunicate Charles VIII and retire with the cardinals into the Kingdom of Naples. The duke's father, Alfonso II, had offered to give the pope the castle of Gaeta north of Naples as his residence, and to pay him an annual subsidy of 50,000 ducats, plus another 10,000 ducats to maintain Jem Sultan, promising at the same time that he would not reach a separate agreement with Charles.

Alexander now feared that he would lose the papacy along with Rome. He had nourished hopes that Emperor Maximilian and Ferdinand of Spain would come to his aid, and even that the Venetians might help him. But these possible allies were all far away, and the French army was almost at the gates of Rome. Thus Alexander finally decided to submit to Charles, and on Christmas morning 1494 he sent his nephew Juan Borgia-Lanzol, Archbishop of Monreale, as an envoy to the French headquarters at Bracciano. Before attending mass at the Sistine Chapel, Alexander summoned the college of cardinals to the Sala del Pappagallo and briefed them on all that had been happening. After mass the pope met privately with Ferrantino and told him of his decision to come to terms with Charles, informing him that the king had demanded that the Neapolitan army be withdrawn from Rome before the French entered the city. Ferrantino led his troops out of Rome that same day under a promise of safe conduct from the French.

That evening three French envoys entered Rome, and by the next day they had come to an agreement with Alexander on the arrangements for the formal French entry into the city. Charles himself would enter Rome on New Year's Eve and take up residence in the Palazzo San Marco. Meanwhile Alexander received the envoys of the foreign powers and the Cardinal of Naples in the Vatican. It was agreed that no Frenchman was to enter the Borgo, the neighbourhood between St Peter's and Castel Sant' Angelo where the foreign colonies were located. The disposal of the troops and the maintenance of order were entrusted to a commission which consisted of the Cardinal of St Denis, the governor and the conservators. On 30 December, Count Gilbert Montpensier, *maréchal* of the French army in Italy, would enter Rome as military governor.

Several points of contention still remained to be settled, but these were put aside to be discussed when Charles and the pope met in Rome. One of these was the question of Jem Sultan's custody. Charles demanded that Alexander unconditionally surrender Jem to him, while the pope was unwilling to give up the Turkish prince until the king was actually ready to embark on his crusade, and even then only for a limited period of time. Charles agreed to respect all the pope's rights, both temporal and spiritual. All of Rome on the left bank of the Tiber was to be occupied by the French troops, while the pope's army, consisting only of 1,000 horsemen and a few soldiers, occupied the Borgo.

Meanwhile Alexander returned to the Vatican, taking Jem with him. There he shut himself in the papal apartments, surrounded by his Catalan bodyguard, ready if necessary to make his way back to the Castel Sant' Angelo by a secret covered passageway.

On 27 December an advance force of 1,500 French troops entered Rome with the permission of the pope. As soon as news of this spread through the city the populace began to display the French arms before their doors. On the morning of 31 December representatives of the citizens of Rome went to meet Charles, as Gregorovius recorded, 'to recommend the welfare of the city to his care and to accompany him thither'. They were accompanied by two papal envoys, the Bishop of Nepi and the pope's master of ceremonies, Johann Burchard, who was to meet the king, 'to inform him of the ceremonial order of his reception'. Charles replied that he wanted to enter the city without undue pomp, whereupon the Roman officials withdrew, and as Burchard wrote,

> King Charles invited me to continue with him, and for four miles or so on the ride, he talked with me, unceasingly asking questions about the ceremonies to be performed, the state of the pope and the cardinals, the power and rank of Cardinal Cesare Borgia of Valencia, and many other things, to all of which I was scarcely able to give appropriate answers.

The French army reached Rome by mid-afternoon and were greeted by cheering crowds as they marched along the Via Lata, which, as soon as darkness fell, was lit with lanterns and bonfires, for it took over six hours for the troops to pass by. At about seven in the evening Charles himself reached the Porta del Popolo, where Pierre de Rohan, the Maréchal de Gié, was given the keys of the city. Charles rode in warlike attitude, his lance at rest, surrounded by an escort of cavalry and bodyguards. By his side were cardinals Giuliano della Rovere and Ascanio Sforza, followed by the men of the Colonna and Savelli. 'Preceding him came some thousand Swiss and Germans, a splendid force of cavalry with broad swords and long lances, in tight, short, and many-coloured uniforms,' wrote Gregorovius. The king himself

> was followed by 5000 Gascons, almost all archers, short, ugly men; then by cavalry, among them the flower of the French nobility, 5000 horse strong ... what excited the greatest admiration was the artillery; thirty-six bronze cannons, each eight feet long, and weighing six thousand pounds, and conveyed in carriages; also culverins [a long cannon] and smaller artillery. The sight of these troops as they passed through Rome by torchlight inspired terror, more especially as the fitful illumination caused men, horses and arms to appear more than their natural size...

The French king took up residence in the Palazzo San Marco, the dwelling of Cardinal Lorenzo Cibo, who greeted Charles and accompanied him to rooms prepared for his reception. Artillery pieces were mounted around the palace; 2,000 cavalry occupied the Campo dei Fiori, and other troops were dispersed throughout the city at strategic points.

Charles dined alone that evening in the palace, according to

Gregorovius, who noted the measures that were taken to make sure that the king was not poisoned.

> When the King retired he caused his slippers to be put on, went into the dining room, seated himself by the fire, had his hair and beard combed and then went alone to table. A chamberlain tasted every dish; after he had partaken of it, the remains were thrown into a miniature silver vessel on the table. The wine was examined by four of the royal physicians; before the King drank, the chamberlain drew a piece of the horn of a unicorn [!], attached to a gold chain, several times through the goblet.

During the days that followed a succession of cardinals and other dignitaries came to the Palazzo San Marco to wait upon the king, who 'received them without honour', according to Gregorovius. Much of the time was spent negotiating a treaty between France and the papacy, for which the pope had entrusted cardinals Carvajal, Pallavicini and Riario with plenary powers. Charles had three principal demands, the first of which was the right of free passage through the papal states, together with the opportunity to buy supplies at fair prices, and a guarantee for the security of his lines of communication, which would involve the surrender to him of a number of fortresses, including Castel Sant' Angelo. Secondly, he wanted the pope to acknowledge his right to the throne of Naples. Finally he demanded custody of Jem, who, he said, was to be the centrepiece of his forthcoming crusade against the Turks.

Whilst these negotiations were going on, Cardinal Raymond Peraudi was involved in discussions on the king's behalf with Andreas Palaeologus, the Byzantine pretender. Andreas was the son of Thomas Palaeologus, despot of the Morea and younger brother of the last two Byzantine emperors, John VIII and Constantine XI. Pope Sixtus IV had given Andreas the title of 'Despot of the Romans' and provided him with a pension. Andreas had fallen into a dissolute life, marrying a Roman prostitute named Caterina, which led the pope to cancel his pension for a time, though it was later renewed. Without seeking the king's consent, Peraudi persuaded Andreas to sell the Palaeologan rights to the Byzantine empires of both Constantinople and Trebizond, as well as to the Despotate of the Morea. In return for this he was to receive an annual pension of 4,300 gold ducats, of which 2,000 ducats was to be paid to him upon ratification. It is quite possible that Andreas and Jem knew one another, if for no other reason that the two of them have been identified in Pintoricchio's painting of the *Disputation of St Catherine* in the Borgia Apartments, the 'pretenders' to the throne of Byzantium and the Ottoman Empire, both of them living under the protection of the pope. And now the French king had come to buy the title of one of them and to carry away the other, intent on conquering the ancestral domains of both men.

Meanwhile, those members of the Curia who were opposed to Alexander – the cardinals Giuliano della Rovere, Sanseverino, Peraudi, Savelli, Colonna and Ascanio Sforza – urged Charles to assert himself as the reformer of the Church and to depose the pope in favour of a more worthy man. The opposition cardinals had already drawn up the decree of deposition, but Charles had no intention of signing it. As Guillaume Briçonnet wrote at the time to Queen Anne of France, 'the King desires the Reform of the Church but not the deposition of the Pope'. And as the chronicler Philippe de Commines remarked, 'the King was young, and his surroundings were not of a nature to fit him for so great a work as the reform of the Church'.

The French occupation of Rome brought on an outbreak of lawlessness, both by the foreign troops and Roman citizens. Burchard, in writing of the public hangings of thieves that took place at this time, recorded that 'Next night, a great part of the outer wall of the Castel Sant' Angelo collapsed over a length of about thirty feet, that is, from the tower to the gate, and with the fall three people, including the keeper, were killed, all crushed by the wall.' This happened just as the pope, Jem, and a number of cardinals, were taking refuge in the building. According to Burchard, 'It was at this time, if I remember rightly, that His Holiness left the Vatican after supper on January 6th and was carried through the cloisters to the Castel Sant' Angelo for greater safety.'

Another section of the walls of Castel Sant' Angelo collapsed a few days later and Charles demanded that the pope surrender, but Alexander refused, saying: 'I will take my stand on the walls of the fortress with the most sacred relics.' Twice Charles ordered his artillery to be directed against the fortress, but no shots were fired, for the king was unwilling to take such an extreme measure with Jem within its walls.

Confident that the pope would eventually capitulate, Charles decided to bide his time. Toward the end of his second week in Rome he emerged from the Palazzo San Marco to make a tour of Rome and in the days that followed he and his entourage took excursions in the environs of the city.

Finally, on 15 January 1495, the pope agreed to Charles's demands, which had been modified in the course of the negotiations. As Sigismondo de' Conti wrote: 'Although the terms were hard in the extreme, the Pope agreed to everything in fear of being attacked.' By the terms of the agreement Cesare Borgia was to accompany Charles's army on its campaigns as 'cardinal legate' (but really as a hostage) for the next four months. Jem was to be handed over to Charles for the expedition against the Turks, though the pope would continue to receive the 40,000 ducats annually for the prince's pension. The cardinals and others who had joined the French were to receive a complete amnesty. Cardinal Giuliano della Rovere was to retain Ostia and all his other possessions and benefices. The pope would agree to give up the port of Civitavecchia to Charles and to guarantee free passage to the French army through the papal states. Governors acceptable to the king would be appointed to the cities in the papal states and the Marche de Ancona. The pope was to keep Castel Sant' Angelo, and, on the king's departure, the keys of the city were to be returned to Alexander. Charles was to profess obedience to the pope, to impose no restraint upon him either in things spiritual or temporal, and to protect him against all attacks.

The agreement mentioned nothing of the demand of Charles for his investiture as King of Naples, nor was there any mention of a reform of the Church, both of these omissions being victories for the pope. Alexander's opponents were furious about this, with Cardinals Ascanio Sforza and Bernardino de Lunate leaving Rome at once in indignation, though Giuliano della Rovere remained with the king.

The pope now invited Charles to take up residence in the Vatican, where some newly built rooms in the Apostolic Palace had been prepared for him. The king moved into the Vatican the following day, after attending mass at St Peter's, and early that afternoon he met with the pope in person for the first time. As Burchard tells the story, the king, having heard that the pope was returning to the Vatican from Castel Sant' Angelo, rushed out to meet him in the palace garden, accompanied by a number of cardinals. The pope, when he reached the entrance to the garden, stepped down from his litter to proceed on foot, as the cardinals led the king toward him. When Charles caught sight of the pope, he

> twice knelt down at suitable intervals when still some eight feet from him, and this His Holiness pretended not to see, but when His Majesty came closer to genuflect a third time, the pope took off his biretta, with his hand restrained the king from kneeling, and kissed him . . . at their first meeting, both men were bareheaded and the king kissed neither the pope's foot nor his hand. His Holiness refused to put his biretta back on his head until King Charles had put on his cap, but eventually both covered their heads simultaneously, the pope stretching out a hand to aid His Majesty with his cap.

Charles took the opportunity to ask that one of his favourites, Guillaume Briçonnet, Bishop of St-Malo, be made a cardinal, and Alexander granted his request on the spot. Alexander then said that he wished to escort Charles back to the royal apartments, but Charles refused to allow him to do so. Instead the king was accompanied by all the cardinals, walking in pairs, as noted by Burchard who then completes his account of this incident by describing the security arrangements for the royal apartments: 'The palace doors and all other entrances to the king's presence were assigned to the Scottish troops chosen to protect him, and these allowed nobody to enter, except for members of his own household, and a select few of our number.' These were the famous Scots archers who served as mercenaries in the French army, renowned for their strength and military prowess, because of which they were assigned to guard the king.

On 18 January, Charles and the pope met to settle one last point of disagreement, namely the guarantees to be given by the king for the restoration of Jem to the pope after an interval of six months. This was finally settled after an argument that, according to Burchard, lasted for three hours. Burchard describes how the pope set up 'two curial chairs' and 'made the king sit down on one, and then seated himself on the other beside him, whilst the rest of the company assembled before them . . . The articles of the settlement were read out, sworn to and signed, the terms being written out in French for His Majesty and in Latin for the pope.'

The agreement specified that the king was to restore Jem to the pope when he left Italy to return to France. Also Charles was to protect the Holy See if Beyazit should make an attack on the Marche de Ancona or any other papal territory. The French 'nobles, lords and prelates' were to pledge 500,000 ducats as surety for Jem's return, and the prince's annual subsidy of 40,000 ducats was also to be paid if the money was not forthcoming from the sultan. What is more, Giovanni della Rovere was to return to the pope the 40,000 ducats he took from Giorgio Bocciardi when he waylaid the papal and Turkish envoys near Senigallia.

The agreement satisfied the pope and represented another victory for him. The negotiations continued during the days that followed, as Jean de Ganay, president of the French parlement, tried to add new terms to the agreement, but for the moment the pope appeared to be winning the diplomatic contest.

On Monday, 19 January, a public consistory was held in the Sala Reale, the hall between the Apostolic Palace and the Sistine Chapel. When the pope was ready to appear, he told Burchard, his master of ceremonies, 'to go to the King of France and instruct him in what to do and say in kissing His Holiness's foot and in swearing allegiance to him'. When Burchard went to the king's apartment, accompanied by the Bishop of Concordia, they found Charles 'standing by the fire in his apartment, dressed in his doublet with his boots still unlaced'. Burchard explained to Charles that the pope was ready and waiting for him; 'but to this the king replied that when he had dressed he wanted first to hear Mass in St Peter's, then to dine, and that following this he would come to His Holiness. Our efforts were unavailing to persuade him to change his mind.'

After keeping the pope and the cardinals waiting for around two hours, Charles finally arrived in the Sala Reale with his entourage. Then, as Burchard wrote, 'King Charles duly knelt in acts of reverence, first at the entrance to the consistory chamber, the second time in front of the papal throne, and lastly at the throne immediately in front of the pope, whose foot and hand he knelt to kiss and who lifted him up for the kiss on the cheek.' Burchard reminded Charles that he must recite his oath of allegiance, and the king replied that he would do so momentarily. At that moment Jean de Ganay stepped forward and knelt before the pope, declaring that the king had come in person to swear allegiance to His Holiness, but that, like any vassal, he first wished to seek three favours from the pope.

[Charles] desired first of all that every privilege given to him, the Most Christian King, to his wife and to his eldest

son, together with all specified grants in deeds, should be
confirmed by the pope; secondly, that he should be invested
with the Kingdom of Naples; and thirdly, that the article
signed on the preceding day concerning the sureties for the
safe return of the brother of the Grand Turk should be
struck out and destroyed.

The pope, in answering the first petition, said that 'he would
immediately confirm all requests of such a nature in so far as
they could be held to be valid'. He held back on the other two
requests including the one relating to Jem, according to Burchard,
by saying that he needed to deliberate about them with his
cardinals. 'He wanted with them, so he said, to give the king
satisfaction as far as possible. His answer . . . was that he wished
to be in complete harmony with His Majesty and the Sacred
College of Cardinals alike, and did not doubt but that they would
all reach agreement.'

In reply the king declared: 'Most Holy Father, I have come to
render homage and reverence to Your Holiness in the same way
as my predecessors the Kings of France have done.' The king's
statement was then elaborated upon by Jean de Ganay, who said
that his master recognized Alexander 'as the Highest Pontiff of
Christians, the True Vicar of Christ and Successor of the Apostles
Peter and Paul'. The pope, holding the king's right hand,
responded briefly and 'spoke of King Charles as his first-born
son', according to Burchard, who then concluded his account of
the consistory.

When he had made his reply, the pope stood up and led
the king by his left hand back to the Pappagallo where he
took off his vestments, and made out that he wished to
accompany His Majesty further. The king, however, declined

his offer, and after thanking His Holiness returned through
the palace to his own apartment, without any cardinals as
his escort.

The following day, at Charles's request, the pope accompanied
him to mass at St Peter's. Afterwards the pope climbed to the
loggia overlooking St Peter's Square, where a huge crowd had
assembled, and there, according to Burchard, 'he solemnly blessed
the people and gave plenary indulgences . . .' Jem watched the
crowd assembling from the upper terrace of his prison, for a
contemporary chronicler noted his reaction: 'And so the Turk in
the Castel Sant' Angelo could see all these people and was very
surprised.'

After dinner that day the pope held a consistory attended by
eighteen cardinals, though Giuliano della Rovere and Raymond
Peraudi boycotted the meeting. Peraudi seemed to be inclined
toward a reconciliation with Alexander, but on 22 January, in
the presence of two other cardinals, he berated Alexander and,
according to Burchard, 'accused him of simony, sins of the flesh,
and maintaining contacts with the Grand Turk'.

On 21 January, Alexander had shown his gratitude to Charles
by making the king's cousin, Philip of Luxemburg, a cardinal.
Then four days later, on the Feast of the Conversion of St Paul,
the pope and the king, accompanied by the college of cardinals,
proceeded together in state from St Peter's to the basilica of San
Paolo fuori le Mura in a public display of friendship. As the
Mantuan envoy remarked, 'Alexander VI endeavours to gratify
the French in every way; all possible expectancies, reservations
and favours of all sorts are bestowed on them.' The Ferrarese
envoy was certain that Charles had secretly received the investiture
of Naples from the pope, as well as being certified by him as

Emperor of Constantinople. Similar rumours circulated through-out Italy and Germany, and Maximilian had written to protest against Charles's supposed intention of assuming the title of *Imperator Graecorum*, which the king had purchased from Andreas Palaeologus. But later historians have established that Charles obtained nothing from Alexander at this time beyond what was laid down in the agreement of 16 January 1495.

On 21 January, the king accompanied the pope to Castel Sant' Angelo. There Charles met Jem for the first time, speaking to him at length through an interpreter in the presence of the pope. Then, according to Marino Sanudo, the pope said to Jem, 'Monseigneur, the King of France is to take you with him, what do you think about it?' Jem apparently answered bitterly, taking exception to the mocking reference to himself as 'Monseigneur', and answered: 'I am only an unhappy slave, deprived of freedom, and do not give any importance to whether the King of France takes me or if I remain in the hands of the pope.' The pope, embarrassed, replied, 'God forbid that you are a slave; you are, as is the King of France, son of a powerful monarch, and as for myself, I am only an intermediary between you two.' Sanudo, in concluding his account of this interview, remarked thus of Jem Sultan:

> The prince is a terrifying person when in war, cruel and very much loved by the Turks. If it had been God's will, and it was not, that Jem defeated Beyazit and became Seigneur of Turkey, and had the inheritance of Mohammed [Mehmet II] been left to him, even if he was younger than his brother, without doubt the whole of Christianity, the whole of the world, would have been inflicted by him, but God had decided everything and Jem is in our power.

The following Saturday, 24 January, Charles moved out of the Vatican and back into the Palazzo San Marco. His staff had reported that the provisioning of the French army in Rome was becoming daily more difficult, and there were incessant disputes between his soldiers and the townspeople. Charles had no reason to linger in Rome, unless it was to obtain the investiture of the Kingdom of Naples, and this seemed unlikely, in the near future at least, given the pope's dilatory tactics on the matter.

So in late January Charles decided to leave Rome and march on Naples. On the twenty-sixth he was received at the Vatican by the pope and six cardinals, including Cesare Borgia, who was to accompany him. Charles then formally asked the pope to hand over Jem Sultan and Jem was brought from the Castel Sant' Angelo into the meeting hall. The king extended his hand to Jem, who kissed him on the shoulder, and then did the same with the pope. The pope addressed the cardinals, saying, according to Marino Sanudo: 'Monseigneurs, I hand over Jem Sultan to the King in your presence, in virtue of our agreement.' Jem then asked the pope to recommend him to the king. Charles responded with grace, assuring Jem that he had nothing to fear, and that he would take him under his protection. Jem on his part thanked Alexander for freeing him, saying, 'The great King of the West and the victorious arms of the Christians would gain him the Ottoman throne.'

The next evening Jem, accompanied by his officers and servants, was taken from the Castel Sant' Angelo and brought to the Palazzo San Marco, where he was formally handed over to King Charles VIII. The following day the king and his entourage rode back to the Vatican to bid farewell to the pope before leaving Rome. There, according to Burchard, the king knelt down bareheaded, and the pope, removing his biretta, kissed him, but refused quite firmly to allow him to smother his feet with kisses, which His Majesty seemed to want to do. The king then departed, mounting his horse at the steps of the gate of the private garden, after waiting for a brief period for Cardinal Cesare Borgia to join him.

As the pope and the cardinals looked on Cesare Borgia appeared

wearing his cardinal's hood, and, with Alexander's permission, mounted the horse beside the king. To His Majesty he presented six exceedingly beautiful horses which stood ready at hand with bridles but no saddles, and then both the king and the cardinal departed, leaving the others watching. King Charles had flatly refused to allow the cardinals as a body to accompany him further because he did not want the delay of a ceremonial departure from Rome . . .

Burchard concluded his account of the departure of King Charles, whose plans called for him and his entourage, including Jem, to spend the night in Marino, the first stage on the road between Rome and Naples.

On that same day, January 28th, His Majesty and Don Cesare [Borgia] rode straight to Marino, and Cardinals della Rovere, Savelli and Colonna, and a Judge of the Chamber, also left Rome at the same time to go with the king. Cardinal Peraudi followed on the same evening with another cardinal riding as his companion as far as the frontier of the Kingdom of Naples. Shortly before the royal departure, Prince Djem too had set out, under a strong guard, to go to Marino and thence travel with the king. When His Majesty had departed from Rome, Cardinal Caraffa came to stay with the pope, and the other cardinals all dispersed to their own homes.

Thus Jem finally left Rome, where he had been a prisoner of two successive popes for five years, ten months and twelve days, now a captive of the French king, heading once more into an uncertain future.

17

From Rome to Naples

O N 22 JANUARY 1495 King Alfonso II renounced his throne and fled from Naples, dying in exile on 10 November of that same year. Alfonso's son Ferrantino (Ferdinand II) was left to rule the ruined kingdom his father had abandoned, with the enemy at the gate. News of Alfonso's abdication reached Rome on the evening of 28 January, just after Charles VIII had led the French army out of the city, and word of Ferrantino's succession to the throne came the following evening. As Burchard writes of this dynastic change in his diary:

> On that same evening, His Holiness learned that King Alfonso had fled from Naples, taking a great amount of the treasure in four galleys in order to sail to Sicily and to recruit forces against the French king. Next day, in the evening, we heard further that Don Ferrantino, the Duke of Calabria, had assumed in marriage Donna Isabella of Aragon, the daughter of his grandfather King Ferrante, and his own aunt. Moreover, it was said, he had ridden through Naples as king, receiving oaths of homage from all, setting at liberty citizens and nobles who had been imprisoned by his father and grandfather, and executing some who were identifying themselves with the French cause.

Charles VIII spent the night of 28 January at Marino. Cardinal Giuliano della Rovere was waiting there with good news, informing him that Alfonso II had abdicated, and that Prince Jem and his guard had already arrived in Marino. The following day Charles directed his hostage, Cesare Borgia, to precede him into Velletri, the next stop along the road to Naples, while the king consulted with his advisors and indulged in a spot of hunting.

Cesare had already put into operation a plan to escape. On his departure from Rome with King Charles, according to Burchard, Cesare

> had arranged for nineteen mules to follow him, laden with his goods and apparently wearing rich trappings; amongst them were two beasts carrying his valuables. On the first day out, however, when his Majesty and the Cardinal were still on their way to Marino, these beasts had remained behind and returned to the city in the evening, whilst the cardinal's servants made the excuse at the king's court that the mules had been seized and despoiled by thieves.

As soon as Cesare arrived in Velletri, he was lodged in the municipal palace by the French, who were already in control of the town and guarding its gates. Aided by a relative named Pietro Sorio Borgia, Cesare disguised himself as a groom. Then under cover of night he was lowered from the walls and mounted a horse that was provided for him, whereupon he made his way back to Rome and went into hiding in the house of Antonio Flores, the nuncio to France.

Charles did not learn of Cesare's escape until the early afternoon of his second day at Velletri. He was sure that Cesare had received help from friends in the town, and so in his fury he ordered that Velletri should be sacked and burned the following morning. Cardinal Giuliano della Rovere, who was Bishop of Ostia and Velletri, intervened on behalf of the terrified inhabitants and persuaded Charles to rescind his order and spare the town. Meanwhile Cesare had left Rome, going first to Rignano and then to Spoleto, while the pope maintained that he knew nothing about his son's whereabouts. Charles sent Philip of Brest to complain to the pope, and Alexander responded by sending the Bishop of Nepi with his apologies. Nevertheless, Alexander did not promise Charles that he would require his son to return as legate to the French, nor did he appoint another cardinal to replace Cesare. According to Marino Sanudo, Charles concluded from this and other such incidents that 'the Italians were a pack of rogues, and the Holy Father the worst of all!'

Meanwhile King Ferdinand of Spain had sent two envoys with a message to Charles, declaring that the French had broken the Treaty of Barcelona by their aggression against the Holy See. However, Ferdinand's real motivation was to try to stop Charles from taking Naples, which belonged to a junior branch of the House of Aragon. The Spanish envoys arrived in Rome just after Charles left, but they caught up with him along the road, presenting their credentials to him on horseback. They told Charles that he must abandon his attempt to take Naples or Ferdinand would declare war on him immediately. Charles summarily dismissed them and the envoys left in a fury, after tearing up a copy of the Treaty of Barcelona in front of the king.

Charles, accompanied by Jem, left Velletri on 2 February, moving over the next few days and nights from Valmontone to Castel Ferentino and on to Veroli, where they remained for two days. Ahead of him the French army had been advancing south-eastward, capturing Montefortina on 31 January and San

Germano on 13 February. Charles entered San Germano in triumph, hailed by the townspeople and greeted by a procession of children dressed in white and carrying olive branches. On the following day he wrote to the Duke of Bourbon, dating his letter from San Germano, which he proudly called 'the first town and city of my kingdom of Naples'.

These reverses forced King Ferrantino to fall back upon Capua. Almost two weeks earlier, on 27 January, Ferrantino had written to his envoy in Istanbul, Camillo Pandone, instructing him to urge Sultan Beyazit to fulfil the promises of military aid he had made to Alfonso II. Letters reaching Venice from merchants in Istanbul, dated 19 January, reported that the Turks were making extensive military preparations in both their army and navy, as well as strengthening their fortifications in the Dardanelles, Negroponte and Valona, all indicating the sultan's fear of the French campaign. Beyazit assured Pandone that he would send aid to Ferrantino, and at the envoy's urging the sultan also said that he would punish Genoa for its alliance with France. He would stop Genoa from trading in the Ottoman Empire, and would also send an expedition against the Genoese in Chios. But time was short and there was little hope that these efforts would save Ferrantino. Beyazit knew this and would have taken great satisfaction in the knowledge that the Christians were fighting one another, for while this was going on the threatened crusade was in abeyance.

Shortly after Ferrantino arrived at Capua he was called away by an urgent message from the queen, who informed him that Naples was on the verge of revolt. As soon as Ferrantino departed, two of the three commanders at Capua, Virginio Orsini and the Count of Pitigliano, withdrew with a handful of loyal troops to Nola, east of Naples, while the third, Trivulzio, went to the French camp and announced that the garrison was willing to surrender.

The French entered Capua on 18 February and two days later Charles was at Aversa. Gaeta had already capitulated, though the garrison still held out in the citadel, and at Nola a French unit accepted the surrender of the Neapolitan troops who had retreated from Capua under Virgilio Orsini and the Count of Pitigliano.

Naples had in the meantime degenerated into a state of anarchy, as mobs sacked the Jewish and Marrano quarters and also plundered government buildings and the palaces of the Aragonese nobility. On 20 February a herald sent by Charles to demand the surrender of the city was welcomed by the townspeople. The following morning a delegation of citizens rode out to Poggio Reale to lay their submission at the feet of King Charles, begging him to delay his entry into Naples until they had time to receive him with appropriate ceremony. But Charles was anxious to take possession of his conquest as soon as possible, and on the afternoon of 22 February he rode into Naples without ceremony through the Porta Capuana, accompanied by a small unit of guardsmen.

ೞ

Jem had accompanied the king's entourage almost as far as Capua. But at Theano, a mile or so from Capua, he complained of feeling weak and ill, saying that his condition had been growing worse for several days. By the time they reached Capua, Jem was unable to ride and had to be carried in a litter. Charles was informed and called in his personal physicians to examine the prince. They found that his face, eyelids and throat were swollen; he had a high fever and had trouble breathing. According to Venetian sources, Jem was suffering from a throat infection and 'catarrh', possibly pneumonia, and the royal physicians treated him according to the best traditions of ancient Greek and Arabic medicine, which included bleeding the patient. When the army moved on Charles provided a carriage for Jem, who was treated by the royal physicians en route to Naples, where it was hoped that the prince could receive better medical attention.

When the party arrived in Naples Jem was taken to the Castel Capuana, a fortified palace just inside the Porta Capuana. The doctors were concerned because Jem's pulse was becoming weak and irregular, and they sent word of this to the king, who came at once. According to Sadüddin, when Charles, speaking through an interpreter, asked Jem how he felt, he replied: 'Thank God, I'm fine.' Then Charles said, 'Be in good spirits, my lord. As soon as you get well you'll find freedom and salvation, so don't be upset any longer about being a prisoner.' When the king departed Jem said to his companions, 'Thank God the words freedom and salvation enter my ears. I have always prayed thus: "Oh God, if the infidels want to take me on the pretext of marching on Muslims, then don't let me see those days, and take my soul first."'

Jem seems to have realized that his end had come, and he dictated his last will and testament to his officers. While his companions wept around him, Jem asked them to honour all his debts and to take his body with them if they ever returned to Turkey, for he did not want the *gavurs,* or infidels, to attack Muslim lands in his name. Jem's will included a letter to his brother, in which Jem asked that his family and companions be brought to Istanbul and treated well, for they had not abandoned him even in the most difficult times.

Jem now lapsed into a coma, and though he occasionally regained consciousness he was unable to speak. During one of his periods of consciousness a companion tried to read to him a letter that had just arrived from Jem's mother in Cairo, but he showed no sign that he understood what was being said to him. He clung to life during the night, but then early in the morning of 25 February Jem passed away, as his grieving companions repeated the Islamic prayer for the dead, 'Truly we belong to God and we will come back to Him, this is the fate of the world.' He was two months past his thirty-fifth birthday when he died, having spent a third of his life as an exile and prisoner of the Christians. As Sadüddin wrote of Jem's death, 'After having emptied the cup of martyrdom, he quenched himself at the spring of eternal life in union with God, forgetting forever all the misfortunes he had suffered in this world.'

Jem's companions, unknown to the *gavurs*, prepared the prince's remains for burial in the Muslim manner. Those who were with Jem included Jelal and probably also Sinan, Ayas, Sadi and Haydar. Jelal boiled water and poured it over Jem's body, which Sinan then washed and used the muslin of the prince's turban to wrap his corpse in a tight shroud. Six or seven of his companions assembled to pray around their master's remains, while another went to inform the king of Jem's death.

When Charles learned of Jem's death he was said to have been deeply pained, partly because of the genuine affection he seems to have felt for the Turkish prince, but far more by the lethal blow this dealt to his hope of a crusade. He ordered that Jem's death be kept a secret, but the Florentine envoy informed his government of the prince's demise that same day. Under orders from the king, the Turkish officers guarding Jem kept up the pretence that he was still alive for three days, but soon everyone in Naples knew that the prince had passed away.

Word of Jem's death reached Rome late on the day that he died, as Burchard noted in his diary, after writing of the escape of Cesare Borgia, 'We learned later on February 25th that Prince Djem had died in the Castel Capuana in Naples, through eating and drinking something unsuitable for him.' Burchard seems to be hinting here that Jem had been poisoned. Indeed, the French swiftly accused the pope of having poisoned Jem out of anger at having lost his valuable hostage, saying that Alexander had given the prince a slow-acting potion in Rome that took effect only when he was well on the road to Naples, reinforcing the image of the Borgias as poisoners which persists to this day. But Burchard, the pope's faithful master of ceremonies, would not have meant his words to have been interpreted this way. He was far too aware of the accusations being levelled against his master, whom he served loyally. It is unlikely also considering that Jem's chief taster, Ayas Bey, was with his master constantly, right to the end. The Venetian Marino Sanudo, hardly a sympathetic commentator on the Borgia pope, wrote in his diary that the accusation against the pope could not be true, for he had nothing to gain in killing Jem: '[Jem's] death was a very great loss to the king of France as to all Italy, and especially to the pope, for it deprived him of the 40,000 ducats of gold which he received every year from his brother [the sultan] by reason of having custody of him.'

Despite all this, the accusation that Alexander Borgia poisoned Jem Sultan persisted, particularly in view of the letter intercepted months earlier supposedly written by Beyazit offering the pope a huge sum to have his brother killed. Historians from the nineteenth century onwards have been inclined to believe that for all his many other sins, Alexander Borgia was innocent of this one: Ludwig Pastor, for example, wrote, 'It is clear that Dschem died a natural death; probably the result of his disorderly life.' And Mallett, writing in the 1960s, says that 'All the indications are that the unhappy Turkish prince died of natural causes.' According to the recent historian of the crusades, Norman Housley, '. . . Jem died, probably of pneumonia . . .' Modern medical opinion believes that Jem died of pneumonia or erysipelas, an acute streptococcal infectious disease of the skin.

One might also have expected suspicion to have fallen on Beyazit, that one of his assassins poisoned his brother, particularly because of the several occasions on which he is known to have tried to do just that. But no one in Europe at the time accused him of having been responsible for Jem's death, not even the Venetians, who were in a far better position than anyone else to know what the sultan was doing.

The earliest Turkish source on Jem's death (aside from the *Vakiat-i-Sultan Cem*, written by one of Jem's close companions) is by the chronicler Idris, writing some fifteen years after the prince's death. Idris based his story largely on what he was told by the Turkish envoy, Mustafa Pasha, soon to be appointed grand vezir. It is clear from his account that Idris did not realize that the pope who signed the non-aggression pact with Beyazit was not the same as the one who last had custody of Jem. According to Idris, writing of the pope's response to the French king's demand for custody of Jem:

> Since the pope considered himself in the religious and worldly affairs the highest authority and successor to Jesus Christ he always rejected the request of the king [Charles VIII] in order not to infringe upon the agreement he had solemnly sworn with the sultan.

He continues: the French king marched 'on Rome, which is equal to Mecca in the eyes of the Christians', whereupon he took Jem by force from the pope, who decided to retaliate:

> It is a widely circulated rumour that the pope secretly instructed a man who came into Jem Sultan's service as a bath attendant and chief barber, and secretly put a deadly poison at the back of a razor. When he shaved Jem with this poisoned razor it caused a fatal disease and the demise of Jem who, until that time, had been a healthy and strong man. He died in this way in the company of the King of France, and, thus, the king's evil plans and ideas came to nothing.

ಖಞ

After the Florentine envoy broke the news of Jem's death to his government, he informed the Council of Ten in Venice, adding that, in his opinion, the cause of death was pneumonia, brought on by the prince's removal from Rome in inclement weather. The Council immediately sent Andrea Gritti with the news on a fast galley to Istanbul, where he arrived on 20 April. Gritti informed Sultan Beyazit of Jem's death, which, he explained, was from natural causes, probably pneumonia. He also told the sultan that the French had captured Naples. When Beyazit heard of his brother's death he said: 'Then it is true; we have already been informed, but did not wish to believe it.' Beyazit then raised his hands, as if giving thanks to God, saying 'Allah, Allah!', and said to Gritti that he was grateful to Venice for informing him and that he would always be a great friend of the Venetians. He told Gritti that he wanted to secure his brother's body, and that he would send an envoy to speak with Charles.

Although Beyazit did not yet know it, he now had nothing to fear from the French campaign, for Jem's death had stopped Charles's plan for a crusade against the Turks in its tracks, marking a watershed in European–Ottoman relations. Sigismondo de' Conti wrote that after the death of Jem Sultan, Charles 'seemed to have abandoned all talk of a war against the Turks'. Although the French had entered Naples, a number of castles in and around the city continued to hold out, most notably Castel Nuovo and Castel dell' Ovo, both of which commanded the port quarter and the harbour. The defence of Castel Nuovo was entrusted by Ferrantino to the Marquis of Pescaro, one of the very few Aragonese generals who had remained loyal to the king in his hour of defeat. Ferrantino himself, along with his family and retainers, took refuge in the Castel dell' Ovo, a massive fortress built on a sea-girt rock joined to the mainland only by a narrow causeway ending in a drawbridge. The fortress was exposed to gunfire from the shore, however, and when the French artillery arrived it was no longer safe for the royal family to remain. And so on 23 February Ferrantino gathered his household together and set sail for the isle of Ischia in the Bay of Naples, and from there he eventually retired to Sicily. Once Ferrantino departed the Marquis of Pescaro fled from Naples, leaving the garrison of the Castel Nuovo to surrender to the French on 7 March. Then on 23 March the Neapolitan garrison in the citadel at Gaeta capitulated to the French, who now had complete control of Naples and its environs.

Charles had in the meanwhile arranged for Jem's body to be embalmed and then preserved in a sealed lead coffin within the Castel Capuana, where it was guarded night and day by the prince's companions. After the French occupied the citadel at Gaeta, Charles decided that Jem's coffin would be more secure there. And so Jem's remains were moved to Gaeta, under the command of Etienne de Vesc, who instructed the prince's Turkish attendants to maintain their guard night and day over their master's coffin. According to Sadüddin, the two companions who were placed in charge of the deathwatch were Jelal and Ayas, who had known Jem better than anyone, having been his companions since they and the prince had played together as children. If ever any question arose about the identity of the deceased Jelal and Ayas would know, for they could identify their beloved master even in death.

Contemporary chroniclers marvelled at the ease with which Charles had marched through Italy and taken the capital of the Neapolitan kingdom, as if, wrote one of them, 'the conquest of Naples was no work of human hands, but was an operation proceeding from the Divine Providence'. As Sigismondo de' Conti was led to remark: 'I have no doubt but what these events will seem to posterity not like facts, but fiction.' And as Francis Bacon wrote more than a century later in his history of the reign of Henry VII, Charles had:

conquered the realm of Naples in a kind of felicity of a dream. He passed the whole of Italy without resistance; so that it was true which Pope Alexander was wont to say, that the Frenchmen came into Italy with chalk in their hands to mark their lodgings, rather than with swords to fight.

Word of the French conquest of the Kingdom of Naples spread through the Muslim world as well, causing universal dismay that this might be the beginning of another crusade, as Arnold von Harff, a German pilgrim to the Holy Land, noted in his journal:

> The Turks and heathens at that time were in great perturbation and anxiety, because King Charles of France had taken Naples, Apulia and Calabria by force, and there were rumours in the land that he was about to cross the sea, in order to march against Jerusalem by force and conquer the Holy Land.

But at the very moment of victory Charles had lost the central figure of the crusade, for which his capture of Naples had supposedly been the springboard. For he no longer had possession of Jem Sultan, the symbolic figurehead for his reconquest of Constantinople and the Holy Land, whose lifeless body was now shrouded within a lead coffin in the citadel at Gaeta. There Jem remained, guarded in solitude by his ever-faithful companions, an exile even in death, as another international struggle developed around him, this time involving the possession of his remains.

18

From Naples to Istanbul

J EM CONTINUED to be a factor in international politics even after his death. The European states knew that Beyazit was anxious to have his brother's body returned to Turkey, and past experience indicated that the sultan would be willing to pay for this, either with money or with pledges not to attack Christendom. And so Jem's coffin was closely guarded in the citadel of Gaeta, where the prince's companions kept up their lonely vigil.

The first attempt to obtain Jem's body was made by Pope Alexander VI not long after the prince's death in February 1495. Alexander sent an envoy to Charles VIII in Naples asking for the prince's body, which he said cynically had 'negotiable value'. Charles refused outright, saying that since he had taken custody of Jem the prince's mortal remains now belonged to him.

The second was made in May 1495, when Beyazit sent an envoy to Naples to negotiate with the French king. The envoy, in the name of the sultan, promised to send Charles several precious relics if he would return Jem's body, but the king turned down the offer, possibly because the price he had in mind was much higher. The envoy then asked for proof that the body so closely guarded at Gaeta was really that of the sultan's brother. He was thereupon brought to Gaeta to interview the prince's companions, particularly Jelal and Ayas, who assured him that they had kept watch over their beloved master since the moment of his death.

Another of Jem's companions, Sinan Bey, had managed to escape in the interim and make his way back to Istanbul to inform Beyazit that his brother was dead, and that his remains were being guarded at Gaeta. But even this assurance did not satisfy Beyazit. He would not be contented, it was said, until Jem's body had been returned to Turkey and buried there.

Sinan Bey's testimony did, however, lead Beyazit to proclaim a three-day period of mourning throughout the Ottoman Empire. This was customary on the death of prominent members of the royal family, and suited Beyazit's purpose of letting everyone know that his rival was no more. All shops in Istanbul were closed for three days, and prayers for the repose of Jem's soul were said in every mosque in the city, while alms were distributed to the poor in the name of the departed prince. Beyazit wore black robes throughout the three days of mourning, at the beginning and end of which all the pashas and other high officials of government came to the palace of Topkapı Sarayı to offer their condolences to the sultan. There are no records of the public reaction to Jem's death, but tradition holds that his passing caused profound sadness in Anatolia, where his following had always been strongest.

During the early days of the French occupation of Naples, Charles and his court had been in raptures with the beauty and abundance of the Kingdom that they had conquered. As Charles wrote to his brother-in-law the Duke of Bourbon on Naples on his first day there: 'So far as I have seen this Kingdom at present, it is a fine and fair country, full of goods and riches; and this city is in every respect as lovely and splendid a town as you can find.' But the mood soon changed, for the arrogance, incompetence and avarice of the French rulers, together with the excesses of their army of occupation, turned everyone against them, from the aristocracy to the ordinary townspeople. The situation was exacerbated by an outbreak of syphilis, which seems to have been introduced into Europe in 1493 by the sailors of Columbus when they returned from the West Indies. Camp followers in the French army probably spread the disease in Italy during the campaign of Charles VIII, particularly in the occupation of Naples. According to the Italian historian Matarazzo, 'As the French were newly come to Italy, the Italians believed that the disease had come from France, whilst the French, to whom it was new, supposed it to be a malady prevalent in Italy; the Italians accordingly called it the French disease, and the French called it the Italian disease.'

While Charles was enjoying himself in Naples, trouble was brewing in the north, where an anti-French coalition known as the Holy League was being formed. The league formally came into being in Venice on 31 March 1495, when a twenty-five-year alliance was concluded between Doge Agostino Barbarigo of Venice, Ferdinand and Isabella of Spain, Maximilian I of Germany, Duke Lodovico il Moro of Milan, and Pope Alexander VI, whose proclaimed goals included the defence of Christendom against the Turks, the preservation of the dignity of the Holy See and the rights of the Holy Roman Empire, as well as the defence of one another's dominions against the attacks of foreign powers. Henry VII of England joined the league in July 1496, making it a truly pan-European coalition against France. Marino Sanudo mentions secret articles in the treaty, which undoubtedly dealt with the expulsion of the French from Italy.

On 5 April the Venetian envoy in Naples officially informed Charles of the league's founding, which infuriated the king, all the more so because he realized that he was trapped. He thereupon decided to leave half of his force in Naples, and with the other half to march swiftly back to France. But he wasted precious time in trying to persuade the pope to grant him the investiture of the Kingdom of Naples. The pope temporized, as always, and in his reply he once again requested that the body of Jem Sultan be returned to him. Charles now realized that the pope had no intention of granting the investiture, and so he had himself crowned in the cathedral at Naples on 12 May, proceeding to and from the church in procession with a splendid retinue, while the hostile townspeople looked on in cold silence. Eight days later the king left the city with half of his army, while the other half remained under Maréchal Montpensier to hold the Kingdom of Naples.

Pope Alexander fled from Rome at the approach of the French, along with the college of cardinals and the diplomatic corps, taking refuge first at Orvieto and then at Perugia. Charles re-entered Rome on 1 June, remaining for just two days before leading his army northwards, gathering up the French garrisons in towns along the way.

The French encountered no resistance until they reached Fornovo di Taro, fifteen miles south-west of Parma at the foot

of the Apennines, where they found their way barred by a fortified camp of the Holy League. The allied army, commanded by
Gian-Francesco Gonzaga of Mantua, far outnumbered the French,
whose force had been reduced to little more than 10,000. The
two armies clashed on the west bank of the Taro on 6 July 1495,
in an intense battle that lasted only an hour but left the field
covered with dead, at least 3,500 on the allied side, only 200 on
the French. Charles fought in the thick of the fray, leading an
Italian historian to write that the king had 'behaved rather as a
common soldier than a general'. Both sides claimed victory, but
more importantly Charles was able to take his army through
the Apennines to safety at Asti, after having been very nearly
surrounded and annihilated by the Holy League.

Charles halted at Asti, for his kinsman the Duke of Orleans
was trapped at Novara, thirty miles west of Milan, where he was
besieged by the Germans and Italians under Lodovico il Moro.
A peace treaty was finally signed at Vercelli on 10 October 1496,
and Orleans evacuated Novara, leaving Charles free to return to
France. Charles finally reached Lyon early in November, after
which, according to Commines, 'he cared only to amuse himself
and make good cheer and tourney'.

Meanwhile Pope Alexander had re-entered Rome on 27 June
with twenty-one cardinals, where he was enthusiastically welcomed by the populace. He threatened Charles with excommuni-
cation for the offences committed by the French in Italy, and
reminded him of the grievous loss which the Christian cause had
suffered in the death of Jem Sultan, which he blamed on the king.
Charles wrote back to the pope to say that he intended to preserve
his Kingdom of Naples, whose capital at the moment was being
defended by Maréchal Montpensier.

King Ferrantino had already begun a campaign to recapture his kingdom, crossing the Strait of Messina and capturing Reggio di Calabria on 20 May 1495, the same day that Charles left Naples. Around that time a Turkish ship arrived in Brindisi bringing an envoy of Beyazit, who offered to send Ferrantino 18,000 troops. There is no record of Ferrantino's response, but it appears that the Turkish envoy was told that the sultan's troops were not yet needed. Beyazit's approach to Ferrantino was triggered, it seems, by fear that Charles might yet embark on a crusade. This is confirmed by a report from Alvise Sagundino, the Venetian envoy to the Porte, who wrote that Beyazit was still not absolutely convinced of Jem's death, and continued to fear that his brother would be used by the Christians in a war against him.

On 6 July 1495, the same day as the battle of Fornova, Ferrantino arrived in Naples with his army aboard a Spanish fleet. By the end of the day Ferrantino's troops had control of all of the city except for Castel Nuovo and Castel dell' Ovo, where Maréchal Montpensier still held out with his garrison. The French also continued to hold the fortress at Gaeta across the gulf to the north-west, where Jem's companions still guarded their master's remains.

Montpensier took the opportunity of a truce to escape to Salerno with 2,500 of his troops, leaving only a skeleton force in the two Neapolitan castles. Castel Nuovo finally surrendered on 8 December 1495, and Castel dell' Ovo capitulated on 17 February 1496, whereupon all of Naples was once again in the control of King Ferrantino, though a French garrison continued to hold out in Gaeta.

On 21 January 1496 Ferrantino signed a treaty with the Signoria, putting the Kingdom of Naples under the protection of Venice.

The Venetians promised to aid Ferrantino with their fleet and an army of 700 men-at-arms and 6,000 infantry, along with financial assistance, for the king was virtually bankrupt.

A Turkish envoy arrived in Gaeta early in February 1496, with instructions from Beyazit to negotiate for the return of his brother's remains. The envoy spoke to the commander of the garrison, the king's favourite Etienne de Vesc, who told him that the French king was ready to sell Jem's body for 5,000 ducats, a sum so small as to indicate that Charles was anxious for ready cash. The envoy was to return within two months with the money, and Etienne de Vesc provided him with a passport and pledge of safe conduct so that he could pass through the French lines. De Vesc then departed for France to obtain supplies and reinforcements for the garrison at Gaeta, which was to be a base for the anticipated French recapture of Naples. As the Turkish envoy and his Greek interpreter left Gaeta, they were arrested by French troops, despite the fact that their papers were in order. The interpreter managed to save himself by offering a bribe, but the Turkish envoy disappeared and was never heard from again.

The garrison at Gaeta continued to hold out, and early in 1496 a French squadron broke through the Aragonese blockade and landed supplies for the fortress, which was reinforced with 2,000 troops, mostly Swiss. By this time Montpensier had begun implementing his plan to gather up the French troops scattered around the country. When this was done Montpensier hoped to recapture Naples, but that summer his forces were trapped by Gonsalvo de Cordoba and he was forced to surrender. According to the terms of the capitulation, the French were to retire to the Bay of Naples and await ships that would evacuate them to France. But while they waited the French were struck by a deadly epidemic of malaria which killed most of them, including Maréchal Montpensier, who died on 5 October.

King Ferrantino was a victim of the same epidemic, succumbing to malaria two days later. He was succeeded by his uncle Federigo d'Aragona, Prince of Altamura, who thus became the fifth king to occupy the throne of Naples within three years, including Charles VIII.

Meanwhile, Etienne de Vesc returned from France with supplies for Gaeta and 800 troops to reinforce the garrison in the citadel, which was being besieged by King Federigo and Prospero Colonna. Despite the reinforcements and fresh supplies, the garrison at Gaeta eventually capitulated on 16 November.

According to the agreement, all of the officers and men-at-arms in the garrison, French and others, were to be allowed to leave unharmed within ten days following 19 November. The last article in the capitulation concerned Jem's remains. It stipulated that the coffin and its guards, the prince's faithful companions, were to be given over to the King of Naples, who would in turn release all French prisoners in his galleys.

The citadel was evacuated on 29 November, whereupon King Federigo and representatives of the Holy League took possession of Gaeta. The Venetian envoy went to see the lead coffin that contained Jem's body, still guarded by Jelal and Ayas, who attested to the authenticity of the remains. Then in December Federigo transported the coffin to Naples, where it was placed in the Castel dell' Ovo, with Jem's companions instructed to continue their vigil over their master's body.

The remaining French units and garrisons in the Kingdom of Naples soon surrendered, the last place to submit being Taranto, which opened its gates to the Aragonese on 18 January 1497. By

March, Don Gonsalvo Fernando of Cordoba succeeding in forcing the French to surrender the fortress at Ostia, so that ships could once again go up the Tiber to supply Rome.

On 8 June Cesare Borgia was appointed by his father as papal legate to Naples, with the responsibility of crowning Federigo in the name of the pope. The mission was delayed by the death of Juan Borgia, who was murdered in Rome on 14 June. Cesare finally left Rome on 22 July, accompanied by a retinue of 300 horsemen, to crown Federigo as King of Naples, a ceremony performed at Capua in mid-August.

This, however, was the highpoint in relations between Federigo and the pope, which began to deteriorate soon afterwards, partly due to a row over custody of Jem's remains. Pope Alexander insisted that Federigo hand over Jem's body to him, but the king refused, having no intention of giving away such a precious possession. The pope had already sent George Buzardo as an envoy to Istanbul, with instructions to negotiate with Beyazit over the return of Jem's body. Federigo now sent his own envoy to Istanbul with a message for Beyazit, offering to sell the sultan his brother's remains. But Beyazit dismissed both envoys, believing that he could force Federigo to return Jem's body without having to pay for it.

When Federigo negotiated for peace with the Porte, his envoy Tommaso Palaeologo Asani was told not to introduce any clause involving the handing over of Jem's remains. The treaty was formally signed in Istanbul on 25 July 1498; by its terms it was to endure only for the lives of the two rulers, and would not be fully confirmed by Beyazit until Jem's body had been returned to Turkey.

Meanwhile Charles VIII had, in the spring of 1498, returned

to his childhood home in the chateau at Amboise, where he supervised the work of reconstruction that had been initiated by his father. He had brought back with him from Naples twenty-two Italian artists as well as 87,000 pounds of loot including paintings, sculptures, tapestries and rare books, assigning his tent-maker Nicolas Fagot to use them to transform Amboise into the Italian paradise that he had been denied.

On the morning of Saturday, 7 April, the eve of Palm Sunday, Charles went out hunting and returned late in the morning, after which he dined and visited the queen's apartment. A temporary tennis court had been set up in the palace moat, and he asked the queen to accompany him to watch a match that was to be played there that afternoon. The approach was through a gallery entered through a low door, where Charles, forgetting to stoop, struck his head. At first he showed no ill effects from the blow, as he sat in the gallery watching the match and talking with his courtiers. But then he suddenly fell backwards and lay uncon-scious, while doctors summoned to the gallery tried to revive him, but to no avail, and soon after sunset he was pronounced dead.

Charles was only twenty-eight at the time of his death. Philippe de Commines wrote of him: 'He was little learned, but so good it was impossible to find a better creature.' Since Charles had no living children the throne passed to the Duke of Orleans, who succeeded as Louis XII, ending the direct line of the Valois and replacing it with the Valois-Orleans.

Pope Alexander sent three apostolic nuncios to France on 4 June to console Louis on Charles's death and to congratulate him on his accession. The nuncios were also instructed to tell him that the pope had, since the time of his own accession, wanted to organize a crusade against the Turks, the 'perpetual enemies of our faith', and that though it had not been possible in the past, the time was again ripe: the accession of Louis, he said, gave him hope that the Christian commonwealth could unite and embark upon this expedition. Knowing that Louis had ambitions in Italy, to exercise his hereditary rights to both the Kingdom of Naples and the Duchy of Milan, Alexander said that he would carefully examine the first claim, but he warned the king against the second one. As the pope wrote in his instructions to his nuncios:

> But if his Majesty decides to reject our counsel and invade the duchy [of Milan], let him carefully consider that so great an effort of war will bring to both the Italian and French nations the destruction of cities, slaughter of peoples, and that [his Majesty] will receive more of calamity and infamy than honour and glory from such a renewal of the tumults of war!

Alexander also instructed the nuncios to remind Louis of his obligations to honour the agreement that Charles VIII had made with the pope concerning Jem Sultan, specifically the payment of the 40,000 ducats that was due for the late prince's 'pension'.

Toward the end of the year, King Federigo of Naples tried to renew negotiations with Beyazit over the return of Jem's body to Turkey. Beyazit's patience was almost exhausted, and he sent the king one final message. Early in January 1499 a Turkish ship landed at San Cataldo, the port of Lecce on the heel of Italy, carrying Beyazit's envoy, who then proceeded to Naples. When he met King Federigo the envoy conveyed Beyazit's warning that if Jem's body was not turned over to his representatives within eight days the sultan would launch an attack on the kingdom. The king was terrified, and on 29 January he submitted to the sultan's demand.

Jem's companions were told that their master's body was finally going to be taken back to Turkey. They thereupon covered the coffin with a gold-embroidered cloth, and then, together with the Aragonese guards, they carried it from Castel dell' Ovo to Poggio Reale. There it was put on an ox-cart to be transported to San Cataldo, where it was to be loaded on a Turkish ship.

The pope was outraged when he heard that Federigo had acceded to Beyazit's demand, and he wrote to the king and reproached him bitterly for moving Jem's remains without papal permission. But Alexander knew that there was nothing that he could now do about the situation, for his captive had finally been taken out of his reach.

Jem's coffin arrived in Lecce in the first week of March, when word was received that a flotilla of seven Turkish ships was anchored in Valona waiting to receive it. A Turkish agent was posted in Lecce to inform the commander of the flotilla as soon as formalities were completed, but difficulties must have arisen, because by 23 April nothing had been decided upon.

Rumours abounded about Turkish military preparations in Valona. Mustafa Pasha, the former envoy to Rome, now Ottoman governor of Valona, was in fact assembling a fleet, having the previous September gone to Istanbul seeking permission to descend upon Apulia. These events frightened the inhabitants of Apulia as well as the Venetian representatives in southern Italy, who were aware that the Porte had designs on Otranto. The Venetians were particularly apprehensive about Otranto, because they had reason to believe that the people there, if they had to choose between being ruled by the Ottoman Empire and the Kingdom of Naples, would prefer the Turks.

Federigo became highly alarmed, and in the early days of May 1499 he sent Giacomo Pignatelli to Lecce with orders to take Jem's body and transport it immediately to Turkey, along with the prince's companions and all of his belongings. Pignatelli supervised Jem's companions as they loaded their master's coffin and possessions aboard a ship in San Cataldo, from where they sailed to Valona. There Pignatelli arranged for transport to take them overland to Turkey, passing through Albania, Macedonia and Thrace, and then finally making their way to Istanbul, where Beyazit was waiting for them.

Beyazit received Pignatelli warmly, presenting him with two sumptuously caparisoned horses, one for the King of Naples and the other for his queen. The sultan then confirmed the peace treaty between the Ottoman Empire and the Kingdom of Naples, instructing Pignatelli to convey his best wishes to King Federigo and thanking him for having sent Jem's remains back to Turkey. Pignatelli returned to Lecce on 15 September and immediately went to Naples to report to the king on the successful completion of his delicate mission.

Thus even in death, Jem played a powerful role in the diplomatic manouevring between the Christian states of Europe and the Ottoman Empire, for the return of his remains to Turkey saved the Kingdom of Naples from being destroyed by Beyazit. But by giving up Jem the Christian princes had lost the greatest deterrent to Ottoman aggression to have existed in centuries.

19

The Last Journey

S OON AFTER Jem's body was returned to Istanbul, Beyazit made preparations to have his brother's remains buried in Bursa. And so Jem began one more journey, his last, accompanied as always by his companions, faithful to the end. His coffin was loaded on to a barge and rowed across the Bosphorus to Üsküdar, where it was placed on a cart to be carried around the Gulf of Nicomedeia to Bursa, passing en route the site near Gebze where Jem's father, Mehmet the Conqueror, had died eighteen years before.

Beyazit had Jem laid to rest at the Muradiye in Bursa, the imperial mosque that their grandfather Murat II had built in 1426, and where he was buried in 1451. The tomb chosen by Beyazit for Jem's interment was in the mosque garden just to the south-west of Murat's mausoleum. This was the tomb of their brother Mustafa, built by their father Mehmet II after his second son had died in Anatolia in 1474. Jem was buried there beside Mustafa, probably in the late summer of 1499. No more exact date can be given, for Jem's interment is not recorded in any Ottoman source, and the inscription on his marble catafalque gives only the Islamic years of his birth and death and the fact that he was a son of Mehmet the Conqueror. The two other marble catafalques in the tomb are those of two sons of Beyazit, Abdullah and Alemşah, the first of whom died in 1483 and the second in 1510.

Now that Beyazit no longer had to be concerned about Jem, he was free to resume the campaigns of conquest that had been interrupted by the death of his father eighteen years before. At a consistory held in Rome on 10 June 1499 Pope Alexander VI had a letter read to the cardinals from Pierre d'Aubusson, dated Rhodes, 30 April. The grand master wrote 'that the Turk himself was getting ready a huge fleet of about three hundred sail to lay siege to the city of Rhodes, where he was expected to arrive for certain sometime in May'. D'Aubusson expected that the siege would be a long one, 'because the Turk [Beyazit] was coming in person to the nearby province of Lycia, where vast preparations were being made of all things essential to a siege'.

D'Aubusson had already alerted all the members of his order to come as soon as possible to the assistance of Rhodes, and he asked the pope for help 'against the perfidious Muslims'. Alexander sent a brief to all the princes in Christendom calling on them to help the Knights of Rhodes. Among the first to respond was Henry VII of England, who sent d'Aubusson several pieces of artillery for the defence of Rhodes, which he suggested might be placed under the charge of the English knights. Henry also sent the grand master a present of purebred horses, which, as he stated in his accompanying letter, had been reared in Ireland and were called Eburi.

But it soon became clear that the target of the Turkish expedition was not Rhodes but Lepanto, the Venetian fortress at the north-west end of the Gulf of Corinth. Beyazit had prepared a fleet of some 240 warships, which set sail from the Sea of Marmara in June 1499, just about the time that Jem's coffin was on the last stage of its journey to Istanbul. The sultan had also mustered two armies, one under his own command and the other led by Mustafa Pasha, his former envoy to Rome, both of which were to move in coordination with the fleet. On 14 August 1499 the Turkish forces attacked Lepanto, and fifteen days later the garrison of the fortress surrendered, a severe blow to Venetian prestige.

The Venetians tried to make peace with Beyazit, sending Alvise Manenti as envoy to the sultan's court at Edirne, where he was received on 17 February 1500. Manenti spoke of Venetian love for the 'Signor Turco' and reminded the pashas of the Serenissima's long-standing good relations with the Porte. He emphasized that during all of the years that Jem Sultan had been in exile Venice 'had never tried to make a move against his Excellency [Beyazit], and had always wanted friendship and peace with him more than with any other ruler in the world'.

One of the pashas responded by saying that Venice was responsible for the war, because its citizens in the Morea and Albania had been attacking subjects of the Porte, 'and we have written to the Signoria to punish them, but it has never done so'. Manenti was then told that the pashas had all urged the sultan to make peace with Venice, 'which they all knew to have been a good and faithful friend of their lord, in the time of Jem Sultan as at other times'. The price of peace would be the cession to the Porte of the Venetian fortresses in the Morea – Navarino, Koroni, Methoni, Monemvasia and Nauplia – as well as an annual tribute to the sultan of 10,000 ducats, 'as was given to his father'. It was then made clear to Manenti that the sultan had 'decided to have the sea as his boundary with the Signoria', meaning that Beyazit wanted the Serenissima to abandon all of her maritime possessions within and around the boundaries of the Ottoman Empire. Manenti replied that such heavy demands could not possibly be met, and the pashas said there was no further point in discussions.

Meanwhile, the Holy See had been celebrating the jubilee year of 1500, in accordance with the decree made by Pope Paul II decades earlier that each twenty-fifth year of the Christian era should be thus commemorated. The celebrations went on in Rome throughout the year, as an estimated 200,000 pilgrims flocked there to gain the plenary indulgence granted by the pope for those who visited the four principal churches of the city, beginning with St Peter's. The pious monk Petrus Delphinus was led to exclaim 'God be praised, who has brought hither so many witnesses to the Faith.' And Sigismondo de' Conti was moved to write that 'All the world was in Rome.'

Among the pilgrims was the young Nicholas Copernicus, who came from Poland to Rome about Easter and remained for a full year. Copernicus gave lectures on the new mathematical astronomy that he had been developing, and which would be published at the time of his death in 1543, proposing that the sun and not the earth was the centre of the cosmos. Among those who attended his lectures in Rome were the sculptor Michelangelo and Cardinal Alessandro Farnese, the future Pope Paul III. The European Renaissance was now in full bloom, particularly in Italy, despite the realization that the Turkish menace was looming once again on the horizon.

The Ottoman attacks on the Venetian fortresses in Greece continued relentlessly. The Turks took Methoni after a six-week siege, led by Beyazit himself, the first time the sultan had commanded his troops in battle, the garrison finally surrendering in August 1500. One of those who died in this campaign was the Turkish captain Barak, who fourteen years before had made his way to Bourganeuf as Beyazit's agent to report on Jem Sultan.

The fall of Methoni soon led the garrisons at Koroni and Navarino to surrender as well, defeats from which Venetian power in the Morea never recovered. The Venetians were forced to sue for peace, on terms agreed to by the sultan in Istanbul in mid-December 1502, a date long remembered in Venice as marking the beginning of the decline of the Serenissima's power.

The fall of Lepanto and the Venetian fortresses in the Morea had already led Pope Alexander VI to make a desperate plea for a crusade against the Turks. But the endless internal conflicts in Europe once again made this impossible. The pope himself participated in one of these disputes when he gave his approval to the kings of France and Spain in deposing King Federigo and dividing the Kingdom of Naples between their two countries. The French and Spanish then declared war against one another over their Neapolitan possessions in the summer of 1502, ending all hopes for a crusade against the Turks.

Pierre d'Aubusson had been elected by the European powers to command the pope's crusade, now aborted, for he had been a champion in the Christian struggle against the Turks all his life, most notably in his heroic leadership of the Knights of St John in defending Rhodes against Mehmet the Conqueror in 1480. He had given refuge to and taken responsibility for Jem Sultan, and had taken a leading part in all of the delicate negotiations between the Christian powers and Beyazit over the custody of the prince, which had deterred the Turks from attacking them. D'Aubusson had been deeply distressed by the events that led to Jem's death, not only because of its effect on the Christian cause, as events were now demonstrating, but also because of his personal affection for the prince, which by all accounts was genuine. The tragedy of Jem's death seems to have led to a decline in d'Aubusson from which he never fully recovered, and he passed away on 30 June 1503. He was eighty years old when he died, having been grand master of the Knights of St John for twenty-seven years. Later that summer the Christian world lost another leader, when Alexander VI died suddenly, aged seventy-three, on 12 August 1503.

On hearing of Alexander's death the nobleman Marcantonio Altieri expressed his satisfaction that now 'all the Borgia have been uprooted from the soil and cast out as poisonous plants, hated by God and noxious to man'. Niccolo Machiavelli wrote of him in *The Prince,* presenting him as an example 'Of Those who by their Crimes become Princes':

> Pope Alexander VI had no thought but of how to deceive and always found material to work on. No man ever had a more effective manner of asseverating, or made more promises with more solemn protestations, or observed them less. And yet, because he understood this side of human nature he always succeeded.

Sigismondo de' Conti was one of the few of Alexander's contemporaries to say anything vaguely positive about him on his passing. 'This pope,' as Sigismondo remarked, 'if he had no children and so much affection for them would have left a better memory of himself.' But recent historians have been inclined to take a more balanced view of Alexander's papacy, as does Michael Mallett in his history of the Borgias.

He brought scandal to the Church by ostentatiously flouting normal conventions of papal behaviour, and yet as Pope his alliance was sought by the great powers of Europe, his army was the strongest in Italy, his capital was a centre of European diplomacy. As a result, on his death the prestige of the Papacy as a force in European politics had probably rarely been higher, but the prestige of the Pope as a spiritual leader can scarcely have been lower.

On 22 September 1503 Cardinal Francesco Piccolomini was elected to succeed Alexander as pope, taking the name of Pius III in honour of his late uncle Aeneas Sylvius Piccolomini, Pope Pius II. The new pope was already in failing health at the time of his election, and he passed away less than a month later. As Sigismondo Tiezo of Siena wrote in a letter at the time: 'The death of Pius III was a great loss to the Church, to the city of Rome, and to us all, but perhaps we deserved no less for our sins.'

A new conclave, the shortest in the history of the papacy, began on 31 October 1503 and ended the next day with the almost unanimous election of Giuliano della Rovere, who became Pope Julius II. As Francesco Guidiccioni wrote of the new pope, who had been a bitter enemy of Alexander VI: 'People here expect the reign of Julius II to be glorious, peaceful, genial, and free-handed. The Roman people, usually so addicted to plunder, are behaving so quietly that every one is in astonishment. We have a pope who will be both loved and feared.'

The decade-long reign of Julius II was an extremely turbulent period, in which the pope tried to revive the temporal power of the papacy and to establish the independence of the Holy See, at a time when Italy was racked by internal wars and under attack by other European powers, most notably France and Spain. The Turks, at least, were less of a threat during that period, for during the years 1500–11 the Ottoman Empire became embroiled in a war with Persia.

The reign of Julius II coincided with the height of the Italian Renaissance, to which he contributed as the patron of Bramante, Michelangelo and Raphael. Bramante began work for Julius on the new basilica of St Peter in 1506; in 1508 the pope commissioned Michelangelo to begin painting the ceiling of the Sistine Chapel; and that same year Raphael and his assistants began decorating the series of rooms in the Apostolic Palace now known as the 'Raphael Stanza'. The latter rooms were the official salons of the new apartments of the pope, who lived in them from 1507 onwards. Paris de Grassis, the pope's master of ceremonies, says Julius moved out of the Borgia Apartments in order 'not to be pestered with reminiscences of Alexander VI'. He is undoubtedly referring to the portrait of Alexander in the *Resurrection* scene in the Room of the Mysteries, not to mention the painting of the *Disputation of St Catherine* in the Hall of the Saints with its central figures modelled on Cesare and Lucrezia Borgia and the young Jem Sultan, hardly the sort of images that Julius wanted to look upon each day in his private apartments.

Julius and Michelangelo became estranged for a time following a dispute in 1506. While they were at odds Michelangelo apparently received an offer to work for Sultan Beyazit, who commissioned him to build a bridge across the Golden Horn in Istanbul. Michelangelo did not go to Istanbul and the bridge was never built, but he did draw up its plans, which are preserved in the Bibliothèque Nationale in Paris.

Meanwhile a renaissance of a different sort had been developing in Istanbul, begun in the reign of Mehmet II, who had built the palace of Topkapı Sarayı on the First Hill of the city and his mosque complex of Fatih Camii on the Fourth Hill. The Conqueror's complex, the largest ever built in the Ottoman Empire, included the great mosque itself, along with eight enormous *medrese*, as well as a refectory, a hospital, a caravanserai, and two domed tombs, one of them for the sultan and the other for his wife Gülbahar, the mother of Beyazit II. This foundation, along with others built by the sultan's pashas, became the civic centres around which the new Islamic capital of Istanbul developed, supplanting the ancient Christian city of Constantinople, some of whose churches had been converted into mosques.

During the years 1501–06 Beyazit built his own imperial mosque complex, the Beyazidiye, on the Third Hill, dominating the central square of the old city, known to this day as Beyazit Meydanı. The mosque itself was larger than that of Fatih Camii, but the rest of the complex was less extensive, though it included a *medrese*, a Kuran school, a public kitchen, a refectory, a primary school, a public bath, and two tombs, one for the sultan and the other for his daughter Selçuk Hatun, who died in 1512. She was one of fifteen daughters of Beyazit, who also fathered eight sons – Beyazit's twenty-three children being a record for Ottoman sultans up to that time and evidence of how much more sedentary his life was compared to that of his father Mehmet II, who only sired eight children.

The city had grown substantially in the half century since the Conquest, for Mehmet II had repopulated it with both Muslims and Christians from the provinces of the empire, while Beyazit had welcomed the Sephardic Jews and Moors who had been evicted from Spain by Ferdinand and Isabella. The commerce of the empire had expanded during the reign of Beyazit, benefiting from nearly two decades of relative peace that had come from the sultan's reluctance to wage war on the Christians while they held his brother Jem captive.

During the latter years of his reign Beyazit left the active direction of military affairs to a succession of grand vezirs, freeing himself to take his ease in seclusion within the walls of his palace of Topkapı Sarayı. This period of Beyazit's reign is described thus by the historian Richard Knolles:

> After so many troubles, Baiazet gave himself unto a quiet course of life, spending most part of his time in studie of Philosophie, and conference with learned men, unto which peaceable kind of life his own natural disposition more enclined than to warres; albeit that the regard of his state, and the earnest desire of his men of warre, drew him oftentimes against his will into the field.

In 1508 Beyazit became so ill that for a time he was not expected to live, and though he improved the following year he remained bedridden until 1511. By that time a three-sided war of succession had erupted among his three sons, with the second oldest, Selim, gaining the advantage when his troops took Istanbul on 23 April 1512. Selim then confronted his father, whom he had not seen in twenty-six years, demanding that he give up the throne to him at once. Beyazit was helpless and was forced to abdicate in favour of his son, who the following day was girded with the sword of his ancestor Osman and took the throne as Selim I, the ninth Ottoman sultan.

Selim had agreed to allow Beyazit to retire to his birthplace at Demotika in Thrace, where a palace had been set aside for his use. The caravan never reached Demotika, for by 26 May Beyazit had become so ill that a halt had to be called at the town of Havsa, a day's journey short of Edirne. Beyazit died there in great agony later that day, his symptoms leading a number of those in his entourage to believe that he had been poisoned by his Jewish physician Moses Hamon on the orders of Sultan Selim.

Selim arranged for his father's remains to be brought back to Istanbul, where they were buried in the royal mausoleum at the Beyazidiye. Beyazit was sixty-four when he died, having reigned for thirty-one years, almost half of which he had been troubled by the fear that his brother Jem would usurp his throne.

Selim was forty-two when he became sultan, having served as provincial governor for many years in Trabzon, the Greek Trebizond. His fierce mien and cruel manner led the Turks to call him Yavuz, or the Grim. The name would seem to be merited, as evidenced by the description that Knolles gives of Selim, so different from his contemplative father:

> But in Selymus his sterne countenance, his fierce and pierc-
> ing eyes, his Tartar-like pale colour, his long mustachios on
> his upper lip, like bristles, frild back to his necke, with
> his beard cut close to his chin, did so express his martial
> disposition that he seemed to the beholder, to have nothing
> in him but mischiefe and crueltie . . .

The Christian powers of Europe enjoyed a respite from Ottoman aggression during Selim's reign, which was distinguished by two victorious campaigns in Asia. In the first of these campaigns Selim defeated Shah Ismail of Iran at the battle of Çaldıran, on 23 August 1514, adding all of eastern Anatolia and western Persia to the Ottoman Empire. In the second campaign Selim conquered the Mamluks of Egypt, capturing Cairo on 20 January 1517, thus extending the boundaries of the Ottoman Empire around the eastern Mediterranean. Tradition has it that at this time the caliph al-Mutawakkil transferred the rights of the caliphate to Selim, whose successors proudly added this to their title of sultan down to the end of the Ottoman Empire.

Selim prepared for a campaign into Europe in the summer of 1520, probably intending to invade Hungary, though he had not divulged his plans to his pashas. The sultan led his army out from Istanbul in early August, but a day's journey short of Edirne he became so ill that the march had to be halted. This was where Beyazit had died a little more than eight years earlier, probably at the hands of Selim, who now met his fate here as well, and after suffering for six weeks he finally passed away on 22 September 1520.

The cause of his death is suggested by the remark of an anonymous European chronicler, who noted that 'Selim the Grim died of an infected boil and thereby Hungary was spared'. The news of Selim's death occasioned services of thanksgiving throughout Christian Europe. As Paolo Giovio wrote of the reaction of Pope Leo X, who had succeeded Julius II in 1513: 'When he heard for a surety that Selimus was dead, he commanded that the litany of common prayers be sung throughout all Rome, in which men should go barefoot.'

Ferhat Pasha, the commanding general, kept Selim's death secret so that Süleyman, the sultan's only surviving son, who was serving as provincial governor in Manisa, could rush to Istanbul to take control of the government and ensure his succession to the throne.

Europe's leaders thought Süleyman to be more amenable than

his father, and they were hopeful that his reign would bring better relations between the Ottomans and Christians, but these hopes were doomed to disappointment, for soon after his accession Süleyman began preparations for a campaign into Europe. The sultan's objective was Belgrade, the gateway to all the lands along the middle Danube, which he captured on 29 August 1521. When word of the fall of Belgrade reached Venice, the doge, Antonio Grimani, wrote to his envoy in England: 'This news is lamentable, and of importance to all Christians.'

Süleyman then began preparing for an expedition against Rhodes, where the knights had been expecting an attack for years. Süleyman began the siege of Rhodes on 28 June 1522, when his fleet of 700 ships crossed the narrow strait from Marmaris carrying a force of some 100,000, vastly outnumbering the knights and their allies. The defenders fought on valiantly for nearly six months, but then on 22 December the grand master, Philip Villiers de L'Isle Adam, was forced to surrender, on condition that he and his men would be allowed to leave the island unharmed, along with all of the Rhodians who chose to accompany them. Süleyman honoured the terms of the surrender, and on 1 January 1523 the grand master and his 180 surviving knights sailed away from Rhodes, along with 4,000 Rhodians. The Knights of St John had held Rhodes for 223 years, blocking Turkish expansion in the eastern Mediterranean, which was now open to Süleyman.

The knights first retired to Crete, and then in 1530 they moved to Malta, where they constructed a mighty fortress that became a bulwark against Turkish incursions into the western Mediterranean. Süleyman sent his admiral Dragut Pasha with a fleet to capture Malta in 1551, but he was driven off by the appearance of a Christian fleet.

Meanwhile the balance of power in Europe had shifted with the rise of the Habsburgs. Charles V, grandson of Maximilian I, had through his inheritances become the most powerful ruler in Europe, his possessions in Spain, the Netherlands and Germany hemming in France. The French king, Francis I, believed that his territories were threatened and that Charles wanted 'to be master everywhere'. Francis was captured after his army was defeated by Charles V's forces at Pavia in 1525. While in captivity Francis wrote secretly to Süleyman asking for help, suggesting that the sultan attack Hungary. Süleyman agreed to the proposal and invaded the country the following year, crushing the Hungarian army in August 1526 at the battle of Mohacs, in which the King of Hungary, Lewis II, was killed. Francis was denounced by his contemporaries for his 'impious alliance' with the Turks, while Eugene F. Rice Jr and Anthony Grafton, writing in 1970, have remarked that 'it was only final evidence of the hollowness of the crusading ideal'.

Three years later Süleyman failed to capture Vienna, the only setback he suffered in more than four decades of campaigning in Europe, while at the time his buccaneering fleets were the terror of the Mediterranean. Süleyman mounted a powerful expedition against Malta in 1565, but the knights defended the island with their usual valour, and the Ottoman forces were forced to withdraw after a siege of nearly four months, having lost as many as 35,000 men, including their commander Dragut Pasha. Their defeat at Malta marked the limit of Ottoman expansion westward along the European side of the Mediterranean, so that the Knights of St John had once more stopped the Turkish advance, as they had in 1480 at Rhodes under Pierre d'Aubusson.

Süleyman died a year later, passing away on the night of

5/6 September 1566, while leading his army in another invasion of Hungary. The Ottoman Empire had reached its peak during his illustrious reign, the longest in the history of the Osmanlı dynasty. The empire began to decline with his death, though it lasted until 1923, when it gave way to the new Republic of Turkey, with its capital in Ankara.

When the last sultan, Mehmet VI, was deposed and sent into exile on 1 November 1922, he was succeeded by his cousin Abdül Mecit Efendi, who held only the title of caliph. The caliphate was then abolished on 3 March 1924, after the creation of the Turkish Republic on 29 October of the previous year, whereupon Abdül Mecit Efendi was deposed and sent into exile. Mehmet died in San Remo in 1926 and Abdül Mecit Efendi became the titular head of the Osmanlı line, living in exile with his family in Nice, where Jem Sultan had begun his own years of exile in Western Europe more than four centuries before.

The Ottoman Empire had lasted for more than six centuries, ruled during that entire time by a single dynasty, the Osmanlı, thirty-six successive sultans and then one caliph representing twenty-one generations of the same family. There are some who would count the total number of sultans as thirty-seven, to include Jem Sultan, though he ruled for only twenty days, and then only at Bursa, where he was finally laid to rest after his long exile.

20

The Parrot Speaks

THUS, THE LONG STRUGGLE between Jem and Beyazit only ended with the two brothers finally at rest in their tombs, Beyazit at his mosque in Istanbul and Jem at the Muradiye in Bursa. By a curious irony this was in keeping with the settlement that Jem had proposed in 1482, that Beyazit rule the European part of the Ottoman Empire from Istanbul, leaving him to reign in Bursa over Anatolia.

Beyazit's tomb is closed to the public, but Jem's is always open and is a place of pilgrimage. The Turkish chronicler Evliya Çelebi made a pilgrimage to the Muradiye in the mid-seventeenth century, and in his *Seyahatname* he tells of how Jem's remains and possessions were brought back to Turkey.

The corpse of Jem, together with his property, amongst which was an enchanted cup, which became brimful as soon as delivered empty into the cup-bearer's hands, a white parrot, a chess-playing monkey, and some thousands of splendid books, were delivered up to Sadi Bey and Haydar Bey, that they might be conveyed to the Sultan. Sadi, being a learned and acute man, first dyed the parrot black, and taught him to say: 'Verily we belong to God, and to him we shall return! Long live the Sultan!' Sadi and Haydar then delivered their master's remains and possessions to the Sultan, including the parrot. But when Beyazit asked, 'Where is the white parrot?', the bird immediately repeated the above-mentioned text, and added, 'Sire, Jem-Shah having entered into the mercy of the Lord, I have put off the attire of an angel clad in white, and clothed myself in the black of mourning weeds.'

And so the loquacious parrot reappeared, seventeen years after it had been presented to Jem as a farewell present by the whores of Nice. The fabulous bird is never mentioned in Western sources, nor are the miraculous cup and the chess-playing chimpanzee, which Turkish tradition has always associated with Jem's exile, and which Evliya now brings on stage again in describing the return of the prince's remains and possessions to Turkey. Evliya then tells a strange tale about Jem's burial in Bursa.

Beyazit ordered the remains of Jem to be buried in Bursa, beside his grandfather Murat II. While they were digging the grave there was such a thunder-clap and tumult in the sepulchral chapel, that all who were present fled, but not a soul of them was able to pass its threshold till ten days had passed, when this having been represented to the Sultan, the corpse of Jem was buried by his order in his own mausoleum, near to that of his grandfather.

Pious Muslim pilgrims still come to visit the tomb of Jem Sultan, part of the cult of emperor worship that lingers on among the peasants of Anatolia. I saw several of them there when I last visited Bursa, half a lifetime after I first went to see the tomb of Jem Sultan. That first visit had inspired me to set off in search of Jem's story, a quest that led me through Turkey and beyond to Cairo, Rhodes, France and Italy, and now back again here to Bursa. The scene was just as I had first seen it in the spring of 1961, for it was April again and the judas trees were flowering in the graveyard garden, dropping their blossoms on the domes of Jem's tomb and those of the other Ottoman princes and princesses buried there, the snow-covered peaks of Mount Olympus of Bithynia gathering clouds above Bursa to the north.

Jem's tomb is also visited by those, like me, who are interested in his remarkable life story, which in recent years has begun to attract renewed interest. In the summer of 1957 a group of French parliamentarians and government officials, including the French ambassador to Turkey and the mayor of Bourganeuf, came to Bursa, in what one Turkish newspaper regarded as a 'new manifestation of French–Turkish amity', a friendship that dates back to the alliance of 1535 between Süleyman the Magnificent and Francis I, who dramatically broke with the other European powers to establish an alliance with the Ottomans at the peak of their power. The tone of the article seemed to suggest that Jem had been in France as an honoured guest of the Knights of St John rather than as their prisoner, the interpretation that Pierre d'Aubusson had tried to put on his custody of the prince.

Evliya Çelebi claimed that there were dynastic grounds to this special relationship between France and Turkey. According to a section in his *Seyahatname* (entitled 'An Explanation of the Relationship between the House of Osman and the King of France'), during the Turkish siege of Constantinople in 1453 the King of France sent his daughter as a bride to Constantine XI, the last emperor of Byzantium, but she was captured by Mehmet II and became the mother of both Beyazit and Jem. In

concluding this tale Evliya says that the French princess never
became a Muslim, and to prove his point he tells a story about
her tomb, which he places next to that of Mehmet II in the garden
of the Conqueror's mosque:

> I myself have often, at morning prayers, observed that the
> clerics appointed to read verses from the Kuran in these
> tombs turned their faces toward the graves of the deceased
> during their recitation, but that they all turned their backs
> upon the coffin of this lady [the daughter of the King of
> France], of whom it is so doubtful that she departed in the
> faith of Islam. I have often seen Frenchmen come and give
> a few aspers to the tomb-keepers to open this mausoleum
> to them, as its gate is always kept shut. There can be no
> doubt that a daughter of the King of France became a wife
> of Mehmet the Conqueror and the mother of Sultan Beyazit
> and Jem Shah.

However, we know that Jem and Beyazit had different mothers,
neither of whom was a French princess: Beyazit's mother
Gülbahar, or 'The Rose of Spring', was of unknown origin, most
likely Turkish, and Jem's mother Çiçek, or Flower, is believed by
many to have been a Serbian princess. There is no record of when
or where Çiçek died, though tradition says that she perished in
a plague in Egypt and was buried in Cairo. One of Jem's daughters,
Gevher Melek, was married at Cairo in 1491 to the Mamluk Sultan
Nasır Mehmet II, son and successor of Kaitbey, and Beyazit sent
wedding presents to the couple. When Nasır Mehmet II was
murdered in 1498 Gevher Melek was promised to a member
of the Kotada family in Egypt, but Beyazit had her brought to
Istanbul, where she married a son of Sinan Pasha, Beylerbey of
Anatolia.

Jem's only other surviving son, Prince Murat, fled from Cairo to Rhodes, because he feared, with good reason, that the Mamluks would surrender him to Beyazit, who would kill him just as he had executed his brother Oğuzhan. Marino Sanudo says that on 5 December 1516 an ambassador of the Mamluk sultan came to Rhodes to demand the surrender of Murat, but the knights refused outright. Murat was given the Chateau de Fondo as his residence in Rhodes, and he showed his gratitude by converting to Roman Catholicism, changing his name to Pierre Mehmet Sayd. Pope Alexander VI created the Principate de Sayd in 1492 as a papal fief for Pierre Mehmet, who was named Viscomte de Sayd by King Ferrantino, as well as being made a patrician of Rome by the Roman Senate. Pierre Mehmet married an Italian woman named Maria Concetta Doria, who bore him four children, a son named Jem and three daughters, whose names are unknown. Little Jem, the grandson of Jem Sultan, was baptized and took the name Niccolo, and eventually inherited his father's title of Viscomte de Sayd.

When Süleyman conquered Rhodes in 1522 he insisted that Jem's son Murat, now known as Pierre Mehmet Sayd, be handed over to him, whereupon he had the prince executed. Turkish sources say that Süleyman also executed Little Jem (Niccolo), but the archives of the Order of St John and of the Vatican record that the boy escaped with the knights and was eventually brought by them to their new headquarters at Malta.

According to an article in the Istanbul newspaper *Hürriyet*, one recent visitor to Jem's tomb in Bursa claimed to be a direct descendant of Jem Sultan. Chevalier George Alexander Said-Zammit from Malta says he can trace his lineage back through seventeen generations to Jem's grandson, Little Jem, and that he has found a record in the archives of the Knights of St John mentioning a 'Nicholas Saytus' who was living in Malta in the 1530s.

The present head of the legitimate Ottoman line is Osman Ertuğrul Efendi, a grandson of Sultan Abdül Hamit II, (r. 1876–1909), born in 1912 in the imperial palace of Dolmabahçe in Istanbul and now resident in New York City. Up until 1992 males of the imperial Ottoman line were not allowed to enter Turkey, but the law has since been changed and Osman Ertuğrul has returned to his homeland several times and has visited the tomb of his ancestors. The Chevalier Said-Zammit recently made contact with Osman Ertuğrul, requesting that he and other descendants of Jem Sultan be reconciled with the legitimate Osmanlí clan. Osman Ertuğrul has acknowledged that Said-Zammit and the other descendants of Jem are descendants of Osman Gazi, founder of the imperial Osmanlí dynasty. But he maintains that their conversion to Christianity and acceptance of titles from the Pope, the King of Naples and other Christian rulers disqualifies the descendants of Jem from being accepted into the legitimate Osmanlí imperial family, who are pretenders not only to the Ottoman throne but also to the title of Caliph of Islam. And so the matter rests.

There are many other intriguing legacies of Jem's life: the Tour de Zizim in Bourganeuf, where Jem spent so much of his imprisonment, has been converted into a museum dedicated to the prince's memory. In 1985 the mayor of the Turkish town of Karaman, capital of the old Ottoman province of Karamania, visited the tower. And as I discovered from the museum's founder, a local artisan named Marcel Chaussade who has been fascinated by Jem Sultan since his youth, for the past quarter of a century there has been a community of Turks living in Bourganeuf. They now number about 300 and come from the area around Karaman to work in the local timber and wood-working industries. Although they have only been in the area since the mid-1970s some French locals still romantically like to believe that they are the descendants of Jem's companions, a story which I have heard repeated myself.

Marcel took me for a drink at the Café Central on Bourganeuf's main square opposite the commandery of the Knights of St John, which was packed with Turkish workers watching Turkey play a consolation match in the 2002 World Cup. I talked to them and learned that they all knew about Jem's story, particularly his imprisonment in the Tour de Zizim. One of them said that Jem was still a hero in Karaman and in fact throughout Anatolia, and that it was a pity that he had not been able to establish a kingdom there, in the heart of Turkey. He then lifted his glass to me and said 'Jem Sultan çok yaşa!' – 'Long live Jem Sultan!', which I repeated with equal enthusiasm.

Indeed Jem's popularity does not appear to have diminished among the Turkish people as a whole. This is despite the fact that in modern Turkish school history books Jem is still described as a traitor who tried to enlist the aid of the Christians against his fellow Turks. It seems that even the name of Jem was excised from the Osmanlı dynasty, as if he had disgraced the royal line by his flight to the Christian world. After the time of Beyazit II, the name Beyazit occurs seven times among the sons and grandsons of the Ottoman sultans, while that of Jem does not appear at all.

But still Jem's appeal endures. The first popular biography of Jem in Turkish, *Sultan Cem* by Ahmet Refik Altınay, was published in 1923 and was still being reissued at the turn of the millennium.

Altınay's biography very definitely takes Jem's side in his struggle against Beyazit, and portrays him as a romantic figure, telling of his love affair with Philippine of Sassenage, and describing his death in Naples in terms appropriate to a tragic hero.

In the summer of 2002, the Museum of Turkish and Islamic Art in Istanbul put on display a beautiful shirt which had been commissioned by Mehmet II for his son, Jem. According to an article on the exhibition in *Hürriyet* by Murat Bardakçı, the designs on its front and back are talismanic symbols of 'the better-known jinns of Islamic demonology, woven by wizards to make the wearer all powerful and immune to the spells of enemies'. Work on the garment was all but finished when Fatih died, but the war of succession that followed prevented Jem from taking possession of the talismanic shirt. If Jem had been able to wear the gown its talismans would have brought him victory in his struggle against Beyazit, or so says Bardakçı, speculating, as many still do, on what might have been.

In fact, during the more than five centuries since his death, Jem has become a folk hero in Turkey. There are those who believe that Jem Sultan might have led the Ottoman Empire in a different path than did Beyazit and his successors, one in which its glory might have remained untarnished by the decay that set in after the reign of Süleyman. His premature death had the effect of preserving his youth eternally, for in the Turkish view Jem is still seen as a handsome young prince in the prime of his life, while his brother Beyazit is depicted as a decrepit old man with a white beard, haunted by the fear of his younger brother.

During Jem's war of succession with Beyazit much of his support came from the heterodox Alevi sect of the Shiites as well as from the dervishes, particularly the Bektaşi. There are said to be

15 million Alevi in Turkey today, most of them in central Anatolia, and countless numbers of dervishes, their orders having been banned in the early years of the Turkish Republic, though they now flourish. Jem is still idolized by both groups, and it is customary among the Bektaşi, when they have almost finished a glass of wine, to drain the last drops on the ground as a libation, saying '*Jem'in hakkı!*', or 'It is Jem's right!'

Jem's popularity has always been greatest in central Anatolia, particularly in Karaman, which he ruled as provincial governor in his youth. Bardic poetry of the type that Jem wrote is still being composed and written there by the wandering minstrels known as Aşıklar, most of whom are Alevi. The origins of the Aşıklar tradition go back to the poetry of Mevlana Jelaleddin Rumi and another thirteenth-century Turkish poet, Yunus Emre, whose best known lines are perhaps those which serve as the epitaph on his tomb in the town of Karaman: 'I love you, so the hand of death can never touch you.'

The story of Jem Sultan is a favourite among these minstrels, and their listeners are often moved to tears by the retelling of his misfortunes and tragic death. The more scholarly of the Aşıklar recite Jem's poems, particularly those that evoke the sadness of his years of exile. The most moving of these is an elegiac ode by Jem that comes to mind when visiting his tomb in Bursa, and this could well serve as his epitaph.

> *Bird of my soul, be patient of thy cage,*
> *This body, lo! how fast it wastes with age.*
> *The tinkling bells already do I hear*
> *Proclaims the caravan's departure near.*
> *Soon shall it reach the land of nothingness,*
> *And thee, from fleshy bonds delivered, bless.*

Such is the story of Jem Sultan, which still resonates today in Anatolia as it does in France, for he is the romantic hero who will never grow old or be forgotten, living on forever in what Homer called 'the country of dreams'. So let the parrot change its colour from mourning black to its original angelic white, and let it speak once again as it did whenever its master entered the room, proclaiming 'Long live Jem Sultan!'

Bibliography

PUBLICATIONS

Alderson, A. D., *The Structure of the Ottoman Dynasty,* Oxford, 1956

Aldridge, James, *Cairo,* Boston and Toronto, 1969

Altınay, Ahmet Refik, *Sultan Cem,* Istanbul, 1924 (reprinted 1999)

Amis du Vieux Poet-Laval, *Le Poet-Laval, Commanderie des Chevaliers de Malta,* Montélimar, 1985

Angiolello, Gian Maria, *Historia Turchesa (1300–1514),* edited by I. Ursu, Bucharest, 1909

Aşıkpaşazade, Dervish Ahmet, *Die altosmanische Chronik des Aşıkpaşazade,* edited by Friedrich Giese, Leipzig, 1929

Babinger, Franz, *Mehmed the Conqueror and His Time,* translated by Ralph Manheim and edited by William Hickman, Princeton, 1978

Barber, Robin, *Blue Guide Greece,* 5th edition, London, 1987

Baysun, Cavit, *Cem Sultan Hayatı ve Şiirleri,* Istanbul, 1946

Bell, Gertrude, *The Thousand and One Churches,* London, 1909

Bellonci, Maria, *The Life and Times of Lucrezia Borgia,* translated by Bernard and Barbara Wall, London, 2000

Blanchard, Paul, *Blue Guide Southern Italy,* 9th edition, London, 2000

Bosio, G., *Del' Istoria della Sacra Religione et Illma. Militi di San Giovanni Gierosolimitano,* 3 volumes, Rome, 1594–1602

Bosso, Matteo, *Familiares et secundae Matthaei Bossi Epistolae,* Mantua, 1493

Boudard, René, *Bourganeuf Au Fil Des Ages . . .*, Bourganeuf, 1980

Bouhours, Fr D., *Histoire de Pierre d'Aubusson*, Paris, 1676

Bradford, Sarah, *Cesar Borgia, His Life and Times*, London, 1976

Bridge, John S. C., *A History of France from the Death of Louis XI*, Volume I, Oxford, 1921; Volume II, Oxford, 1924

Brockmann, Eric, *The Two Sieges of Rhodes, 1480–1512*, London, 1969

Brooton, Jerry, *Trading Territories, Mapping the Early Modern World*, Ithaca, New York, 2002

Brown, Rawdon (ed.), *Calendar of State Papers and Manuscripts Relating to English Affairs Existing in the Archives and Collections of Venice and other Libraries of Northern Italy*, Volume I, 1202–1509, London, 1894

Burchard, Johann, *Alle corte di cinque papi* (Diary, 1483–1506, of Johann Burchard, translated from the Latin by Luca Bianchi), Milano, 1988

——*At the Court of the Borgia, Being an Account of the Reign of Pope Alexander VI written by his Master of Ceremonies Johann Burchard*, edited and translated by Geoffrey Parker, London, 1993

Cantemir, Dimitrie, *The History of the Growth and Decay of the Othman Empire*, translated by M. Tindal, London, 1734–5

Caoursin, Guillaume, *Obsidionis Rhodiae Urbis Descriptio*, Venice, 1480, translated by John Kaye, Laureate to King Edward IV, published by Caxton in 1496 under the title: *The Dylectable newessee & Tithyngs of the Gloryoos Victorye of the Rhodyns Agaynst the Turke*

——*Opera*, Ulm, 1496

Caron, Marie-Thérèse, and Denis Clauzel (eds), *Le Banquet du Faisan*, Arras, 1997

Chevrier, Jean-Marie, *Zizim, Grand Sultan Ottoman, Exilé Volontaire à Bourganeuf*, adapted in comic book format by Jean-Marie Chevrier, Limoges, n.d.

Clement, Clara Erskine, *Naples, The City of Parthenope and its Environs*, Boston, 1894

Coles, Paul, *The Ottoman Impact on Europe*, London, 1968

Commines, Philippe de, *Mémoires*, Paris, 1843

Conway-Morris, Roderick, *Jem, Memoirs of An Ottoman Secret Agent*, London, 1989

Creighton, M., *A History of the Papacy, from The Great Schism to the Sack of Rome*, Volumes III and IV, 2nd edition, London, 1919 and 1923

Davies, Norman, *Europe, A History*, Oxford and New York, 1996

Duruy, Victor, *A Short History of France*, Volume I, London, 1873

Elliot, J. H., *Imperial Spain, 1469–1716*, London, 1963

Erlande-Brandenburg, Alain, *La Dame à la Licorne*, Paris, 1989

Ertaylan, Ismail Hikmet, *Sultan Cem*, Istanbul, 1951

Evliya Çelebi, *Narrative of Travels in Europe, Asia and Africa [the Seyahatname]*, translated by Joseph von Hammer, London, 1834–6

Eyice, Semavi, 'Sultan Cem'in Portreleri Hakkinda', Türk Tarih Kurummu Belleten XXXVII, Sayı 145, January 1973, pp. 1–49

Faroqhi, Suraiya, *Pilgrims and Sultans, The Hajj under the Ottomans, 1517–1683*, London, 1994

Fisher, Sydney Nettleton, *The Foreign Relation of Turkey, 1481–1513*, Urbana, Illinois, 1948

Freely, John, *Istanbul, The Imperial City*, London, 1996

——*The Companion Guide to Turkey*, 2nd edition, London, 1996

——*Inside the Seraglio; Private Lives of the Ottoman Sultans*, London, 1999

Gaspare da Verona, *Le vite di Paolo II*, edited by G. Zippel, *Rerum Italicarum Scriptores*, new series, XVI, 3, p. 39, Cite di Castello, 1904

Gessi, Leone, *The Vatican City*, 6th edition, Rome, 1956

Gibb, E. J. W., *A History of Ottoman Poetry*, Volume 2, London, 1906

Gregorovius, Ferdinand, *History of the City of Rome in the Middle*

Ages, translated from the German 4th edition by Annie Hamilton, Volume VII, Part I (1421–1496), London, 1900

Hale, John, *The Civilization of Europe in the Renaissance*, London, 1993

Hammer-Purgstall, Joseph, *Geschichte des Osmanische Reiches*, Graz, 1963, 10 volumes (reprint of 1827–35 edition)

Hay, Denys, *Europe in the Fourteenth and Fifteenth Centuries*, 2nd edition, London and New York, 1989

Höfler, C. von, *Don Rodrigo de Borja (Past Alexander VI) und seine Söhne . . .* , Vienna, 1890

Housley, Norman, *The Later Crusades, 1274–1580*, Oxford, 1992

Ibn Battuta, *The Travels of Ibn Battuta, AD 1325–1354*, 2 volumes, translated by H. A. R. Gibb, Oxford, 1959–62

Imber, Colin, *The Ottoman Empire, 1300–1481*, Istanbul, 1990

——*The Ottoman Empire, 1300–1650, The Structure of Power*, London, 2002

Inalcık, Halil, *The Ottoman Empire; The Classical Age, 1300–1600*, translated by Norman Itzkowitz and Colin Imber, London, 1973

——'A case study in Renaissance diplomacy: the agreement between Innocent VIII and Bayezid II on Djem Sultan', *Journal of Turkish Studies* 3 (1979), pp. 209–33

——'Djem', in *Encyclopedia of Islam*, New Edition, 1960, Volume III, pp. 529–31

——'Ahmad Pasha Gedik', *Encyclopedia of Islam*, New Edition, 1960, Volume I, pp. 292–3

Infessura, Stefano, *Diario della citta di Roma*, Rome, 1890

José, Marie, *La Maison de Savoie*, Paris, 1956

Kiang, Dawson, 'Josquin Desprez and a Possible Portrait of the Ottoman Prince Jem in Cappella Sistina Ms. 41', *Southern California Early Music News*, XXIV, no. 7 (March 2000), 1, pp. 18–24

Kitchin, W., *A History of France*, Volume II (1453–1624), Oxford, 1896

Knolles, Richard, *The Lives of the Othoman Kings and Emperors*, 2 volumes, London, 1610

Kritovoulos of Imbros, *History of Mehmed the Conqueror*, translated by Charles T. Riggs, Princeton, 1954

Lamansky, Vlad, *Secrets d'Etat de Venise*, St Petersbourg, 1883

Lamartine, Alphonse de, *History of Turkey* (3 volumes), translated from the French, New York, 1855

Lane, Frederic C., *Venice, A Maritime Republic*, London and Baltimore, 1973

Lane-Pool, Stanley, *A History of Egypt in the Middle Ages*, London, 1901

Lefort, Jacques, *Documents Grecs, dans les archives de Topkapı Sarayı, contribution à l'histoire de Cem Sultan* (in French, Greek and Turkish), Ankara, 1981

Lewis, Bernard, *The Muslim Discovery of Europe*, New York, 1982

Luchinat, Cristina Acidini, *Pintoricchio*, translated by Huw Evans, Milan, 1999

Luttrell, Anthony, 'The Hospitallers at Rhodes, 1306–1421,' in Kenneth M. Setton, *A History of the Crisades*, Volume III, Madison, Wisconsin, 1975, pp. 278–313

Lyle-Kalças, Evelyn, *Bodrum Castle and its Knights*, Izmir, 1984

Machiavelli, Niccolo, *The Prince*, translated by Robert M. Adams, New York, 1977

Malipiero, D., *Annali Veneti dell' anno 1457 al 1500 . . .*, Florence, 1843

Mallett, Michael, *The Borgias; The Rise and Fall of a Renaissance Dynasty*, London, 1969

Manfroni, C., *Storia della marina Italiana della caduta di Constantinopoli alla battaglia de Lepanto*, Rome, 1897

Masson, Georgina, *The Companion Guide to Rome*, 3rd edition, London, 1972

Ménage, V. L., 'The Mission of an Ottoman Secret Agent in France in 1486', *Journal of the Royal Asiatic Society*, 1985, pp. 112–32

Merriman, Bigelow Merriman, *The Rise of the Spanish Empire in the Old World and in the New*, Volumes I and II, New York, 1918

Minorsky, V., and C. E. Bosworth, 'Uzun Hasan', in *Encyclopedia of Islam*, New Edition, 1960, Volume X, pp. 936–7

Muir, William, *The Mameluke or Slave Dynasty of Egypt, 1260–1517*, London, 1896

Okur, Mustafa, *Cem Sultan, Hayato ve Şiir Dünyası*, Ankara, 1992

Pastor, Ludwig, *The History of the Popes* (5th edition), Volumes IV, V and VI, edited by Frederick Ignatius Antrobus, London and St Louis, Missouri, 1950

Peirce, Leslie, *The Imperial Harem, Women and Sovereignty in the Ottoman Empire*, New York and Oxford, 1993

Pettegree, Andrew, *Europe in the Sixteenth Century*, London, 2002

Pitcher, Donald Edgar, *An Historical Geography of the Ottoman Empire, from earliest times to the end of the sixteenth century*, Leiden, 1972

Porcius, Hieronimus, *Commentarius*, in L. Thuasne (ed.), *Burchardi Diarium*, Paris, 1883–5

Porter, Whitworth, *The Knights of Malta or the Order of St John of Jerusalem*, 3rd edition, London, 1884

Poutiers, Jean-Christian, *Rhodes et ses Chevaliers, 1306–1523*, Bruxelles, n.d.

Reumont, Anton von, *Geschichte der Stadt Rom*, Volume III, Berlin, 1867–70

——*Lorenzo de' Medici il Magnifico*, Volume II, Leipzig, 1883

Rice, Eugene F. Jr, and Anthony Grafton, *The Foundations of Early Modern Europe, 1460–1559*, New York, 1970

Robertson, Ian, *Blue Guide France*, 4th edition, London, 1997

Rossi, Ettore, 'The Hospitallers at Rhodes, 1421–1523', in Kenneth M. Setton, *A History of the Crusades*, Volume III, Madison, Wisconsin, 1975, pp. 314–39

Russell, Dorothea, *Medieval Cairo, and the Monasteries of the Wadi Natrun*, New York and Toronto, 1962

Sablier, Edouard, *Le prisonnier de Bourganeuf: Djem Sultan, 1459–1495*, Paris, 2000

Sadüddin, *Tacü-i-tevarih*, Istanbul, 1863/64

Sanudo, Marino, *Diarii*, 58 volumes, Venice, 1879–1903

Setton, Kenneth M. (general editor), *A History of the Crusades*, Volume III, edited by Harry W. Hazard, Madison, Wisconsin, 1975

——*The Papacy and the Levant (1204–1571)*, Volume II, Philadelphia, 1978

Sigismondo de' Conti da Foligno, *Le storie de' suoi tempe dai 1475 al 1510*, Rome, 1883

Spandounes, Theodore, *On the Origin of the Ottoman Emperors*, translated and edited by Donald M. Nicol, Cambridge, 1997

Stavrides, Theoharis, *The Sultan of Vezirs; The Life and Times of the Ottoman Grand Vezir Mahmud Pasha Angelovic (1453–1464)*, Leiden, Boston, Köln, 2001

Thuasne, L., *Djem Sultan, Fils de Mohammed II, Frere de Bayazid II (1459–1495)*, Paris, 1892

——(ed.), *Burchardi Diarium*, Paris, 1883–5

Vatin, Nicolas, *L'Ordre de Saint-Jean-de-Jérusalem, l'Empire orientale entre les deux sièges de Rhodes (1480–1522)*, Paris, 1994

——*Sultan Djem, Un prince ottoman dans l'Europe du XV siècle d'après deux sources contemporaines: Vakıatı Sultan Cem, Oeuvres de Guillaume Caoursin*, Ankara, 1997

Yılmaz, Muammer, *Cem Sultan*, Ankara, 2001

Zinkeisen, J. M., *Geschichte des Osmanischen Reiches in Europa*, 2 volumes, Gotha, 1840–55

Index

P.S.

Ideas,
interviews
& features . . .

About the author

About the book

Read on

Sailing the Seven Seas
Louise Tucker talks to John Freely

You have been captivated by Turkey for forty-five years. When did you first visit, and what were your first impressions?
I first came to Turkey with my wife Dolores and our three children in September 1960, when I began teaching physics at Robert College in Istanbul. We fell in love with the city at once, because of its beauty and the depth of its history, and also because its relaxed way of life was so much more congenial to us than the programmed materialistic world we had left behind in the US. We left Istanbul twice, first in 1976 and then in 1991, but on both occasions we returned, after living and working in Athens, Boston, London and Venice. Since 1993 I have been teaching astronomy and the history of science in Istanbul at Bosphorus University, which was founded in 1971 in the buildings and grounds of the old Robert College. Istanbul and Turkey have changed considerably since we first arrived, but life here is still extremely interesting and pleasant, and we feel that we have escaped from the worst of the modern world, though there are signs that it is catching up with us even here on the shores of the Bosphorus.

You were born in the US, grew up in America and Ireland, but live in Turkey. Where is home, and why?
Istanbul, because this is where we have lived a good part of our life and where most of our friends live, though we have many other dear friends around the world. People have more time for friendship here and there is more

communal life than we have found in the US in recent years, and I say that remembering the very rich communal life that I enjoyed in my youth in Brooklyn and in my earlier childhood in Ireland. I do miss New York, but I think that what I miss no longer exists except in my memory.

What did you want to be when you grew up?
I wanted to sail the seven seas and write about the places I saw, and I've been very fortunate to have been able to do that, though in a very different way than I first imagined, as a university lecturer rather than a merchant seaman.

Did your family background influence your career in any way?
My great-grandfather Thomas Ashe was wounded in the Crimean War and recuperated in Florence Nightingale's hospital in Istanbul. During the part of my transatlantic childhood that I spent in Ireland I was taught to read by my maternal grandmother, and one of the books I read was a travelogue that Thomas Ashe had bought in Istanbul, which I first knew of as Constantinople, and which seemed to embody all that was romantic about the East.

As someone who served in the Second World War, did Jem Sultan's desire to defend and protect his country and his freedom resonate with your own military experience?
Jem Sultan's desire was to regain the empire ▶

6 I first came to Turkey with my wife Dolores and our three children in September 1960. We fell in love with Istanbul at once, because of its beauty and the depth of its history, and its relaxed way of life. 9

Sailing the Seven Seas *(continued)*

◀ he had lost to his brother Beyazit, but he was doomed to failure and lost his freedom forever once he put himself in the hands of Pierre d'Aubusson, Grand Master of the Knights of St John. This hardly resonates with my own military experience, which began when I joined the US Navy at the age of seventeen in May 1944, less out of patriotism than from a desire for adventure, which I got more of than I bargained for serving with a commando unit in the Pacific, India, Burma and China during the last year of World War II and then on troopships in the Indian Ocean, the Mediterranean and the North Atlantic in the following year. My military career ended exactly a month before my twentieth birthday, ending two years of service that gave me enough stories of war and adventure to last me the rest of my life.

Your books span a wide range of subjects, from travelling in Greece to Ottoman history, and yet you are by trade a physicist. How do you combine such a wide range of interests, and is there any crossover between science and humanities in your work? Physicists have traditionally had a wide range of intellectual interests, partly because in their conversations with non-scientists they can hardly talk about their own abstruse researches in physics. I have always been deeply interested in history, and after I obtained my doctorate in physics I did a year of post-doctoral research at Oxford in the history of science, which I have been teaching for the last forty years. Our university press has just published my *Emergence of Modern*

⟨ Physicists have traditionally had a wide range of intellectual interests, partly because in their conversations with non-scientists they can hardly talk about their own abstruse researches. ⟩

Science, East and West, and I am now working on a book about medieval Islamic science.

As well as writing forty books you have also taught physics in various universities around the world. How do you find the time to do both, and have you ever been tempted to give up teaching to write full time?
I did all of my graduate studies at night while I was working full time as a research physicist, and so I had to apportion my time very carefully, which I still do, except now all of my spare time is spent writing, which I'm able to do since my wife Dolores has always taken care of all the practical details of our household. I have thought about giving up academic work to write full time, but it was never possible, even now, and besides I so much enjoy the intellectual stimulus of teaching and personal contact with students that I can't even imagine retiring from the university here.

Among the many books that you have written, which one is your favourite and why?
My first book, *Strolling Through Istanbul*, published in 1972, which I wrote in collaboration with the late Hilary Sumner-Boyd, my colleague at Robert College. As the Catalan scholar Petrus Gyllius wrote of Istanbul in the mid-sixteenth century: 'While other cities are mortal, this one will endure as long as there are men on earth.'

What has been the most satisfying part of your career? And the most frustrating?
The most satisfying has been the last twelve ▶

‘ Travel always inspires me, particularly to out-of-the-way places that I have read about for years, such as Albania. ’

LIFE
at a Glance

BORN

New York, 26 June 1926;
early childhood back and
forth between US and
Ireland (joint US–Irish
citizenship)

MILITARY

US Navy 1944–6; combat
service with a commando
unit in the Pacific, India,
Burma and China

EDUCATED

New York University, PhD
in physics; Oxford, post-
doctoral studies in the
history of science

MARRIED

1951 to Dolores Stanley;
three children: Maureen,
Eileen and Brendan

CAREER

Research physicist,
Princeton (1955–60);
Professor of Physics,
University of the
Bosphorus in Istanbul
(formerly Robert College)

Sailing the Seven Seas *(continued)*

◄ years, which brought me back to Istanbul
and the University of the Bosphorus, and in
which I began writing works of history and
biography rather than guide books. The most
frustrating began when we left Istanbul for
the first time in 1976, after which we moved
in turn to Athens, Boston and London, when
I taught long hours in secondary schools
in order to survive, trying to write during
lunch hours or physics labs or late at night,
dreaming that one day we might be able to
return to Turkey and Greece.

What motivates you to write?

My deep interest in human history, and the
people and places involved in this endless
drama. I am fascinated by the spirit of place
and the perpetuation of cultures, and by the
questions of what differentiates one human
society from another and what endures in
them despite change, thoughts that have
always been in my mind during my travels
around the world.

Where do you go for inspiration?

Travel always inspires me, particularly to
out-of-the-way places that I have read about
for years, such as Albania, which we finally
visited at the turn of the millennium in
search of the tomb of Sabbatai Sevi, the lost
messiah, about whom I wrote in my last
book. That same year we also travelled to
south-west China, which I had last seen fifty-
five years before during the last weeks of the
Second World War, when I was attached to a
unit of the Chinese army. I travelled there to
do research on the matriarchal societies that

still flourish in Yunnan province, part of a book on the Amazons that I have been contemplating for many years, inspired by the regiment of women warriors who were in action with our unit in the summer of 1945.

Who are your influences as a writer?
I suppose that I have been most deeply influenced by Homer, whose *Odyssey* I first read in a prose translation just before joining the navy in 1944. When I came back from the war the first book I read was Chapman's translation of the *Odyssey*, and the lines that I recall best are those describing Odysseus' first sight of Crete, which I myself saw for the first time in October 1945 from the deck of the troopship that took us back from Calcutta to New York. 'In the middle of the sable sea, there lies an isle called Crete, a ravisher of eyes . . .' Forty-two years later I quoted those lines at the beginning of a book that I wrote on Crete, which is as direct an influence as you can find of one writer on another, though separated by some twenty-seven centuries, and I have quoted them again in a book on the Greek islands that I have just completed.

What do you do when you're not writing/working?
Dolores and I sit down in the evening before supper and talk, often about the places we have been to in times past or which we will visit in the future, many of which I have written about and which she has depicted in her paintings. At least once a week we have dinner at one of our favourite restaurants ▶

LIFE *at a Glance*
(continued)

(1960–76,1993–present); also lived and worked in New York, Boston, London, Athens, Venice, Asian Turkey, Crete, the Greek islands and Ireland

BOOKS (A SELECTION)
Strolling Through Istanbul (with Hilary Sumner-Boyd) (1972); *Stamboul Sketches* (1974); *The Western Shores of Turkey* (1988); *Classical Turkey* (1990); *Sinan, Architect of Süleyman the Magnificent* (with A.R. Burelli, photos by Ara Güler) (1992); *The Bosphorus* (1992); *Istanbul, The Imperial City* (1996); *Inside the Seraglio: Private Lives of the Sultans in Istanbul* (1999); *The Lost Messiah: In Search of the Mystical Rabbi Sabbatai Sevi* (2001); *The Byzantine Monuments of Istanbul* (with Ahmet Çakmak) (2004); *The Emergence of Modern Science, East and West* (2004); *John Freely's Istanbul* (2004)

Sailing the Seven Seas *(continued)*

◄ in Istanbul, joined by friends and
sometimes by one or more of our three
children and six grandchildren who may be
passing through town, talking about other
friends, some of them now gone forever
except in our memories.

What are you writing now?
One of the books I am working on is entitled
*Aladdin's Lamp: How Greek Science Came
to Europe via Islam.* Another is my travel
autobiography, *Around the World in Eighty
Years,* which I hope to finish in the thirteen
months between now and my eightieth
birthday, June 26, 2006, though there are
a couple of places I want to revisit in the
interim, particularly my mother's birthplace
on the Dingle peninsula in south-western
Ireland, where I first dreamt of sailing the
seven seas and writing about the places I
had seen. ■

Top Ten
Favourite Books

1. **The Odyssey**
   Homer

2. **The Histories**
   Herodotus

3. **The Dialogues**
   Plato

4. **Don Quixote**
   Miguel de Cervantes

5. **The History of the Decline and Fall of the Roman Empire**
   Edward Gibbon

6. **Moby Dick**
   Herman Melville

7. **Ulysses**
   James Joyce

8. **The Sleepwalkers**
   Arthur Koestler

9. **The Cyclades, or Life Among the Insular Greeks**
   James Theodore Bent

10. **Narrative of Travels**
    Evliya Chelebi

A Writing Life

When do you write?
Whenever I have the opportunity.

Where do you write?
At my desk in my study.

Why do you write?
Because that is my creative life.

Pen or computer?
I type on a computer with the rubber end of a pencil, and in that way I keep one foot (or hand) in the pre-electronic age and the other in the modern world.

Silence or music?
Silence.

What started you writing?
I started writing in 1966 when I had a fellowship at Oxford, for that was the first time in my life that I had any spare time. I wanted to write about Istanbul, where I had been living for six years, and that was the beginning of the process that led to my collaboration with Hilary Sumner-Boyd in writing *Strolling Through Istanbul*.

How do you start a book?
I am very disorganized, so I start by clearing my desk, which gives me the feeling that I am organized, at least for the moment.

And finish?
I finish by clearing my desk again, for the same reason that I did when I started.

Which living writer do you most admire?
Patrick Leigh Fermor.

What or who inspires you?
The human spirit.

If you weren't a writer what job would you do?
I would do what I have been doing for the past forty-five years, teach, for that is the noblest and most satisfying of professions.

What's your guilty reading pleasure? Favourite trashy read?
Reading the sports pages of the *International Herald Tribune.* ■

An Unfinished Tale

By John Freely

IN WRITING ABOUT the Ottoman dynasty, both in *Jem Sultan* and *Inside the Seraglio*, I have found that the story goes on after I have finished my book, and now for the first time I have the opportunity to pick up the thread of an unfinished tale in a postscript.

Part of this story concerns the history of the imperial Turkish dynasty after the fall of the Ottoman Empire, when the last rulers were deposed and sent off into exile, most of them totally without resources. As Princess Ayş Osmanoğlu, a daughter of Sultan Abdül Hamit II, wrote in her memoirs: 'We are a group of human beings without fatherland, without a home, without shelter. The history of our family in exile was just a sequence of tragic deaths.'

The last four Ottoman sultans were all sons of Abdül Mecit I (r. 1839–69). The first of the four half-brothers (they all had different mothers) to reign was Murat V (r. 1876), who succeeded after the death of his uncle Abdül Aziz (r. 1861–76). Murat was deposed after three months because of his insanity. He was succeeded by his brother Abdül Hamit II (r. 1876–1909), who confined Murat to the palace of Feriye Sarayí on the European shore of the Bosphorus, where he lived until his death in 1904. Abdül Hamit was deposed in 1909 and succeeded in turn by his brothers Mehmet V Reşat (r. 1909–18) and Mehmet VI Vahidettin (r. 1918–22), the last sultan, who was deposed and exiled on 1 November 1922. His cousin Abdül Mecit II succeeded, but only as caliph, and then he was exiled and deposed on 3 March 1924 after the creation of the Turkish Republic on 29 October of the previous year.

When Mehmet VI died in 1926 Abdül Mecit II became the titular head of the Osmanlí line, and when he passed away in 1944 the title passed to the oldest male of the dynasty, Ahmet Nihat (1884–1954), a grandson of Murat V. The title then passed in turn to Osman Fuad (1895–1973), another grandson of Murat V; Mehmet Abdül Aziz (1901–77), a grandson of Abdül Aziz; Ali Vasib (1903–84), a great-grandson of Murat V; Mehmet Orhan (1909–94), a grandson of Abdül Hamit II; and Osman Ertuğrul (b. 1912), another grandson of Abdül Hamit II, who now lives quietly in retirement in New York City.

The males of the imperial Osmanlí line were not permitted to return to Turkey until 1992, when the ban was lifted and Mehmet Orhan visited Istanbul as the guest of President Turgut Ozal, staying in the luxury hotel that had been built on the ruins of Çirağan Sarayí, the Bosphorus palace in which he had lived as a young prince. Osman Ertuğrul returns to Turkey at least once a year, and in the summer of 2004 he came on a Turkish passport that had been issued to him earlier that year, the first titular head of the Ottoman line to have his nationality restored, seven centuries after his ancestor Osman Gazi founded the imperial Osmanlí dynasty.

Early in the fall of 2004 I met Beyzade (Prince) Osman Selaheddin Osmanoğlu, a grandson of Sultan Mehmet V Reşat and ▶

❛In writing about the Ottoman dynasty, I have found that the story goes on after I have finished my book. ❜

An Unfinished Tale *(continued)*

◀ great-great-grandson of Murat V. Beyzade Osman's paternal grandfather Ahmet Nihat and his father Ali Vasib were successively titular head of the Osmanlí line. Beyzade Osman was born in Alexandria in 1940 and in 1958 moved to England; he now lives in Oxford, though he is renovating a second home in Istanbul, where he plans to spend a good deal of time every year.

When I gave Beyzade Osman a copy of my *Jem Sultan*, he smiled and said that his fourth grandson, born in High Wycombe in England on 1 July 2004 (two weeks before the publication of *Jem Sultan*), had been given the name Turan Jem. The child is the first of his line to bear the name Jem since Jem Sultan himself, for after Jem's exile the official view was that he had disgraced the imperial dynasty by his flight to the Christian world. Beyzade Osman told me that Jem Sultan had always been a hero to him, and that he was pleased that his newest grandson had been given that illustrious name.

I spent part of the summer of 2002 visiting the various French chateaux where Jem Sultan had been imprisoned, particularly the tower that still bears his name at Bourganeuf. When I returned to Istanbul later that summer I learned that I had missed an opportunity to meet the Chevalier George Alexander Said-Zammit, a Maltese aristocrat who claims to be a descendant of Jem. The Chevalier traces his descent through Jem Sultan's son Murat, who took the name Pierre Mehmet Sayd when he converted to Christianity and was ennobled by Pope Alexander VI. Said-Zammit made a

❝ The males of the imperial Osmanlí line were not permitted to return to Turkey until 1992. ❞

pilgrimage to Jem Sultan's tomb in Bursa, which was reported in one of Istanbul's leading newspapers, reviving an apocryphal story that Jem had converted to Christianity during his imprisonment in the Vatican.

The Chevalier subsequently approached Osman Ertuğrul, the present titular head of the Osmanlí dynasty, suggesting a rapprochement with the descendants of Jem. The present head of the House of Said, as the direct descendants of Jem Sultan are known, is Prince Giuseppe Said (b. 1949), who settled in Australia in 1947 and now lives in semi-retirement there and in Malta. In 2002 Osman Ertuğrul recognized the Prince as being in the line of direct descent from Osman Gazi, founder of the imperial Osmanlí dynasty.

This coming summer I am planning to visit the tomb of Jem Sultan in Bursa together with Beyzade Osman Selaheddin Osmanoğlu, who is hoping to bring his grandson Turan Jem along with him. Turan Jem represents the twenty-seventh generation of the imperial Osmanlí dynasty that began with Osman Gazi, whose tomb is also in Bursa, and we will pay a visit there after our pilgrimage to Jem Sultan's tomb. When Turan Jem is old enough to understand, I hope that Beyzade Osman will tell him the story of Jem Sultan's parrot, so that he too can say 'Jem Sultan çok yaşa!' ■

Have You Read?

Other books by John Freely include:

Strolling Through Istanbul
'A guide-book that reads like a novel!'
WILLIAM BUCKLEY, *New York Times*

Strolling Through Athens
'If you want a cultural guide to the ancient
city, this is the one for you.'
ANTHONY SATTIN, *Sunday Times*

The Western Shores of Turkey
'John Freely's enchanting guide to the
western shores of Turkey ... is a work of
genuine scholarship, lightly worn and
charmingly conveyed.'
PAUL BAILEY, *Sunday Times*

Istanbul, The Imperial City
'If you're thinking of paying Istanbul a
visit, don't go without reading this book
from cover to cover at least twice.'
ARMINTA WALLACE, *Irish Times*

**_Inside the Seraglio: Private Lives of the
Sultans in Istanbul_**
'A richly-coloured, highly-entertaining book
that I wished I'd had in hand when I strolled
around the Topkapi.'
LAWRENCE JAMES, *The Times*

**_The Lost Messiah: In Search of the Mystical
Rabbi Sabbatai Sevi_**
'The first popular biography of Sabbatai to
appear for many years and a jolly good one
at that. Everything in it is astonishing.'
Mail on Sunday

If You Loved This,
You Might Like . . .

Turks: A Journey of a Thousand Years,
600–1600
Filiz Cağman, Nazan Olcer, David J.
Roxburgh
The sumptuous catalogue of the recent
much-praised exhibition at the Royal
Academy of Arts in London, UK.

My Name is Red
Orhan Pamuk
Sixteenth-century Istanbul is the backdrop
for this historical novel which is at once a
detective story and a tale of the conflict
created by the rise of the West contrasted
with the decline of the Ottomans.

Istanbul
Orhan Pamuk
Pamuk's portrait of himself as artist against
the backdrop of the city where he grew up
and now lives.

The Turks Today: After Ataturk
Andrew Mango
A respected specialist introduces
contemporary Turkey.

The Fourth Crusade and the Sack of
Constantinople
Jonathan Phillips
Throughout the reign of Jem Sultan, the
planned crusades never take place. However,
in 1204 the Fourth Crusade did, with
devastating consequences.

The Turks in World History
Carter V. Findley
Two thousand years of Turkish history
presented for the first time in one volume.

Find Out More

USEFUL WEBSITES

www.fast.net.au/tancarville/libro %20d'oro/said.html
This website has a summary history of the Ottoman Empire as well as a section on the descendants of Jem Sultan.

www.maltagenealogy.com.libro% 20d'oro/said.html
This website gives all the currently available genealogical information about the descendants of Jem Sultan.

OR VISIT . . .

- Palace of Zizim in the Castle of the Knights, Rhodes
- Tour de Zizim, Bourganeuf
- Borgia Apartments in the Vatican, Rome
- Castel dell'Ovo, Naples
- Topkapí Sarayí palace, Istanbul
- Mosque and Tomb of Beyazit II, Istanbul
- Tomb of Jem Sultan, Bursa